UNMASKING THE POWERS

OTHER FORTRESS PRESS BOOKS
BY WALTER WINK

The Bible in Human Transformation:
Toward a New Paradigm for
Biblical Study
(1973)

THE POWERS SERIES

Naming the Powers:
The Language of Power in
the New Testament
(1984)

Engaging the Powers:
Discernment and Resistance
in a World of Domination
(1992)

WALTER WINK

UNMASKING THE POWERS

The Invisible Forces That Determine Human Existence

THE POWERS • VOLUME TWO

FORTRESS PRESS   PHILADELPHIA

Cover art: Pomona Hallenbeck
Cover design: Terry Bentley

Library of Congress Cataloging-in-Publication Data

Wink, Walter.
  Unmasking the powers.
  (The Powers; v. 2)
  Includes index.
  1. Powers (Christian theology) I. Title. II. Series:
Wink, Walter. Powers; v. 2.
BS2545.P66W56 1984 Vol. 2 [BT962] 235   85–45480
ISBN 0–8006–1902–1

Printed in the United States of America   1-1902
96   95   94   93   6   7   8   9   10

For June

Whisper of running streams, and winter lightning.
The wild thyme unseen and the wild strawberry,
The laughter in the garden, echoed ecstasy
Not lost, but requiring, pointing to the agony
Of death and birth.

T. S. Eliot, Four Quartets

Contents

Preface

Much of this book emerged not from solitary research or introspection, but from group dialogues over biblical texts. Some of the most fundamental insights I owe to seminars with the Guild for Psychological Studies. The very process of communal, Socratic biblical study that I have been championing these past fourteen years is integral to the results that find their way onto these pages. I would not have come by many of them any other way. I want to thank the hundreds of you who have made contributions every bit as significant as those acknowledged in the notes. This book and its companion volumes are in a real sense your books, and I am proud to be your scribe.

Two people, Carl G. Jung and Elizabeth Boyden Howes, have had a particularly profound impact on the themes developed here. On the strength of a first reading by Morton Kelsey, Robert T. Fortna, Barbara Wheeler, Dwayne Huebner, John B. Cobb, Jr., and James A. Forbes, Jr., I redrafted the entire book. Special thanks are due to John Pairman Brown, who criticized it with a thoroughness and care that was as gracious as it was helpful. Others read parts: on Satan and the Gods, Elizabeth Boyden Howes and Sheila Moon; on the Gods, Brewster Beach; on the Demons, M. Scott Peck, Nan Merrill, and Tilda Norberg; on the Angels of the Churches, Carl Dudley; on the Angels of Nations, Coleman Barr Brown; on the Angels of Nature, David Ray Griffin and Douglas Sloan; on the Elements, George A. Riggan, Barbara Thain McNeel, and Douglas Sloan. John A. Hollar of Fortress Press again ably orchestrated the editorial process. Despite its many evident flaws, this book is immeasurably better thanks to the care of each of you, and I am profoundly grateful.

The further I have probed into the themes of this book, the more I have become aware of how little we really know. What clarity I may have achieved may even prove deceptive, since the reality may in fact be far more complex and confusing. Consider this then the work of a person describing as faithfully as possible what little comes to light on a mountain wreathed in thick fog.

Abbreviations

ANF	*The Ante-Nicene Fathers*, ed. A. Roberts and J. Donaldson (Grand Rapids: Wm. B. Eerdmans, 1951)
ANRW	*Aufstieg und Niedergang der römischen Welt*, ed. H. Temporina and W. Haase (New York and Berlin: Walter de Gruyter)
APOT	*Apocrypha and Pseudepigrapha of the Old Testament*, 2 vols., ed. R. H. Charles (Oxford: At the Clarendon Press, 1912)
au. trans.	Author's translation
BDF	F. Blass, A. Debrunner, *A Greek Grammar of the New Testament*, trans. and ed. R. W. Funk (Chicago: University of Chicago Press, 1961)
IDB	*Interpreter's Dictionary of the Bible*, ed. G. A. Buttrick (Nashville: Abingdon Press, 1962)
ILL	*An Inclusive Language Lectionary, Year B* (Philadelphia: Westminster Press, 1984)
JB	Jerusalem Bible
Jung	Collected Works (CW), Bollingen Series XX (Princeton: Princeton University Press, 1954–1978)
KJV	King James Version of the Bible
LCL	Loeb Classical Library
LXX	The Septuagint (Greek translation of the Hebrew Scriptures)
NEB	New English Bible
NIV	New International Version of the Bible
NPNF	*Nicene and Post-Nicene Fathers*, ed. Philip Schaff (Grand Rapids: Wm. B. Eerdmans, 1956)
NT Apoc.	*New Testament Apocrypha*, 2 vols., ed. Edgar Hennecke and Wilhelm Schneemelcher (Philadelphia: Westminster Press, 1965)
OT Ps.	*Old Testament Pseudepigrapha*, vol. 1, ed. James H. Charlesworth (Garden City, N.Y.: Doubleday & Co., 1983)
RAC	*Reallexikon für Antike und Christentum*, ed. Theodore Klauser (Stuttgart: Anton Hiersemann, 1950–)

RSV   Revised Standard Version of the Bibl-

TDNT   *Theological Dictionary of the New Testament*, ed. G. Kittel and G. Friedrich, trans. G. W Bromiley (Grand Rapids: Wm. B. Eerdmans, 1964–74)

TEV   Today's English Version of the Bible

Introduction

One of the best ways to discern the weakness of a social system is to discover what it excludes from conversation. From its inception Christianity has not found it easy to speak about sex. Worse yet, it could not acknowledge, even privately, the continued existence of inner darkness in the *redeemed.* Because Gnosticism attempted, often in bizarre forms, to face sex and the inner shadow, it was declared heretical and driven underground, where it ironically became symbolic of the very repressed contents that it had attempted to lift up into the light. Gnosticism became Christianity's shadow.

Nineteenth-century science could not deal with the "secondary qualities" of objects—color, taste, smell, texture—or the emotions of people, which were merely subjective and not a part of the objective, analyzable world. In reaction to this arbitrary exclusion of soul from the universe, the Romantic movement attempted to redress the balance, only to lend, by its failure, an even greater sense of legitimacy to the ideology it opposed.

What does late twentieth-century Western society exclude from conversation? Certainly not sex; at least in more "sophisticated" circles accounts of sexual exploits scarcely raise an eyebrow. But if you want to bring all talk to a halt in shocked embarrassment, every eye riveted on you, try mentioning angels, or demons, or the devil. You will be quickly appraised for signs of pathological violence and then quietly shunned.

Angels, spirits, principalities, powers, gods, Satan—these, along with all other spiritual realities, are the unmentionables of our culture. The dominant materialistic worldview has absolutely no place for them. These archaic relics of a superstitious past are unspeakable because modern secularism simply has no categories, no vocabulary, no presuppositions by which to discern what it was in the actual experiences of people that brought these words to speech. And it has massive resistance even to thinking about these phenomena, having fought so long and hard to rid itself of every vestige of transcendence.

Why then trouble secular materialism by "the return of the repressed," these "spiritual hosts . . . in the heavenly places," and all their ilk, both good and evil? There are several compelling reasons. The first is that materialism itself is terminally ill, and, let us hope, in process of replacement by a worldview capable of honoring the lasting values of modern science without succumbing to its reductionism. In that emergent worldview, spirituality will be perceived as the interiority of material, organic, and social entities, as I have suggested in volume 1 of The Powers (*Naming the Powers*).

Having repressed the spiritual so long, however, we no longer have ready access to it. The wells of the spirit have run dry. We can scarcely rediscover in a few generations what it has taken the race millennia to learn by costly trial and error. So we find ourselves returning to the ancient traditions, searching for wisdom wherever it may be found. We do not capitulate to the past and its superstitions, but bring all the gifts our race has acquired along the way as aids in recovering the lost language of our souls.

A second reason for approaching these old symbols with new respect is that true individuation seems to take place only when thought, feeling and behavior are integrated around a central myth-system at the core of the self.[1] To a degree far beyond current recognition, the myth of materialism has served as such an integrating agent for modern society, but it has been an integration bought at the cost of what is most human, most aesthetic, and most meaningful in life. Alternative myth-systems are not easily come by, however. Western civilization has in all its centuries known as few as seven.[2] With the collapse of materialism, many people sense an acute spiritual hunger and are reaching out, at times blindly and in every direction, for adequate sustenance. Often, however, they react not only against materialism itself but against the Judeo-Christian myth that seems to have proven so ineffective in stemming materialism's advance. Some look to the East, not recognizing that the contents of their own unconsciouses are still to a great extent conditioned by the biblical myth. Even when insights of exquisite worth are discovered in Eastern thought, it is not possible to integrate them fully until they have found a niche in one's core myth, or until one's core myth has been altered to accommodate them. Since virtually all religions in all cultures have spoken of angels, spirits, and demons, the traditional religions are in some sense all natural allies against materialism and can mutually enrich each other. But mere spiritual nomadism—that aimless wanderlust that characterizes so much of the current ferment—will scarcely prove any more effective against entrenched, senescent materialism than Romanticism before it. Only the revitalization of a powerful countermyth, capable of incorporating the valid aspects of materialism while jettisoning the rest, will be capable of securing the "new age" that so many neoromanticists are heralding.

There is at least one more reason for dusting off these old terms and asking what they might have designated in the actual lives of real people. Teilhard de

Chardin[3] has eloquently evoked the picture of human evolution as no longer physical but social, no longer the product of random events but increasingly the consequence of choice and invention. Humanity has gradually begun to become aware of itself as an entity. Two world wars, in all their horror, illustrate this infolding of humanity upon itself, this shrinking of the world through communication, economic and military dependency, scientific cooperation and even tourism. What our century has thus far survived to witness is the staggering speedup of this socialization process. But this global totalization has been going on for several thousands of years. We see a sharp increase in critical consciousness in classical Greece, and simultaneously in Israel, India, and China. We observe the spread of Greek culture and its intersection with Israel and the East through Alexander the Great and his successors, and then the pervasive establishment and institutionalization of this culture under the Pax Romana.

Hellenization: the term has hitherto referred to the imposition of Greek culture, the collapse of the Greek city-states and their replacement by a cosmopolis, and the breakdown of traditional religions and their incorporation in religious forms and cults capable of universal vision. It is time that we also see Hellenization as a large groundswell in the rising tide of human destiny, when for the first time—in the West at least—this infolding process, due to sufficient density of population and a sufficiently universal vision of humanity, *began to be perceived.* And it was perceived the way artists and seers always perceive the dark new shapes of things—through the language of symbol. They spoke of angels, of demons, of principalities and powers, of gods and elements of the universe, of spirits and Satan. This was not simply a hangover from an even more remote antiquity. Much of this language was new, and what was not new was altered.[4] It was the amorphous, vague but descriptively accurate language of a new awareness, the awareness of powers operative *among and between people*: not transcendent like God, but higher than humans. "Intermediate beings" they seemed, and the names for them mattered little, *so long as one knew they were there.*

That rough and ready phenomenology of the infolding social dimension of reality served well for almost two millennia. Its survival and even revival today (in fundamentalism, Satan cults, tongue-speaking, visions, exorcism, and renewed belief in the devil) is testimony to both its descriptive effectiveness and its profound symbolic power. If the modern age saw fit to renounce such categories of experience, it was because they were thought to be insufficiently precise, and because their residual symbolic power was experienced not as helpful but as a tyranny. Between the use of the Satan image to excuse irresponsibility and its use to terrify people into compliance to sectarian mores, there was little left to commend it. But the modern world threw out the reality with the words, and now finds itself without an adequate vocabulary for powers even more real today than two thousand years ago, due to the ever-tightening compression of the human infolding. *Without a vocabulary*—yes, we have no single language for speaking of the total phenomenon the ancients knew as "the Powers"; but also, *too many vocabularies*—the languages of quite unrelated disciplines each vie in a Babel of technical, esoteric tongues to account for their own discrete sectors of reality. It would be my hope that as more comprehensive languages are developed for describing these intermediate powers which so largely determine personal and social existence, we will recover a degree of respect for the monumental spiritual achievement of our forebears—an achievement that we have not yet overtaken. With a proper humility, perhaps we can more soberly ask ourselves what it was that came to expression in these archaic terms, and what we might be able to learn from them today.

In *Naming the Powers* I developed the thesis that undergirds all three volumes of this work: that the New Testament's "principalities and powers" is a generic category referring to the determining forces of physical, psychic, and social existence. These powers usually consist of an outer manifestation and an inner spirituality or interiority. Power must become incarnate, institutionalized or systemic in order to be effective. It has a dual aspect, possessing both an outer, visible form (constitutions, judges, police, leaders, office complexes), and an inner, invisible spirit that provides it legitimacy, compliance, credibility, and clout.

In the ancient world people discerned and described the interiority of things by the only means available to them: symbolic projection. They were able to monitor the actual impact of the spirituality of an institution like the Roman Empire or the priesthood by throwing it up against the screen of the cosmos in the form of visual images in which the interiority of the social entity was perceived as a personal entity: an angel, demon, or devil. For many this approach still works, but at the cost of considerable mystification. The material or institutional sources of distress often escape notice while the actual spirituality is split off and fought as a separate demonic agency "in the air." Some analysts of this phenomenon have tended to debunk the spiritual as a smokescreen masking the real material determinants: the economic system, the state apparatus, the power elite. This was no doubt often the case. But a proper understanding of the dynamic of symbolic projection leads to quite a different conclusion: every economic system, state apparatus, and power elite *does* have an intrinsic spirituality, an inner essence, a collective culture or ethos, which cannot be directly deciphered from its outer manifestations (they, in fact, may be deliberate attempts to deceive people through propaganda, image making, and advertising). The corporate spirits of IBM and Gulf+Western are palpably real and strikingly different, as are the national spirits of the United States and Canada, or the congregational spirits ("angels") of every individual church. What the ancients called "spirits" or "angels" or "demons" were actual entities, only they were not hovering in the air. They were incarnate in cellulose, or cement, or skin and bones, or an empire, or its mercenary armies.

In the present volume we will be focusing on just seven of the Powers mentioned in Scripture. Their selection out of all the others dealt with in *Naming the Powers* is partly arbitrary: they happen to be ones about which I felt I had something to say. But they are also representative, and open the way to comprehending the rest. Nor are they the end of the story. For while the Powers dealt with in this volume—Satan, demons, angels of churches, angels of nations, gods, elements, angels of nature—are instances of the hidden interiority of reality, volume 3 (*Engaging the Powers*) will provide an occasion to look at some of their more visible, institutionalized forms. The list of possible candidates for examination there is virtually endless: economics, militarism, propaganda, education, language, ideologies, rules, roles, values, the legal system, politics, sports, religion, families—all of social reality falls under the category of the Powers, and a good slice of physical and psychic reality as well.

We will begin in this volume with the more immediate personal experience of evil (the devil, demons) and gradually bring into focus the issue of worldview or cosmology. It is not my intent to defend the biblical worldview, for it is in many ways beyond being salvaged, limited as it was by the science, philosophy, and religion of its age. This very relativity of the biblical cosmology to its historical epoch led many theologians earlier in our century to discount cosmology as unimportant altogether, a husk to be stripped from the kernel and cast aside. We can now see, however, that such an approach simply meant acquiescing without a struggle to the worldview of modern materialism. That uncritical capitulation is the cause in large part of the split that runs through so many religious people today, who want to hold two utterly incompatible things together: belief in God as the Creator of the world and Sovereign of the Powers, and belief in the materialistic myth of modern science, which systematically excludes God from reality.

Cosmology is not gospel. It is not the core proclamation, not the revealed truth of human existence. But cosmology certainly determines how that message can be spoken and how heard. It is not the Word made flesh, it is its cradle. But it is a very important cradle. It is not a matter of indifference that the New Testament proclamation was couched in the language, thought-forms and concepts of the Greco-Roman world, even as it poured new and finally shattering contents into them. At one level, Christian evangelists sought only to convert people, but at another, they sought to claim an epoch, to take captive an entire culture, to mediate a new way of seeing the world. They accomplished these objectives so thoroughly that the question of cosmology could be dropped from the theological agenda for fifteen hundred years. *The gospel had become its own cosmology.* With the rise of the worldview of scientific materialism, however, that cosmology became first problematic, then dubious, and finally unintelligible. And because the gospel had become indistinguishable from the cosmology in which it was couched, it faced compounded difficulties in addressing the whole life of modern people meaningfully.

What increasing numbers of people are now realizing, both inside and outside organized religion, is that Christianity's lack of credibility is not a consequence of the inadequacy of its intrinsic message, but of the fact that its intrinsic message cannot—simply, categorically, cannot—be communicated meaningfully within a materialistic cosmology. Some, sensing the irresolvable contradiction, have simply abandoned religion. Others have dismissed modern science altogether—a sacrifice of the intellect made all the sadder by the fact that modern science need not have, and never should have, wedded itself to the mechanistic images and materialistic philosophy of Democritus in the first place. Still others have attempted a desperate compromise, in blind faith that two things that seem so true, science and religion, must be finally reconcilable, even if it is not yet evident how.

This book attempts to go beyond these alternatives. It is not simply a commentary on New Testament cosmology, though that is inevitably our starting point, but an attempt to contribute toward a new, postmaterialist cosmology, drawing on biblical resources. I will not argue that all of the Powers featured in this volume are equally weighted in Scripture. Satan holds a prominent place in most of the books of the New Testament, but demons are more frequently encountered in the Synoptic Gospels, and gods, elements, and the angels of nature, nations, and the churches make only infrequent appearances. It is not my purpose to argue that they were central aspects of the gospel. What I wish to argue, however, is that recovery of these concepts and *a sense of the experiences that they named* can play a crucial role in eroding the soil from beneath the foundations of materialism. At the same time they can provide a language for naming these experiences in the new worldview that is emerging. Just as the materialist paradigm cannot tolerate the mere *possibility* of ESP, clairvoyance, psychokinesis, or spiritual healing, even when scientific evidence is piled up in their favor, so it cannot account for the kinds of spiritual experiences identified by the traditional terminology of Satan, demons, gods, and angels. It is precisely their incompatibility with the dominant scientific mind-set, their incomprehensibility within its rubrics, that makes these biblical categories so important today. They are a scandal, a stone of stumbling, a bone in the throat of modernity. They represent a worst-case test of its capacity to give an account-ing of the whole compass of human experience. Properly understood, they expose the soft underbelly of a philosophical system which has attempted to banish God from the earth; and not God only, but all spirits from the earth; and not spirits only, but our own spirits as well.

More intimately, a reassessment of these Powers—angels, demons, gods, ele-ments, the devil—allows us to reclaim, name, and comprehend types of experi-ences that materialism renders mute and inexpressible. We have the experiences but miss their meaning. Unable to name our experiences of these intermediate powers of existence, we are simply constrained by them compulsively. They are never more powerful than when they are unconscious. Their capacities to bless us are thwarted, their capacities to possess us augmented. Unmasking these Powers can mean for us initiation into a dimension of reality "not known, because not looked for," in T. S. Eliot's words. In the new world of quantum physics and the new sciences of life and consciousness, these antiquated, repudiated, and neglected Powers can open new awareness of the richly textured plenitude of life, its abysses as well as its ecstasies. The goal of such unmasking is to enable people to see how they have been determined, and to free them to choose, insofar as they have genuine choice, what they will be determined by in the future.

We are living through a watershed period intellectually, a vast sea-change in the metaphors with which we describe and make our home in the world. This work is but one of many that are questioning the adequacy of the materialist metaphor and groping for its replacement. As is so often the case with things that are new and thus have no history of failures, there is in many of these attempts a naive utopianism, as if all that is faulty is the old metaphor and not me. Such approaches lack seriousness about the intractability of evil, and believe that education, or meditation, or a new worldview, or an ecological atti-tude, or the application of science to human values, is all that it will take to bring in a time of peace and plenty. Once again, the deep wisdom of the past must figure in the emergence of the new, or else we will be consigned to repeat or even augment the evils of the past.

One note on method. In attempting to recover the inner meaning of the first-century worldview, one is not limited to New Testament texts. Virtually any scrap of papyrus, however dubious its literary or religious value, can help us recover the basic cosmology of the epoch. A cosmology is quite different from ideas, beliefs, or opinions. It represents the largely unconscious assumptions and shared images held by parties on *all* sides of a debate. It is enshrined in their presuppositions and premises, not their declared convictions. There is scant reference to the angels of nature in the Bible, for instance, but they abound in the intertestamental writings and in later Christian apocalypses, and where they are mentioned (in the Book of Revelation), the references are so offhand as to make it clear that they are assumed to be part of the background belief of the age. My preoccupation with noncanonical literature should not be construed as lack of commitment to canonical Scripture. On the contrary, I have the highest regard for canon—so high, in fact, that I refuse to elevate any part of it, such as the indubitably Pauline writings, to implicit supremacy as the "canon-within-the-canon," as so many scholars do, or to write off Colossians or Ephesians, Hebrews or Revelation as irrelevant because they might be un-Pauline.

The real test of the canon of Scripture is whether it has the power, in each new age, to evoke life, to strike fire, to convey the stark reality of God's hunger to be known. This book is a wager, taking the worst of odds, by virtue of the very alienness of its subject matter, that Scripture still has that power.

1. Satan

Nothing commends Satan to the modern mind. It is bad enough that Satan is spirit, when our worldview has banned spirit from discourse and belief. But worse, he is evil, and our culture resolutely refuses to believe in the real existence of evil, preferring to regard it as a kind of systems breakdown that can be fixed with enough tinkering. Worse yet, Satan is not a very good intellectual idea. Once theology lost its character as reflection on the experience of *knowing* God, and became a second-level exercise in *knowing about,* the experiential ground of theology began to erode away. "Although mythologically true," Morton Kelsey writes, "the devil is intellectually indefensible, and once it was realized that the conception of the powers of evil was 'only' a representation of peoples' experience, no matter how accurate, the devil began to fade. . "

> With only sense experience and reason to go on, and with no rational place for an evil first cause, enlightened people simply dropped the devil from consideration. With direct psychic experience no longer admissible as evidence of his reality, the devil was as good as dead.[1]

Nor is this picture essentially altered by polls that show belief in Satan to be sharply on the increase. As we shall see later, such belief is most frequently a component of neurotic religion, and the remarkably subtle character of Satan is collapsed into a two-dimensional bogeyman that has only vague similarities with the biblical devil. The Satan image, even where it lingers on, has been whittled down to the stature of a personal being whose sole obsessions would seem to be with sexual promiscuity, adolescent rebellion, crime, passion, and greed.[2] While not themselves trivial, these preoccupations altogether obscure the massive satanic evils that plunge and drive our times like a trawler before an angry sea. When television evangelists could try to terrorize us with Satan and then speak favorably of South African apartheid, we should have sensed something wrong. When the large evil went undetected, when the symbol no longer attracted to the fact, when evil ran roughshod through corporate boardrooms and even churches, unnoticed and unnamed, while "Satan" was

9

relegated to superego reinforcement and moralistic scare tactics, then we should have caught the stench—not of brimstone, but of putrefaction. Not that we had progressed beyond evil. On the contrary, *the evil of our time had become so gigantic that it had virtually outstripped the symbol and become autonomous, unrepresentable, beyond comprehension.*

We had killed Satan. For those who never mourned his passing, who even met it with relief, I offer this awkward and perhaps unwelcome parody, pilfered (satanically) from any number of poets:

> Killed Satan!
> Hardly the words are out
> before we notice the sky has darkened,
> not into perpetual night,
> but into unending grey.
>
> Satan dead!
> and we scarcely even missed him,
> that old tempter with whom we toyed
> and lost, enjoying the thrill of transgressing
> *something* that could be transgressed.
> Now, without Satan,
> Where's the thrill?
>
> So Satan is gone!
> And now how will we recognize evil
> before it has us already in its maw?
> How will we know we have crossed the boundary,
> beyond human return,
> without Him there to say,
> "Oh, come on across."
>
> Every point gives vertigo,
> we reel, dizzy and sick,
> every spot on earth a mount of temptation,
> without a tempter, without bounds,
> with no stakes left, nor obedience,
> nothing but survival into that grey,
> never-ending, dawnless day.

While the symbol may have fallen on hard times, the reality to which it gave expression has become all the more virulent. Satan did not begin life as an idea, but an experience. The issue is not whether one "believes" in Satan, but whether or not one is able to identify in the actual events of life that dimension of experience the ancients called "Satan." Nor is the metaphysical question, Does Satan really exist? of any real urgency, unless the question is asked in the context of an actual encounter with Something or Someone that leads one to posit Satan's existence.

Without a means of symbolization, however, evil cannot come to conscious awareness and thus be consciously resisted. Like an undiagnosed disease it rages through society, and we are helpless to produce a cure. *Evil must be symbolized precisely because it cannot be thought.*[3] Is there any way we can resymbolize evil? Thought cannot resuscitate Satan, but only committed persons consciously making choices for God, as we will see. But thought can perhaps roll away the stone. Then perhaps, if we can live through that dark interval between Satan's death and resurrection, we may yet see Satan functioning again—as a servant of the living God!

Satan as a Servant of God

We are not accustomed to thinking of Satan as God's servant. But when Satan makes his late appearance in the Old Testament, that is precisely what he is.

The faith of early Israel actually had no place for Satan. God alone was Lord, and thus whatever happened, for good or ill, was ascribed to God. "I kill and I make alive," says the Lord, "I wound and I heal."[4]

So it was not inconsistent to believe that Yahweh might call Moses to deliver Israel from Egypt and then, on the way, attempt to murder him. The text, much neglected by preachers, is Exod. 4:24–26a. "On the journey, when Moses had halted for the night, Yahweh came to meet him and tried to kill him. At once Zipporah, taking up a flint, cut off her son's foreskin and with it she touched the genitals of Moses. 'Truly, you are a bridegroom of blood to me!' she said. And Yahweh let him live" (JB). Perhaps Moses had fallen critically ill, or had been almost killed by an attack or fall or avalanche, or had somatized his terror at the enormity of his task. In any case, the attack was ascribed, not to natural causes, but to God.[5]

The God who led Israel out of Egypt, however, was a God of justice. How then could God demand justice, be just, and still cause evil? Had not Abraham challenged God with the question, "Shall not the Judge of all the earth do right?" (Gen. 18:25)? This problem was the terrible price Israel had been forced to pay for its belief that Yahweh was the primary cause of all that happens. Morally, the cost was unbearable. Gradually Yahweh became differentiated into a "light" and a "dark" side, both integral to the Godhead, with Yahweh transcending both as the unity that encompasses multiplicity.[6] The bright side came to be represented by the angels, the dark by Satan and his demons.

Yet this process of differentiation was completed so late that Satan makes only three appearances in the Old Testament.[7] In 2 Sam. 24:1 Yahweh in anger against Israel had incited David to carry out a census (the basis of taxation and military conscription). But in Chronicles, a postcaptivity revision of Samuel and Kings, this same passage is changed to read, "*Satan* stood up against Israel, and incited David to number Israel" (1 Chron. 21:1). The Adversary has assumed the function of executor of God's wrath. Satan is an *agent provocateur* who plants oppressive ideas in a mortal's mind. He does not represent disorder, chaos, or rebellion here, but rather the imposition of a suffocating bureaucratic order (the census). Satan furthers God's will by visiting wrath on disobedient mortals, and in so doing carries out the will of God.

In Zech. 3:1–5 we find "the satan" in the role of accuser or prosecuting attorney.

> Then he showed me Joshua the high priest standing before the angel of the Lord, and Satan (*ha satan*) standing at his right hand to accuse him. And the Lord said to Satan, "The Lord rebuke you, O Satan! The Lord who has chosen Jerusalem rebuke you! Is not this a brand plucked from the fire?" Now Joshua was standing before the angel, clothed with filthy garments. And the angel said to those who were standing before him, "Remove the filthy garments from him." And to him he said, "Behold, I have taken your iniquity away from you, and I will clothe you with rich apparel." And I said, "Let them put a clean turban on his head." So they put a clean turban on his head and clothed him with garments; and the angel of the Lord was standing by.

The scene is set in the heavenly council, with the accuser at the right of the accused, Joshua.[8] The high priest, representing the whole people of Israel, is dressed in filthy garments, symbolic of the sins that Israel's prophets had identified as the cause of Israel's exile in Babylon. The vision is dated around 520 B.C.E.; this means that upward of three generations of Jews had lived with the belief that they had gone into captivity in 585 as punishment for their infidelity to Yahweh. Joshua bears all that collective guilt.[9] The Adversary merely reiterates what the accusing conscience of the people has been affirming all along. The guilt is real, and it is deserved. Only God's undeserved grace causes the case to be quashed.

Satan is clearly not demonic here. If anything, Satan echoes what everyone knows to be the attitude of *God* toward Israel, prior to God's unexpected reversal of the judgment. Satan merely repeats what the prophets had been saying all along! Nevertheless God intervenes. Israel is a "brand plucked from the fire"; it will be consumed by guilt and succumb to hopelessness unless it experiences forgiveness soon. Satan is thus not merely a mythological character invented out of whole cloth; the "adversary" is that actual inner or collective voice of condemnation that any sensitive person hears tirelessly repeating accusations of guilt or inferiority. And indeed, there is often a degree of truth in the charges.

But Satan's demand for strict justice, untempered by mercy, can crush the spirit of a person or a people. This "voice" is a phenomenological fact;[10] its mythic conceptualization makes it possible to isolate it, lift it to consciousness, and ask whether it is indeed the voice of God.

The final Old Testament reference to Satan is in the prologue to Job. "Now there was a day when the sons of God (*bene elohim*) came to present themselves before the Lord, and Satan (*ha satan*) also came among them." Here again, Satan is not a fallen angel but a fully credentialed member of the heavenly court. "The Lord said to Satan, 'Whence have you come?' Satan answered the Lord, 'From going to and fro on the earth, and from walking up and down on it.' " His role is somewhat like that of a district attorney, zealously seeking out law-breakers to bring before the bar of divine justice. "And the Lord said to Satan, 'Have you considered my servant Job, that there is none like him on the earth, a blameless and upright man, who fears God and turns away from evil?' " Satan has indeed considered him well: "Then Satan answered the Lord, 'Does Job fear God for nought? Hast thou not put a hedge about him and his house and all that he has, on every side? Thou hast blessed the work of his hands, and his posses-sions have increased in the land. But put forth thy hand now, and touch all that he has, and he will curse thee to thy face.' And the Lord said to Satan, 'Behold, all that he has is in your power; only upon himself do not put forth your hand.' So Satan went forth from the presence of the Lord" (Job 1:6–12).

This is more than simply prosecution, however. It is entrapment. Not content merely to uncover injustice, Satan is here, as in 1 Chron. 21:1, an *agent provocateur,* actively striving to coax people into crimes for which they can then be punished. Excessive zeal for justice always becomes satanic. All Job's oxen, asses, camels, sheep, and servants are slain; then finally all his sons and daugh-ters. Yet Job holds piously to his faith (1:21).

When next they meet, God chides Satan for his failure: Job " 'still holds fast his integrity, although you moved me against him, to destroy him without cause' " (2:3). What kind of God is this, that trifles with the lives and flesh of human beings in order to win a bet? This God is too bent on sheer power to mark the sufferings of mere people. The author seems to be deliberately lifting up the God of a degenerate Deuteronomic theology to ridicule. That God (represented by Job's three "comforters"), who rewards the wealthy landed aristocrats with riches and long lives and curses the poor, is the butt of a merci-less lampoon that issues from the outraged sensibilities of a writer who has acutely observed how the oppressed and infirm suffer undeserved evil at the hands of the powerful and rich. Those God has not blessed, who have no such vast herds and spacious houses, but barely subsist on the land, must relish seeing this rich man stripped of his props and reduced to their level. And they must have chuckled with delight at the storyteller's artful repetition in 2:1–3, where God behaves like a forgetful potentate unable to recall the job description of his own appointee![11]

Job's Satan, in short, while no friend of Job's, is in fact humanity's best friend, who lures God into a contest that will end by stripping *God* of the projections of the oppressors. Satan has already persuaded God to act arbitrarily ("to destroy him without cause"). Now Satan compounds the murder of Job's children with the torture of Job's own body: " 'Put forth thy [!] hand now, and touch his bone and his flesh, and he will curse thee to thy face.' And the Lord said to Satan, 'Behold, he is in your power; only spare his life' " (2:5–6).

In all this Satan manifests no power independent of God. Even when Satan slays, it is not Satan who does so, but God who slays through Satan ("the fire *of God*," 1:16; "you moved me against him," 2:3; "put forth thy hand," 2:5). God alone is supreme; Satan is thoroughly integrated into the godhead in a wholly nondualistic fashion. Satan is not evil, or demonic, or fallen, or God's enemy. This adversary is merely a faithful, if overzealous, servant of God, entrusted with quality control and testing. Satan, in fact, prompts God and humanity (in the person of Job) to explore the problem of evil and righteousness at a depth never before plumbed—and seldom since.

These three passages exhaust the references to Satan in the Old Testament, and even in these Satan is more a function ("the adversary") than a personality. It is only in the period between the Testaments, and even more in the period of the New Testament and early church, that Satan gains recognition. Soon he will become known as the Enemy of God, the Father of Lies, the Black One, the Arch-Fiend, and assume the stature of a virtual rival to God. We will come to all that. But first we must do justice to those passages in the New Testament where Satan continues to function as a servant of God. So accustomed are most of us to thinking of Satan as purely evil that we tend to read this interpretation into passages where there is nothing of the kind. If we suspend that bias, the evidence points toward a strikingly different picture.

Luke 22:31–34. Jesus is speaking: " 'Simon, Simon, behold, Satan demanded to have you [plural], that he might sift you [plural] like wheat, but I have prayed for you [singular] that your [singular] faith may not fail; and when you have turned again, strengthen your brethren.' And he said to him, 'Lord, I am ready to go with you to prison and to death.' He said, 'I tell you, Peter, the cock will not crow this day, until you three times deny that you know me.' " Satan is God's sifter, the left hand of God, whose task it is to strain out the impurities in the disciples' commitment to God. Had Peter been fully conscious of his frailty and flightiness, he would never have responded with such bravado. Had he been able to say, "Yes, Lord, I am weak and impulsive; pray for me to stand through this trial," perhaps such sifting would not have been necessary. But it is clear that nothing Jesus has been able to do has weaned him or the rest from egocentricity. Satan has made a legitimate request; they deserve to be put to the test. *Jesus has to grant Satan's request.* He does not pray that they be delivered from the test, but only that their faith may not fail through it. *Satan is depicted here as able to accomplish something that Jesus had himself been unable to achieve during his ministry.* If we refuse to face our own evil, and take refuge, like Peter, in claims to righteousness, our own evil comes up to meet us in the events triggered by our very unconsciousness. Satan is not then a mere idea invented to "explain" the problem of evil, but is rather the distillate precipitated by the actual existential experience of being sifted. When God cannot reach us through our conscious commitment, sometimes there is no other way to get our attention than to use the momentum of our unconsciousness to slam us up against the wall. Heavenly jujitsu, practiced by God's "enforcer," this meat-fisted, soul-sifting Satan—servant of the living God![12]

1 Corinthians 5:1–5. A man in the Corinthian church is sleeping with his step-mother. Paul writes:

> Let him who has done this be removed from among you.
> For though absent in body I am present in spirit, and as if present, I have already pronounced judgment in the name of the Lord Jesus on the man who has done such a thing. When you are assembled, and my spirit is present, with the power of our Lord Jesus, you are to deliver this man to Satan for the destruction of the flesh, that his spirit may be saved in the day of the Lord Jesus.

This reads uncomfortably like a text from the Spanish Inquisition. Is the man to be ritually murdered?[13] The language is extreme, but apparently Paul only means that they should excommunicate him (5:2, 13), thus forcing him to choose between his sexual preoccupation and his faith in Christ. Destruction of the "flesh" would then refer, not to his body, but as is usual in Paul, to the whole life-orientation that his actions betray him to be mired in, body, soul, and spirit: a world reduced to the limits of sensual gratification. Satan is to work him over through the choice forced upon him by the act of ceremonial exclusion (and possibly shunning), "that his spirit might be *saved*"—at least on Christ's return, but possibly, through Satan's good offices, rather immediately.

Apparently the man did repent, for 2 Cor. 2:5–11 seems to relate the outcome of the punishment. Ironically, however, the very congregation that had tolerated his sin as an expression of Christian freedom from the law now refuses to forgive him and receive him back. And the same Paul who chastised them with the full force of his spiritual authority now must plead with the congregation to forgive and comfort him lest he be overwhelmed by excessive sorrow.

Such self-righteous, judgmental behavior manifests the very qualities we saw associated with Satan in Zech. 3:1–5. Their new-found zeal for justice is as overweening and one-sided as their previous indifference. Paul wants to "keep Satan from gaining the advantage over" them (2 Cor. 2:11), an advantage that would be won, not through their tolerance of sin, but by their refusal to forgive!

Satan's role here is remarkably fluid. Satan is again God's holy sifter. Using the momentum of the man's sin, Satan casts him into the annealing fire of a solitude in which he is given precisely what he thought he wanted—and absolutely nothing else besides. But the choice could have gone either way. Had he chosen for the woman and against the church, Satan would have appeared to have been the instrument of his damnation.

Again, if the church had refused to tender its forgiveness to the man, Satan would have caught them in a charade of self-righteousness, thus "gaining the advantage over us" (2 Cor. 2:11). By refusing to forgive, the church plays the role of Satan in Zechariah 3, reiterating an accusation that God is prepared to drop Satan is thus not an independent operative, but rather *the inner and actual spirit of the congregation itself when it falls into the accusatory mode.* So Satan cannot be described here as "good" or "evil." It is *our choices* that cause him to crystallize as the one or the other.

And most astonishing of all, Paul does not say that Satan enticed this man to sin; rather, Satan is the means of his deliverance! This understanding of Satan has little in common with the irremediably evil Satan of popular Christian thought.

1 Timothy 1:20. The writer of 1 Timothy says (in the name of Paul) that he has delivered the heretics Hymenaeus and Alexander "to Satan that they may learn not to blaspheme." Apparently the writer does not mean that he has damned them to hell for eternal punishment. He really seems to expect them to learn to stop blaspheming and return to the fold. Once we acknowledge that Satan is a devoted servant of God, the meaning is transparent: these men, like the fellow in 1 Corinthians 5, are to be excommunicated in order to force them to recover a sense of "conscience" (1:19) and abandon their libertine ways.[14]

Matthew 4:1–11 (Luke 4:1–13). Jesus has just left his baptism where he has heard God declare him his beloved son. The dovelike Spirit that came upon him there now leads him out into the wilderness "to be tempted by the devil." What kind of collusion is this? Why, if he needs testing, does the Spirit not provide it? Why place him in ultimate jeopardy by throwing him into the hands of Satan? It makes no sense at all—if Satan is evil personified. But if he is the heavenly sifter, the setter of choice, then we have a different story altogether.[15]

"And the tempter came and said to him, 'If you are the Son of God, command these stones to become loaves of bread.' " What is so wrong about that? Later he will feed the five thousand. The fast of forty days has ended (*"afterward* he was hungry," v. 2); now he must eat or die. If he could demonstrate such power to meet the basic needs of the masses, surely he could generate an instant following. Moses had cried to God and God had sent manna to the people of Israel; how much more ready should God be to perform mighty works on behalf of Jesus? People would recognize him as the New Moses, the prophet of the end time, the deliverer of Israel, and flock to his banner.

Jesus refuses. Is it because such acts violate the nature of the "Father" revealed to him at his baptism? Or is it because of that sticky "*if* you are the Son of God," with its taunt to prove his sonship by a miracle?—an act that could only prove his mistrust. For whatever reason, he turns the temptation aside by means of Deut. 8:3. He will not live by bread alone, but "by every word that proceeds from the mouth of God." He will live by what God says, and God had said at his baptism, "Thou art my beloved son."

Nothing exposes one to temptation more dangerously than a successful rebuff of temptation. Satan seizes upon the very answer as the next temptation. You mean to live by every word that proceeds from the mouth of God? Very well, then, here is one such word. "*It is written,* 'He will give his angels charge of you,' and 'on their hands they will bear you up, lest you strike your foot against a stone' " (Ps. 91:11–12). Put God to the test. Trust God's promises. "If you are the son of God, throw yourself down" from the pinnacle of the temple in Jerusalem. Surely the courtyard will be teeming with people. They will instantly recognize in such an amazing rescue God's stamp of approval on the Chosen One of God.

What could be appealing to Jesus in such a suicidal fantasy? He is being tempted to prove himself invulnerable, indestructible, a superhuman being immune to the threat of death. Having just forsworn the shortcut of feeding the masses, what guarantee has he that God will protect his life on the more difficult path of making disciples? He has received an immense calling; what will become of his mission if he is prematurely killed? Will God intervene to guarantee his survival until he has accomplished his task?

This temptation takes place at the temple, where Malachi had prophesied that the Lord would suddenly appear to cleanse it of pollution and purify the priesthood (Mal. 3:1–4). Is he perhaps called to be the Priestly Messiah who would restore true worship in Israel?

Jesus again refuses. "Again it is written, 'You shall not tempt the Lord your God.' " To live by what one has heard from God does not mean biblical proof-texting. It means listening to what God says to us about the specific life-tasks to which we are called. The word of God must be found and heard among all the welter of voices of Scripture, tradition, creed, doctrine, experience, science, intuition, the community; but God's word is none of these alone, or perhaps even all of them together. Jesus is being nudged by God toward a new, unprecedented thing, for which no models existed. No one else could have helped advise him. Scripture itself seemed loaded in the opposite direction—toward messianic models of power, might, and empire. The dominant image was—but let Satan say it:

> Again, the devil took him to a very high mountain, and showed him all the king-doms of the world and the glory of them; and he said to him, "All these I will give you, if you will fall down and worship me." (Matt. 4:8–9)

Satan is offering him the kingdom of David, grown to the proportions of world empire. Scripture was rife with this hope. Israel seethed with longing for some form of its fulfillment. Jesus could not but have internalized that desire: free-dom from Roman oppression, restoration of God's nation, the vindication of Yahweh's honor. This is no bald seduction. What is Satan tempting him with here and in each of these "temptations," if not *what everyone knew to be the will of God?* Mosaic Prophet, Priestly Messiah, Davidic King—these were the images of redemption which everyone believed God had given them in Scrip-ture. (And in no time at all they would be the titles given Jesus by the church: Prophet, Priest, and King.) What irony: everyone in Israel knew the will of God for redemption—except Jesus. He was straining with every nerve to hear what it was *as if he alone did not know it.*

And Satan's function in all this? He is no archfiend seducing Jesus with offers of love, wealth, and carnal pleasures. Satan's task is far more subtle. He presents Jesus with well-attested scriptural expectations which everyone assumed were God's chosen means of redeeming Israel. Satan throws up to Jesus the collective Messianic hopes, and by so doing brings them for the first time to consciousness as options to be chosen rather than as a fate to be accepted. Tested against his own sense of calling, they did not fit. Jesus could perceive them to be "yester-day's will of God," not what was proceeding out of the mouth of God.

Satan offers him, in short, not outright evils but the highest goods known to Israel. That is when the satanic is most difficult to discern—when it offers us the good instead of the best. That does not mean Satan is benign. By no means! We have so moralized him that we fail to see that the most satanic temptation of all is the temptation to become someone other than ourselves. When people try to "be good Christians"—what is that but Satan's crowning victory? For "being a good Christian" is always collectively defined by some denomination or strong religious personality or creed. One does not need to "live by every word that proceeds from the mouth of God" in order to be a "good Christian"; one need only be pliant, docile, and obedient. Is it not easier to "let Jesus do it all for us," or imitate Christ, rather than embark on the risky, vulnerable, hazardous journey of seeking to find God's will in all its mundane specificity for our own lives? That harder way will certainly entail mistakes and failures, false starts, and sin masquerading as innovation. Perhaps the collective way is better—but what am I doing, my friends? With whose voice am I speaking?

So Satan again appears to be a strange servant of the living God. When Jesus is depicted as leaving the wilderness and moving "with a sure, fierce love towards Galilee,"[16] he does so not so much knowing who he is and what he will do, as who he is not and what he will not do. The rest will emerge through interruptions (most of the stories in the Gospels are accounts of interruptions), through listening, through being true to the baptismal voice as the entelechy of his being. As Rivkah Schärf Kluger puts it, "The human will becomes conscious through its collision with the divine will, by coming up against the adversary. Thus, behind the deadly threat of the divine opposition there is also hidden a positive, purposeful aspect; the adversary, as such, is at the same time the creator of individual consciousness."[17] In short, the conscious devil is useful; the unconscious devil is perilous.

John B. Cobb, Jr., has defined the eternal Logos (the divine Word) as the lure that attracts us to "that specific actualization which is the best outcome for the given situation."[18] Held up against the divine Logos, Satan here would represent the lesser lures and promptings that appear alongside the lure of the highest. Some of these lures are flagrantly evil; most are not intrinsically evil but merely trivial, less than best: a diversion, a waste. In another situation or for another person they might in fact represent the "will of God"—the persuasive call to creative transformation. But here, now, with this person or event, they would mean a diminishing of the potential for creative novelty in the world, a regression to collective tendencies, a settling for an old novelty that has exhausted its creative strength—in short, *yesterday's will of God*.

Satan, our adversary, is the one who puts the question at the leading edge of possibility—right at the place where the creative potentiality can be suffocated. The issue then is what we bring to the encounter. If we relate to choice unconsciously, it can become for us "evil" (even if our choice is, as so often for Christians, to be "harmless"). But if we bring consciousness to choice, along with commitment to doing God's will in the situation, Satan serves us and God by bringing to consciousness those unconscious roles and expectations that prompt so much regressively habitual action.[19] Related to properly, Satan can be the centrifuge by means of which what is not essential to selfhood or society is precipitated out. Satan is not gentle; if we relate to him unconsciously we can be destroyed. Satan plays for the highest stakes of all, but for those who bring the light of the image of God to the struggle for choice, Satan is "Lucifer," light-bearer—a very brilliant servant of God.

Am I belaboring the point? I shall labor even more, to rectify two millennia in which Satan has been so persistently maligned. Satan served Paul personally, caught as Paul was in his own proclivities for boasting, as the next text shows.

2 Corinthians 12:1–10. "And to keep me from being too elated by the abundance of revelations, a thorn was given me in the flesh, a messenger of Satan, to harass me." Three times he asked God to remove it; the third time God spoke: " 'My grace is sufficient for you, for my power is made perfect in weakness.' " Did Paul *need* a disability in order to combat a pride too powerful for him to master? We cannot even begin to guess what his "thorn" was; what is clear is that what might have been merely a satanic affliction is made, by Paul's faithfulness in confronting it, a means by which his own chronic tendencies to inflation were continually kept in check. How kind of Satan to assist—as he is always ready to do—when we cannot consciously let some part of our egos die![20]

1 Corinthians 7:5. Some couples in the church at Corinth are abstaining from sex. Paul responds: "Do not refuse one another except perhaps by agreement for a season, that you may devote yourselves to prayer; but then come together again, lest Satan tempt you through lack of self-control." Satan operates like a thermostat: when a husband and wife have abstained from sex for the sake of prayer for too long, temptations arise, signaling that piety has become foolishness, and that conjugal relations should be resumed, "lest Satan tempt you through lack of self-control." It is worth noting, as Trevor Ling points out, that Satan is depicted here as having to wait until we present him with an opportunity, and that *not sexuality but an abnormal abstinence from it* provides the satanic occasion.[21] The image of a thermostat is especially pertinent, because Satan seems to operate at both extremes, and acts as a negative constraint prepared to exploit both our ascetic silliness and our libertine excesses.

Ephesians 4:26–27. "Be angry but do not sin; do not let the sun go down on your anger, and give no opportunity to the devil." Note this: the anger is not caused by the devil. The author regards it as absolutely essential, even going so far as to *command* his hearers to express it: "Be angry."[22] But one must then deal with it, and not let it sink into the unconscious, where it can connect up with all sorts of autonomous complexes and balloon into a murderous wrath. We work with our anger consciously, or else the devil works evil by means of it. There is no escape from anger, either way. How sharply this contrasts with the belief of so many people that anger *itself* is satanic, rather than how we *deal* with it.[23]

James 4:7. "Submit yourselves therefore to God. Resist the devil and he will flee from you." This is not the devil of popular fantasy, that virtually omnipotent enemy of our race. This devil knows his place! St. Ignatius Loyola understood this with clinical precision. "It is the nature of our enemy to become powerless, lose courage, and take to flight as soon as a person who is following the spiritual life stands courageously against his temptations and does exactly the opposite of what he suggests. On the contrary, if a person begins to take flight and lose courage while fighting temptation, no wild beast on earth is more fierce than the enemy of our human nature as he pursues his evil intention with ever increasing malice."[24] In short, *we* elicit Satan's demonic aspect by our refusal to face the regressive alternative he poses.

Jude 8–9 (2 Peter 2:10–11). In light of all this, we should not revile Satan. "But when the archangel Michael, contending with the devil, disputed about the body of Moses, he did not presume to pronounce a reviling judgment upon him, but said, 'The Lord rebuke you' " (see Zech. 3:2). Some lost legend lies behind this, alluded to in the *Assumption of Moses:* When God sent Michael to bury the body of Moses, the devil laid claim to it on the ground that Moses had murdered the Egyptian.[25] Here again Satan is characterized by an excessive zeal for strict, merciless justice. Michael calls on God to rebuke Satan, not because Satan is evil, but because he is a legalist.

Nevertheless, Michael shows respect, unlike the "revilers" in Jude's church, for Satan has a thankless job which should not be made more miserable by vilification. Or, as the writer of Ecclesiasticus put it with deep psychological insight, "When the ungodly curseth Satan, he curseth his own soul" (21:27).[26] For it is not Satan's fault when we refuse to learn from the dark side of God about the dark side of ourselves.

Do not unfairly revile Satan. When one rabbi preached that Satan acts only from the highest motives, the Talmud relates, Satan came and kissed his feet in gratitude (*T. B. Baba Batra* 15b–16a)! When one has the task of God's enforcer, prosecutor, sifter, *agent provocateur,* tester, presser of choice, catalyst of consciousness, advocate of strict justice, and guardian of the status quo, though one be ever so faithful a servant of the living God, one gets little appreciation.

This aspect of Satan as God's servant is stated with wonderful simplicity in the following dialogue between Sidney Harris and his daughter:

My little nine-year-old girl said to me, "Daddy, there's something peculiar about the whole story of God and the devil and hell. It just doesn't hold together." "Oh," I said, "and why doesn't it hold together?" "Well," she continued, "God is supposed to love good people, and the devil is supposed to favor bad people. Right? The good people go to God, but the bad people go to hell, where the devil punishes them forever. Isn't that the story?" When I agreed that it was, she continued, "It doesn't make sense. In that case, the devil couldn't be the enemy of God. I mean, if the devil really was on the side of the bad people, he wouldn't punish them in hell, would he? He'd treat them nicely and be kind to them for coming over to his side. He'd give them candy and presents and not burn them up." "You've got a point," I said. "So how do you work it out?" She thought for a moment, and then she asserted, "It seems to me that if the whole story is true, then the devil is secretly on the side of God, and is just pretending to be wicked. He works for God as a kind of secret agent, testing people to find out who's good or bad, but not really fighting against God." "That's remarkable!" I exclaimed. "Do you think there's any proof?" "Well," she concluded, "here's another thing. If God is really all-powerful, no devil would have a chance against him. So if a devil really exists, it must be because he's secretly in cahoots with God!"[27]

But there is another side to Satan, one more familiar to most of us, and far more chilling. How did Satan pass from being God's servant—to God's enemy?

Satan as the Evil One

Already we have seen Satan in his role of *agent provocateur* (1 Chron. 21:1; Job 1—2; Matt. 4:1-11 par.). A curious feature of such agents all through history is the way they tend to overstep their mandate. Recall in this connection the activities of the FBI in instigating murders that it ostensibly existed to prevent. Viola Liuzzo was gunned down during the civil rights struggle by an undercover FBI informer, and anti-Vietnam war groups were infiltrated and incited to violence by FBI operatives. The FBI even deceived a succession of U.S. Presidents by withholding data on the John F. Kennedy assassination and setting illegal wiretaps in an attempt to blackmail Martin Luther King, Jr. The FBI director, J. Edgar Hoover, also appears to have acted against his own chief executives by keeping blackmail files on presidents in order to prevent them from firing or retiring him. Add to this revelations about the clandestine activities of the CIA, and we find ourselves possessed of a secret and virtually autonomous government within the government which threatens the very basis of our democratic system.

The comparison is particularly apt, for Satan also seems to have evolved from a trustworthy intelligence-gatherer into a virtually autonomous and invisible suzerain within a world ruled by God. The original model for the figure of Satan may actually have been the oriental spy, who in the absence of a state police apparatus served as a "mobile inspector," the "eyes and ears" of the king.[28] The prologue of Job had already portrayed Satan as capable of causing sickness, catastrophes, pillage, and death. It would not take the popular imagination long to turn this free operative into "the god of this world" (2 Cor. 4:4).

Another element in Satan's transformation from a servant of God into the epitome of evil was the need for a more adequate explanation of the origin of evil. The story of the fall of Adam and Eve simply could not account for *undeserved* evil, such as that rained on Job. Nor could the figure of Satan as God's tester render noneducative or nonredemptive sufferings intelligible. The sheer massiveness of evil in the world pointed to a more malevolent source than the isolated infidelities of puny human beings. The ancient allusion to a "fall" of the angels through their intercourse with women (Gen. 6:1–4) provided the seedbed of a whole new species of ideas about evil that proliferated wildly and finally narrowed to that of Satan and his fallen angelic hosts.[29]

These elements: the overzealous *agent provocateur*, the fall of the angels, and the later, postbiblical myth of Satan's fall, have formed the backdrop for Christian understandings of Satan. They have been augmented by other New Testament passages so familiar that they scarcely need elaboration. Satan is called "the devil" (a *false* accuser, slanderer, calumniator), "the evil one,"[30] "the ruler of this world,"[31] "the prince of the power of the air,"[32] "Belial,"[33] "Beelzebul,"[34] "the god of this world,"[35] "the Destroyer,"[36] "a murderer from the beginning,"[37] and "the enemy."[38] These are titles virtually unknown to Pharisaic Judaism.[39] According to this strain of New Testament imagery, Satan is the chief of the demons,[40] who prevents shallow people from hearing the gospel.[41] He binds people in prison[42] or under disease,[43] hinders Paul in his journeys,[44] provokes lies,[45] attempts to destroy the church,[46] and enters into Judas in order to lead him to betray Jesus.[47] He is the father of unbelieving Jews.[48] All pagans are under Satan's power; their worship of idols is really worship of Satan.[49] God will (or has) cast Satan out of heaven[50] and will chain him in the bottomless pit and later burn him in unquenchable fire.[51] Jesus encountered these aspects of Satan in the collective messianic expectations, in the possession of demoniacs, in the defection of Judas, as a regressive pull against consciousness, as a dynamic agency that seized upon the personalities even of the disciples, and as a will to destroy God's emergent purpose.

It would be difficult to develop a systematic picture from all this. Some of it is plainly repugnant: there is a straight line from John 8:44 (you Jews "are of your father the devil") to the persecutions and pogroms directed at Jews by Christians; and the scorn with which "pagan" religion is regarded in these passages will haunt us into the future.

There is a terrible splitness in these images of Satan as evil. Satan appears to have virtually no relationship with God, serves no redemptive functions, not even negatively, and strains the outer limits of the notion that there is but one ultimate, benevolent Reality in the world. But there is also something existentially accurate here. For Satan's fall did in fact take place, not in time or in the universe, but in the human psyche. Satan's fall was an archetypal movement of momentous proportions, and it did indeed happen every bit as much as the Peloponnesian War, but it happened in the collective symbolization of evil. "The whole world is given over to the evil one" (1 John 5:19, au. trans.): Satan has become the world's corporate personality, the symbolic repository of the entire complex of evil existing in the present order.[52] Satan has assumed the aspect of a suprapersonal, nonphysical, spiritual agency, the collective shadow, the sum total of all the individual darkness, evil, unredeemed anger, and fear of the whole race, and all the echoes and reverberations still vibrating down through time from those who have chosen evil before us.

The image of Satan is the archetypal representation of the collective weight of human fallenness, which constrains us toward evil without our even being aware of it. It is a field of negative forces which envelops us long before we learn to think or even speak, and fills us with racial, sexual, and role stereotypes as if they were indubitable reality itself. Satan is "the god of this world" (2 Cor. 4:4) because we human beings have made him god as a consequence of willfully seeking our own good without reference to any higher good, thus aligning our own narcissistic anxiety with the spirit of malignant narcissism itself. But since narcissism is antithetical to the needs of a harmonious and ecological universe, Satan has become, by our practice of constantly giving over the world to him, the principle of our own self-destruction.

When in Luke 4:6 Satan declares that he can give Jesus all the kingdoms of the world and their glory, he is not lying; "for it has been delivered to me, and I give it to whom I will." God *permits* Satan such power, but has not handed it over to him; *we have delivered it,* as a consequence of all the consciously or unconsciously evil choices we have individually and collectively made against the long-range good of the whole. Satan thus becomes the symbol of the spirit of an entire society alienated from God, the great system of mutual support in evil, the spirit of persistent self-deification blown large, the image of unredeemed humanity's collective life.[53]

All this runs the risk of personifying Satan, however, and personification was the subtle poison by which Satan's theological assassins did him in. Personification is too rationalistic to deal with archetypal realities. It merely uses the word "Satan" as a shorthand sign for a cluster of ideas—ideas that could fare quite well without the name.

If Satan has any reality at all, it is not as a sign or an idea or even an explanation, but as a profound *experience* of numinous, uncanny power in the psychic and historic lives of real people. *Satan is the real interiority of a society that idolatrously pursues its own enhancement as the highest good.* Satan is the spirituality of an epoch, the peculiar constellation of alienation, greed, inhumanity, oppression, and entropy that characterizes a specific period of history as a consequence of human decisions to tolerate and even further such a state of affairs.

We are not dealing here with the literal "person" of popular Christian fantasy, who materializes in human form as a seducer and fiend. The Satan of the Bible is more akin to an archetypal reality, a visionary or imaginal presence or event experienced within. But it is more than inner, because the social sedimentation of human choices for evil has formed a veritable layer of sludge that spans the world. Satan is both an outer and an inner reality.

It is not then a question of whether we "believe" in Satan or not, but of how the archetypal and/or social reality of evil is currently manifesting itself in persons and in society. Perhaps we should distinguish between the *archetypal images of Satan* that are served up in actual encounters with primordial evil (what M. Scott Peck calls the extraordinarily willful spirit of malignant narcissism[54]), and the *theological use of the term* "Satan" for speaking about such experiences and reflecting on their meaning. "Belief" in Satan serves only to provide a grid that one can superimpose on the actual experiential phenomenon in order to comprehend it, and even then the wrong kind of belief in Satan may do more harm than good, since it is usually so one-sided.

But the phenomenon itself is there, named or unnamed. We wake up screaming, terrified by an image in a dream.[55] We watch our feet walking straight into acts which we consciously know risk everything we most value over the long haul. We encounter a landlord who deliberately attempts to blow up an apartment building full of tenants by opening a gas main in order to end their rent strike. Or we hear of a teenager trying to get off drugs whose "friends" spike her candy with a fatal dose. Here the issue is not whether there is a metaphysical entity called Satan, but how we are to make sense of our actual experiences of evil. In that sense, Satan is an archetypal image of the universal human experience of evil, and is capable of an infinite variety of representations.[56] The archetype itself is unfathomable; the primordial power of evil is as much more than our images of it as God is more than our images of God.

If some literal-minded person were to pick up the jargon of Transactional

Analysis and conclude that there "really is" a being designated by the term "the negative parent," that would probably parallel what has happened to Satan: the name given to the personal reality that *functions* as an accuser, slanderer, inner critic, was granted metaphysical status as an actual being. This worked fine as long as the metaphysical entity was still experienced as an aspect of the process of living. Once the experiential dimension was lost, however, Satan became a "being" in whom one was free to believe or disbelieve, quite apart from the phenomenology of everyday life. That is why in this study I am relatively uninterested in the metaphysical question, Is there a Satan? If we do not encounter the experience that came to be named "Satan," we really have no further need for the word.

Beliefs about Satan are matters of debate. The experience of Satan is a brute and terrifying fact. A couple very dear to us lost their ten-year-old son to cancer after a heroic and utterly devastating nine-month fight. Some time after the death they went to the beach to try to restore themselves from the ordeal. One night, on the ninth floor of the hotel, the husband had this dream: He was standing by a great bog. He knew it was his own inner evil, and that he couldn't run from it, so he just jumped in. With that he woke up. As he lay there at two in the morning, a voice said to him, "Why don't you go to the balcony and jump?" My friend said no, thinking he must still be dreaming. But the voice insisted. "Go ahead, you won't hurt yourself. You'll land in the trees; they'll break your fall." He got up, went to the bathroom, dashed water on his face, trying to break out. He went back and sat on the edge of the bed. The voice assailed him again. "You can jump to the swimming pool." No, I'd never make it, and anyway, the nearest part is the shallow end. "But if you jumped you would see your son." At that moment a vision of his dead son seemed to hang in the room. For the first time the idea of jumping became appealing. He resisted, and the voice began to scream: "Jump! Jump! Jump!" relentlessly. Then it got very quiet. "Why don't you just go out and sit on the balcony?" This went on for more than two hours. Finally, he woke his wife and asked her to hold him. The moment she did, the assault ceased.

No doubt such an experience is susceptible to a variety of explanations. The satanic voice could be interpreted as the "voice" of a part of this man that felt defeated and despairing after the long and futile struggle for his child's life. Or it could be considered an external malevolent power attempting to exploit a father's grief as a way of destroying him. The problem is that this question cannot in principle be settled, and from a phenomenological point of view need not be. Whether Satan be located inside or outside, what matters is that the experience actually happened and could have led to suicide. What this man experienced as "Satan" was an actual force of evil craving annihilation, however it be conceived, and is far more pervasive in human experience than most people are aware.

Where does this life-quenching power come from? Why does it desire murder (the devil is "a murderer from the beginning," John 8:44)? Why does it seek to suck us down into feelings of worthlessness and despair ("Beliar," one of Satan's names, is a corruption of *Belial*, "worthless," 2 Cor. 6:15)? To this day I know next to nothing about the devil, despite all that I have heard and read. Yet I am familiar with the voice of that "slanderer." It is the voice that whispers to us, just when we most need to marshal all our abilities in order to perform an important task, "You're no good, and you never will be any good." "You're not smart enough, you'll never succeed in this job." "You deserved this, you had it coming, this is what you get." "You're ugly, fat (or skinny), and unlovable." Do you recognize that voice? It is the voice that railed at Joshua, smearing him with Israel's guilt in Zech. 3:1–5. No doubt it gains leverage from every flaw, every grain of remorse, every impossible perfectionist demand and unachievable ego ideal we lay upon ourselves, and flays us with them. These are all aspects of the unreality we have embraced, and by our own connivance in illusion we give life to "the real spirit of unreality"[57] and deserve to be worked over by it until we dare to face the truth. Satan could well prove to be God's servant in such a role. But this does not explain the sheer destructiveness, the wanton hatefulness of this "voice." It wants to persuade us that we ought to die—not in order to overcome the illusions of the ego or to liberate us from perfectionism, but simply to exterminate us. The fact that in some this voice is raucous and shrill, and in others scarcely even heard, indicates that the structure of the individual personality or the extremity of the circumstances has a great deal to do with its effectiveness.[58] But does that mean that Satan is a product of our neuroses, or does Satan gain entry by means of them?

This "spirit of worthlessness" tells lies, and is the father of lies (John 8:44), because in God's sight we are precious, beautiful, beloved, of infinite worth, and gifted with untapped potentialities of almost infinite reach. We ourselves are totally responsible for whether we listen to this spirit or not. Once we know—really know personally, existentially—of God's inexhaustible love for us, then this voice only continues to have whatever power we choose to give it.

And yet, where does all this resistance in us come from? Where do we get this ineffable magnetic attraction toward non-being, toward human diminution, toward being a fraction of ourselves? Whence this imploding black hole in moral space, sucking up life and energy and giving back no light whatever? Freud himself finally posited a *Thanatos* (death) instinct to account for it; it would have been as scientific to have called it Satan.

I am oppressively aware of the hazards involved in labeling things satanic; yet there are some evils too horrendous to be labeled otherwise. And naming something correctly can sometimes help us see it in the right light. When we label the nuclear arms race satanic, for example, we realize that the struggle is not between the administrations in Washington and Moscow, but that *both are on the same side.*

Whether we call it death or evil, Satan or the satanic, there seems to be some irreducible power which cannot finally be humanized, cured, or integrated, but only held at bay. And it is never more diabolical than when it has become linked in a pact with human beings. "We are driven to conclude that the Devil too would incarnate in and through man."[59] There is a concentration of evil in a directional pull counter to the will of God. And however intolerable it is when encountered personally, its manifestations are most disastrous when they are social.

There is something sad in the moralistic tirades of fundamentalist preachers terrifying the credulous with pictures of Satan lurking in the shadows, coaxing individuals to violate rules which are often enough satanic themselves and deserve to be broken, while all the time ignoring the mark of the cloven hoof in economic or political arrangements that suck the life out of *whole generations* of people. The media have made a sensation out of a few rare cases of possession of pubescent youth, with no comprehension whatever of Satan's grip on our entire civilization. Why should Satan reveal himself more often in individual cases, when he can, from invisibility, preside over an entire global culture that spreads out over the whole surface of the planet like a cancer: a civilization that systematically erodes traditional religions, that treats people as robots for producing and serving things, that denies not only the spiritual but even the poetic, the artistic, the inner, that propagates belief in the ultimate power of money, and that organizes an economic system exploitative of most of the peoples of the world and anchored in a permanent war economy?

Liberal Christianity has so reacted against the misuse of the Satan-image in fundamentalist circles that it has tended to throw out the notion altogether. The absence of any really profound means of imaging radical evil has left us at the mercy of a shallow religious rationalism that is naive, optimistic, and self-deceiving. We need not return to medieval superstition in order to appreciate the power of the Satan-image, *not* as an explanation of evil—for Satan explains nothing—but as a way of keeping its irreducible malignancy before our eyes.

How are we to evaluate, for example, the proposal first conceived by J. D. Bernal in 1929 and renewed by D. E. Wooldbridge,[60] that the brain of a living human being be removed and rehoused in a short cylindrical container that not only would keep it alive but whose apparatus the brain itself could direct? This being would be a completely effective mentally directed person "mechanized for science rather than for aesthetic purposes." Through such technology Bernal looked forward to a time when the masses would be kept in "a perfect docility under the appearance of perfect freedom."[61] There is no indication that he himself planned to submit to the operation; he would be needed to direct all these automatons in the proper actions.

How can scientists of such stature even conceive of such things? Because, says Wooldbridge, he and his kind are "strongly attracted by the idea of a lawful universe," in which "all we can observe or feel is caused by the operation of a set of inviolable physical laws upon a single set of material particles." We must, he argues, abandon even the small vestige of claim to human uniqueness left to us by the discoveries of Galileo and Darwin, and know ourselves to be nothing but machines. This is the price we must pay, he says, "for a world view in which all human experience is lawful and orderly."[62]

Wooldbridge seems to feel no twinge of regret at having become dehumanized, and even fewer compunctions over surgically dismembering some living person's brain. (The experiment has already been successfully performed on animals.) As the physicist Walter Heitler warns, "When once we have got to the stage of seeing in man merely a complex machine, what does it matter if we destroy him?"[63]

No doubt the vast majority of scientists simply passed this off as absurd. But it is worse than absurd. Bertrand Russell was able to name it rather precisely. He called this kind of misuse of science devil-worship. Noting that we seek knowledge of an object either because we love it or desire power over it, Russell observed in 1949 that in the development of science the power impulse has increasingly prevailed over the love impulse. As physics has developed, it has deprived us step by step of what we thought we knew concerning the intimate nature of the physical world. "Colour and sound, light and shade, form and texture . . . have been transferred from the beloved to the lover, and the beloved has become a skeleton of rattling bones, cold and dreadful." Thus, reasoned Russell, "disappointed as the lover of nature, the man of science is becoming its tyrant." More and more, science has "substituted power-knowledge for love-knowledge and as this substitution becomes completed science tends more and more to become sadistic."

Russell was therefore apprehensive about the desirability of a society controlled by science. He thought it probable that its sadistic impulses would in time justify more torture of animals and humans by surgeons, biochemists, and experimental psychologists. "As time goes on," he warned, "the amount of added knowledge required to justify a given amount of pain will diminish." In short, *"the power conferred by science as a technique is only obtainable by something analogous to the worship of Satan, that is to say, by the renunciation of love.*"[64]

It is not my intention to single out science as satanic. I am profoundly grateful for many of its discoveries, and not a little awed by its competence. My choice of Bernal and Wooldbridge as examples is largely arbitrary; we could easily have focused instead on human or animal torture, or the pesticide or tobacco industries, or the nuclear arms race.

Indeed, a nuclear holocaust would beggar every other evil imaginable. How could Satan benefit from such a catastrophe? Whitehead once described evil as "the brute motive force of fragmentary purpose, disregarding the eternal vision."[65] As the principle of fragmentation, Satan can never achieve the totalization of evil it desires; there is a contradiction built into the very nature of evil that prevents it from ever gaining complete ascendancy. The whole is too harmonious in its foundations and fabric, and evil must always be conceding too much to the good, since it must mimic the good and pass itself off as desirable in order to win adherents. But a nuclear holocaust—that is as close as we could come to totalizing fragmentation.

"We"? Did I say "we"? When we tear away the mask from Satan, do we then find—ourselves? Have we, after all, breathed life into this image and kept it alive by our continually stoking the fires of Armageddon? Does that mean then that there is a retrogressive pull in us that fears the creative possibilities of self-transcendence, and which would finally blow everything up to avoid *that* pain? Is it our own willful refusal of abundant life that has turned Satan from a servant into a monster? Was this our counterattack on God, whereby we seduced God's seducer and won him to our side? Must Satan then after all be redeemed, freed, delivered—not from his own overweening pride, but from *ours?*

Satan as Chameleon

Satan has been called a snake. Better he had been called a chameleon. For Satan is never quite the same from moment to moment, but changes his colors according to circumstances. How Satan appears to us will then be at least in part a function of how *we* have responded to the choices set before us. If we drift with the collective roles and expectations, or yield to regressively instinctual behavior, or are caught in egocentric strategies for self-aggrandizement without reference to the whole, or actually opt for what we know to be wrong, we augment Satan's power as a force for evil. We reinforce the sheer bulk of collective unconsciousness and shadow that presses down on events, and help to set off a train of consequences that can only wreak evil on ourselves and others. If, however, we respond to choice with a conscious commitment to creative transformation, if we use the encounter with the voice of the shadows as an occasion for self-discovery and pruning, if we are willing to risk the uncertain path of seeking God's will, and to allow our egos to undergo the mortification necessary to allow the greater self to emerge, then Satan appears as God's Servant, and even our mistakes and wrong choices can become the catalysts of our transformation (Rom. 8:28).

All that is true on the individual level. But the history of evil does not begin with us. We enter a world already organized for evil. The satanic is already crystallized in the institutional values and arrangements in which we find ourselves. The victims of the bombings of Hiroshima and Hamburg and the Plain of Jars were not fully responsible for the evil they suffered. Africans seized by slavers or forced into townships were not faced with a choice between the good and the better, but between death-in-life and death. There are evils that God can redeem; Solzhenitsyn goes so far as to assert that no great literature can exist apart from suffering.[66] But there are events of torture, psychosis, suicide, and violence for which there is no apparent redemption this side of the grave. There are experiences, to be sure, when we encounter Satan as sifter. But there are others in which we come face to face with an evil so raw, so malevolent, so unredeemable, that Jesus could only counsel us to pray to be delivered from the encounter.[67] But this then raises the question: How can these two poles be held together within one godhead, without splitting it into an absolute dualism?

Earlier we saw that Israelite religion originally had no place for Satan. God alone was the source of everything, good or ill. As Yahweh was ethicalized, good and evil were differentiated within the godhead, and Satan became the prosecuting attorney in the heavenly council. This idea seems wholly incompatible with the later notion of Satan as God's Enemy, who possesses no apparent redeeming functions whatever. Yet it was only this latter tributary that emptied into mainstream Christianity. Diagrammed, the development would look something like this:

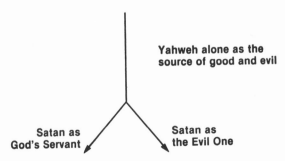

Yahweh alone as the
source of good and evil

Satan as
God's Servant

Satan as
the Evil One

It would be tempting to conclude that what we find here are two competing and mutually exclusive interpretations of Satan, and to opt for one or the other on the basis of personal theological preference. But that easy solution is denied us by the fact that the early church seems to have seen some inner connection between the contrary views, for *both representations of Satan appear in the same document or from the hand of the same author.*

Servant	*Evil One*
Luke 22:31	Luke 10:18; 13:16; Acts 5:3; 13:10; 26:18
Matt. 4:1–11 par.	Matt. 12:24–29 par.
1 Cor. 5:1–5; 7:5 (Paul)	1 Thess. 2:18; 2 Cor. 11:14–15 (Paul)[68]

This duality is nowhere more vivid than in Luke's version of the temptation narrative, where Satan simultaneously claims (with sufficient empirical justification) to have authority over all the nations, and yet serves, in the very act of revealing this fact, to bring Jesus to awareness of other alternatives (Luke 4:1–13).

Perhaps then we should think of a continuum:

Satan **as** ◄	**our**	► **Satan as** **the**
Servant	**choices**	**Evil One**

and of our responses to the satanic occasion as the determining factor in how Satan is constellated. When we combine this continuum with the following schema of historical development, the apparent contradiction would appear to be resolved.

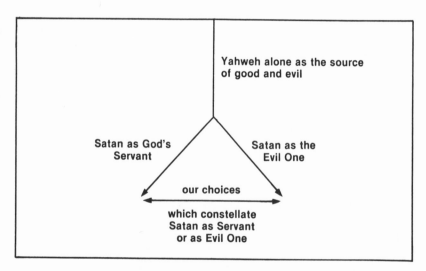

This would help to account for Satan's incredible pliability ("and no wonder, for even Satan disguises himself as an angel of light," 2 Cor. 11:14). He can be described by one writer as "the suspended superego," the seducer into sin (the psychologist David Bakan[69]), and by another as the polar opposite: the harsh superego, the voice of condemnation, the rigorous legalist who lashes and flails us with laws which, in some cases, should never have been decreed (Norman O. Brown[70]). No doubt both are right. One moment the devil lures us to boundlessness, the next to moralistic rigidity. We all know him as licentious; he can also be a pursed-lipped prude. In Bishop Bossuet's words, he follows the current of our inclinations and presses us and overthrows us on the side to which he sees we are leaning.[71]

The difficulty then lies precisely in discerning God's will in a field where Satan appears prepared to suit up for either team. But precisely that is his service: *Satan prevents our presuming, on the basis of theology, Scripture, tradition, custom, reason, science, instinct, or intuition, that we can know the will of God, apart from listening acutely for every word that proceeds from the mouth of God.* Hence the shock of those who had prophesied and cast out demons and done stunning miracles, all in Christ's name, when he turns to them and declares, " 'I never knew you; depart from me, you evildoers' " (Matt. 7:22–23). They were doing what "everybody knows" is the will of God. But they had not consulted God. They had substituted activity for a relationship. Perhaps God intended something quite different for them, and they had never stopped to listen.[72]

That is why we must never attempt to straitjacket Satan in rigid doctrinal categories. Satan is not a fixed, unnuanced figure. The tendency of some Christians to regard Satan as unambiguously evil breeds a paranoid view of reality. It justifies the demonizing of opponents. It prevents our loving our enemies. It legitimates violence against those whom we regard as irredeemably evil. It conceals from us our own shadow and our ambivalence toward evil. The rejection of Satan altogether by others has scarcely worked better. It induces blindness to the radicality of evil, trivializes the struggle for conscious choice, and drives the satanic underground, converting the unconscious into a cesspool of erupting nightmares.

Perhaps in the final analysis Satan is not even a "personality" at all, but rather a function in the divine process, a dialectical movement in God's purpose which becomes evil only when humanity breaks off the dialectic by refusing creative choice. Whether one "believes" in Satan is thus not nearly as important as that one recognizes the satanic function as part and parcel of every decision.[73] Occasionally people (yes, still today—though they are not likely to tell you about it) encounter the satanic in dreams, auditions, apparitions, or visions. The image of Satan can be male or female, a supernatural power, a monster, or a pulsing blob of energy. We recognize the satanic, however, not by conventions of dress (the familiar red suit and horns), but by the numinous, dreadful, uncanny terror the image evokes. Even such experiences have an "as if" quality, however; they are not literal representations of Satan but archetypal images appropriate to the aspect of Satan we are encountering on any given occasion.

When we fail to bring a committed ego to struggles for choice, and yield ourselves to compulsive gambling, or to overeating or drinking, or to sexual promiscuity, or to compliance with corporate directives we know are unethical—then to a degree we place ourselves in the power of autonomous complexes in the psyche or idolatrous institutions in the world. We do their bidding and are at their mercy, and as the popular expression says, "the Devil made us do it." But this is only because we have delivered ourselves straight into his hands. When we fail to make conscious, committed choices for God, we default on our "dominion" over the world, and Satan becomes like a holding company that has taken over billions of mortgages in arrears through foreclosure. The satanic is actualized as evil precisely by our *failure* to choose, and has no more power than we continue to give it. Hence it would be truer to say, "*We made the devil do it*"![74]

We do not "create" Satan by our choices, however. Satan is an autonomous spirit that rises out of the depths of mystery in God. But by our choices we *do* determine which side Satan is on.

Origen was condemned as a heretic for arguing that Satan might finally be redeemed.[75] His humanitarian impulses certainly deserve respect, but that way of putting things leaves the real issue buried in eschatological myth. The truth of what he was saying is that *we must redeem Satan,* by bringing conscious, committed choice to the encounter. Only thus can Satan be freed from the sheer burden of unconsciousness, shadow and projection that an irresponsible humanity has laid on him.[76] *We made Satan evil. Only we can restore him to his rightful role at God's left hand.*

Evil is finally irrational. Our attempts to comprehend it are an odd mix of pastoral sensitivity and intellectual anxiety. Perhaps I have long since overspoken, and the only appropriate stance is silence before the mystery. But I must risk one more observation. Milton, in his *Paradise Lost,* portrayed Satan as such a complex, rebellious, Promethean spirit that despite all the punishments a just heaven might rain down on him, the readers' secret sympathies could scarcely help being attracted to him. Milton's God, by contrast, is a bit boring, too busy being Almighty to be very interesting. What got left out was the complexity and wiliness of *God.* Perhaps then we should distinguish four "moments" in the manifestation of the divine in reference to Satan:[77]

1. God as God
2. God as "Satan"
3. Satan as "God"
4. Satan as Satan

The unequivocal revelation of God or Satan in experience (1 and 4) is unambiguous, however much it may still require interpretation. The problem arises in distinguishing the second from the third. A great deal that is creative or innovative is initially resisted as evil, and God's new creation is rejected as the work of the devil (God as "Satan"). When Jesus turned aside the current messianic roles as satanic, and began to act on the basis of just those words that were proceeding from the mouth of God, the authorities declared him an enemy of God. When he cast out demons and declared this to be a sign of the inbreaking kingdom, he was accused of being in cahoots with Beelzebul.[78] When he unmasked the evil of those blinded by the efficient normality of a satanic world, they said he was mad,[79] or possessed by demons.[80] When he declared sins forgiven he was called a blasphemer,[81] and when he violated the Sabbath he was damned as a law-breaker.[82] When he treated women as equals,[83] or took children seriously,[84] or ate with taxgatherers, or identified himself with harlots,[85] how else could others regard him but as "satanic"?—*as long as they accepted the world as it was*. The God beyond god—that reality that lures us to ever greater creative transformations in order to liberate life to its fullness—instigates what those who obey "the god of this world" can only regard as evil.

In such a time, what is of Yahweh and what is of Satan becomes devilishly hard to unravel. Where are we experiencing evil disguised as the divine? Where are we experiencing the divine perceived by everyone as evil? How can we discern the difference? The struggle is most redemptive when if one enters it fully committed to discovering and doing the will of God to the very limit; that is, to seeking the creative transformation latent in the situation in which one finds oneself at any given moment. It is the "satanic" aspect of God's will—justice, mercy, and truth misperceived as evil by the Powers That Be—that constitutes the threat and, simultaneously, the effectiveness of nonviolent civil disobedience. It is what produces horror among the "godly" when those whom they have judged outside the pale—blacks, Hispanics, gays—recognize their humanity and clamor for equal rights and recognition. It is this "satanic"-seeming aspect of the divine call that paralyzes our moral nerve when the question is raised about *our* joining a picket line outside a nuclear weapons plant, or going to jail for our beliefs. For how can we be certain that the voice we call "God" is not rationalized rebelliousness, or an unredeemed power complex, or an egoistic passion for publicity?[86]

For Satan can also masquerade as God, and with so many masks (2 Cor.

11:14)! William Blake made the classic statement of the problem of Satan as "God":

> Man must and will have Some Religion: if he has not the Religion of Jesus, he will have the Religion of Satan, and will erect the Synagogue of Satan, calling the Prince of this World, God, and destroying all who do not worship Satan under the Name of God. Will anyone say, "Where are those who worship Satan under the Name of God?" Where are they? Listen! Every Religion that Preaches Vengeance for Sin is the Religion of the Enemy and Avenger and not the Forgiver of Sin, and their God is Satan, Named by the Divine Name.[87]

Blake is not talking about Satanism (more on that shortly) but about Christian churches that behave satanically under the banner of Christ. To his criterion for discerning satanic "Christianity" we might add these: hostility toward those who are different; projecting evil out on others who are then demonized; claiming doctrinal certitude; breeding psychic dependency, unconsciousness, stagnation, fear, guilt, or hatred; depicting God as a monster (as in ascribing the death of loved ones to God). Satanic Christianity can be rigidly legalistic or morally slack—in either case substituting its view of morality for a living relationship with the God revealed by Jesus. But these are characteristics of much of what passes as Christianity![88]

The cost involved in the ethicalization of Yahweh was, as we saw earlier, the differentiation of "the Adversary" as an agent of divine justice and wrath. When, under the impact of apocalypticism, Satan became increasingly evil, the tendency to split Satan off altogether from the godhead became acute. Only if Satan's role as Evil One could be held in tension with his role as Servant could a genuine dualism be averted. In the history of Christianity, unfortunately, that tension snapped, and Satan became virtually an evil, rival God.

No such parallel development took place in Pharisaic Judaism in the same period, so we must ask what it was in the unique constitution of Christian faith that led to Satan's becoming so evil. Perhaps, as Jung has argued,[89] the identification of Jesus as the Christ who is all goodness and light led to a conception of God so bright-sided that the earlier complementarity of good and evil within God was obliterated, and Satan had to be pressed into service as the polar opposite of Christ, an antidivine force bent on destruction, sucking goodness and light into the abyss of everlasting night.

Justin Martyr (d. 165 C.E.) marks the turning point in that development. In Justin's theology, Satan was made responsible for every kind of evil in the world. Heretics are inspired by him; pagan rites that appear to be similar to Christian ones (baptism, eucharist), far from drawing from the same archetypal well, are conceived of as satanic parodies to confuse unbelievers. Satan is the cause of the persecution of Christians, the father of magic, the source of lust, the prince of demons.[90]

Something has gone wrong with the Christian archetype of God. Satan is now virtually autonomous from God. All paganism is diabolical; pagan gods are demons; demons operate in dreams. Evil, having been excluded from the now "perfect" godhead, is driven into the unconscious. Dreams, those oracles of *God* in the Old Testament,[91] now become instruments of Satan, and the archetypal images cast up in sleep (the "gods") are devilish. No more clear statement of the collective psyche of Christendom would ever be articulated, though the split would continue to widen for two centuries.

Those Gnostics who sensed intuitively what was happening and reacted by stressing the dark side of God, or sexuality, or the feminine, were driven beyond the pale. *Gnosticism now became the Christian unconscious,* and would erupt in every century (the Catharii, the Albigensians, witchcraft, satan worship). This repression of the dark side accounts for the remarkable voyeuristic quality in treatises on Satan, from the early theologians until today. Writer and reader alike are titillated by the "return of the repressed" under the safe guise of a pious exposition of Satan's perfidies. Indeed, Epiphanius (d. 403) was so awash with unconscious fascination with the forbidden evils of the gnostic groups he wrote to refute that the editors of the *Nicene and Post-Nicene Fathers* refused to translate his exhaustive and deliciously obscene descriptions of the Gnostics' licentious practices. A great deal of his *Refutation of All Heresies* was, at an unconscious level, pornographic.

By the High Middle Ages, many people seem to have regarded the devil as a more insistent reality than God. Abbot Richalm of Schöntal (early thirteenth century) had the gift of seeing demons. He saw them everywhere. They swarmed his monastery, interfered with devotions, caused the Abbot to nod and sleep in the choir, provoked the celebrant to wrath or indignation just before the hour of mass, or caused troublesome thoughts, snorting, coughing, or spitting. They plastered up the ears so that the brothers could not hear the reading of the monastic Rule.[92] All one's personal resistances, ambivalence, shadow, and unbelief are here conveniently repressed, projected, and reappear as hallucinated powers exterior to and other than the self, so that one need take no responsibility for or work on them directly. The spiritual life amounts to reinforcing repression and fighting the demons in the open field.

Witchcraft also reflects this peculiar split in the Christian psyche, aggravated by an even more basic split: the repression of women. One constant feature of the "confessions" of "witches" (almost invariable under torture) was the priests' insistence that they elaborate in great detail about their "intercourse" with

Satan. It does not take advanced training in psychoanalysis to catch the scent of voyeurism here. By projecting on witches their own desires for illicit sex, these (celibate) inquisitors could live out in fantasy their own repressed desires while at the same time keeping them in check by the severity of the penalty visited upon their victims.

There is another side to witchcraft, however. Once God had been split off into "good" only, and Satan had been made totally evil, it was inevitable that certain people would gravitate toward the worship of the one side and not the other. To women who were denied access to power, especially to ordination to the priesthood, or who were not willing to suppress their sexuality, or who were rebellious against male authority, or who hated God for a particular evil suffered ostensibly at God's hands, or were angry at the church, or frustrated at the inability to use their talents except at "women's" work, or greedy to the point of selling their souls to the devil in return for success, or who wanted revenge over a rival or a love potion for a lover, witchcraft and Satan worship represented an attractive gesture of defiance to a patriarchal God and to a male-dominated society. And it provided a means of seizing power against them.[93] Besides all that, much of what was called witchcraft was simply the underground continuation of immemorial fertility cults, now shaped and colored in reaction to the dominant Christian religion.

It is in this context that we must view the surprising revival of Satan cults today. At least a part of their appeal derives from a reaction against the "God" of Christendom. Satanists do not doubt God; they *hate* God. But the "God" they hate is in certain respects deserving of hatred, insofar as the God-image has been used by moralistic Christians as a kind of introjected police power to censure and stifle aspects of peoples' own authentic creativity. In reaction to Christianity, Satanism is a kind of adolescent rebellion, a decomposition product of repressive Christianity. Its very one-sidedness, its sheer *dependence* on God to fuel its discontents, prevents it from ever achieving autonomy. For that reason Satan cults experience a high rate of turnover and a serious problem with backsliders, who simply outgrow the stage of rebellion and move on to something else.[94]

Satanism also is a continuum. Its milder form is represented by Anton LaVey, who has capitalized on the "Playboy" mentality and franchised a middle-class Satanist "denomination" that practices enough ritual sexuality to make it exciting and yet affirms a negative form of the golden rule (do not do unto others what you do not want done to you) to garner a certain respectability and stave off chaos.

The extreme forms of Satanism, however, involve the conscious, deliberate identification with evil as an act of religious devotion. Adolescent rebellion against God can be a necessary and freeing moment in a person's life-journey toward the God beyond the gods. But those who freely choose to embrace, worship, and surrender themselves to raw, senseless evil become the instruments of a primordial elemental force in themselves and the universe which has been darkened by millennia of wrong decisions, and which now, like a great blob of protoplasm constantly fed by the effluents of society, represents a power so horrendous that the very future of the planet hangs in the balance.

Satan's End

Origen's desire to see Satan redeemed at the final consummation was far more generous than the usual visions of Satan's eternal punishment. We have to hold the myth open to the possibility of Satan's conversion in order to honor the divine gift of freedom and the hope of the ultimate reconciliation of all things. But historical experience suggests a far more pessimistic climax. The degree of human commitment and consciousness necessary to redeem Satan is hard to envision as happening. Yet without such a response, how can we speak of the reign of God coming at all?

Perhaps the whole matter should be approached a different way. One of the climactic visions of the Book of Revelation (20:10) may provide the very clue we need:

> And the devil who had deceived them was thrown into the lake of fire and brimstone where the beast and the false prophet were, and they will be tormented day and night for ever and ever.

This represents a second attempt at a final solution to the problem of evil. The first had been to chain Satan for a thousand years in the bottomless pit, "that he should deceive the *nations* no more." Satan's heart has always been in international politics. "After that he must be loosed for a little while" (Rev. 20:3). The image of being chained in the bottomless pit could scarcely be more clearly one of psychological repression: out of sight, out of mind. And, as with all unconscious repression, it does not last: "He must be loosed."

That is what makes the second attempt so remarkable, both as a symbol of the achievement of individuation in John of Patmos, and of the sublimation of evil into the godhead. For this time Satan will not be consigned to the pit—which is precisely where repressive Christian theologies have tried to keep him—but to the lake of fire. The question that has not been asked is, *Where* is this lake? The assumed answer has been, In the underworld. But that is where Satan was consigned the first time around, and that did not work. A search through Revelation supplies the answer: those who worship the Beast "shall be tormented with fire and brimstone *in the presence of the holy angels and in the presence of the Lamb"* (Rev. 14:10). And where are they? Right before God's throne. The lake of fire bubbles and spews in the very presence of God! The lake of fire is nothing less than the sea of glass "mingled with fire" that stands before the throne of God (Rev. 4:6; 15:2). Satan and his unredeemed hosts crackle in the fires, not of the deep unconscious, where they inevitably must explode with volcanic fury (see what happens after Satan emerges from the bottomless pit in Rev. 20:7–10!), but in the fires of the heavenly throne room itself, visualized as the heavenly counterpart of the Jerusalem temple.

> And I saw what appeared to be a sea of glass mingled with fire, and those who had conquered the beast and its image and the number of its name, standing beside the sea of glass with harps of God in their hands. And they sing. . . . (Rev. 15:2–3a)[95]

What do these symbols mean? The satanic energy here burns in a perpetual transformation of satanic libido into heavenly passion (fire).[96] If Satan is not so much a person, a being, a metaphysical entity, as a function in the divine economy, then the issue is not the inhuman torture of Satan as a person, but the transformation of Satan as an archetype. Does this not represent for the godhead what Freud declared to be the goal of all analysis: to move from the unconscious repression of negative elements to the integration of what can be redeemed and the *conscious repression* of what cannot?[97] The craving of the addict may never be healed, but the addiction itself can be stopped. Inappropriate sexual desires may never cease, but their expression can be checked. The sense that one is unlovable, unworthy, or inadequate may never fully disappear, but we can refuse to let that drive us to perfectionism, despair, or overwork. Satan sublimated, burning forever in the lake of fire, the crystal sea: transformation comes not through the denial and repression of our evil, but by naming it, owning it, and lifting it up to God.

In our own selves, this faithfully portrays the goal of all our striving: to face our own evil as courageously as we can; to love it into the light; to release the energy formerly devoted to restraining it; and to use that energy for the service of life. But there is also a residue of evil that can neither be cured nor integrated nor humanized. *That* we can only bring before God to be burned forever (for it never burns up altogether; it is in fact a kind of fuel), trusting God to transform even our irredeemable evil into fiery light.

> And all shall be well and
> All manner of thing shall be well
> When the tongues of flame are in-folded
> Into the crowned knot of fire
> And the fire and the rose are one.[98]

2. The Demons

Satan is not an independent agent. He has his own satanic host. He is "the prince of demons." Demons, however, are the drunk uncle of the twentieth century: we keep them out of sight. Modern psychiatry had explained them all away as primitive approximations of mental illnesses now more exactly named, if not, arguably, better treated, by modern drugs and therapies.

Then, just when everyone thought demons were finished, William Peter Blatty's novel and later movie, *The Exorcist,* catapulted them back into public view. On its heels followed a whole procession of movies, books, and television programs about possession. Some surprising, deep, unconscious need is being met here. Why should people want to believe again in demons?

If the matter were simply one of popular credulity and superstition—and it surely is that in part—sweet reason might be the prescribed cure. But the demonic is an inescapable fact of the twentieth century, perhaps its most characteristic trademark and perverse attainment. No intelligent person *wants* to believe in demons, but the utter failure of our optimistic views of progress to account for the escalating horrors of our time demands at least a fresh start at understanding the source and virulence of the evils that are submerging our age into night, leaving us filled with such a sense of helplessness to resist.

In this chapter I will attempt to reconcile two contradictory views of the origin of the demonic. One is held by liberation theologians, Marxists, and a wide spectrum of social theorists, who contend that personal pathology, distress, and alienation are not due to a flawed personal psyche but are instead caused by the capitulation by the person to oppressive structures of power. The other view, held by the vast majority of people in the United States, is that while structures and systems may contribute to personal breakdown, psychopathology is primarily the consequence of personal developmental malfunctions.

According to those who see the cause in *society*, people are held in submission to alienating structures and ideologies and cannot be liberated by personal insight, unless that insight includes the ways in which their inner demons are the internalized product of real external demons of brute institutional power.

According to those who see the cause in the *individual*, on the other hand, social influences count, but cannot explain why some people become dysfunctional while others in similar circumstances are able to transcend negative heredity and environment and live creatively in a fallen world. The one attempts exorcism, without acknowledging as much, through social struggle, reform, or revolution. The other, also without acknowledgment, endeavors to exorcise through personal analysis, behavioral modification, or life style changes. The one sees demons as outer, the other as inner.

From the perspective of the inbreaking new order of God declared by Jesus, each position is correct, but only in tension with the other. The alternatives are vicious if made exclusive, and deform their proponents as well as distort the truth. The notion that people are solely the victims of outer oppressive structures is materialistic, and denies human capacities for self-transcendence. The view that psychopathology is rooted exclusively in the person is individualistic, and isolates people from the social matrix, without which human existence is impossible.

A truer understanding of persons sees them in cybernetic or systemic terms, as the network of relations in which they are embedded. This means that the individual can never be considered in isolation from the political, economic, and social conditions in which the person was gestated and by which the person has been to a significant degree formed. Wilhelm Reich, one of the few psychotherapists to do justice to the social dimension, put it this way: "The character structure is the congealed sociological process of a given epoch."[1] Increasing numbers of therapists are recognizing that personal healing is impossible to attain if it ignores the political, economic, and social conditions that helped produce the craziness in the first place. Increasing numbers of liberation theologians are recognizing that long-term struggles for justice require not just the tools of political analysis and a praxis or strategy for social transformation, but also therapies capable of removing "all the flaming darts of the evil one" (Eph. 6:16) that have carried the toxins of self-doubt, fatalism, and docility before the Powers directly into the bloodstream of the oppressed. We are beginning to witness a convergence of these two orientations, so long locked in fruitless antagonism.

The unity of the outer and inner demonic runs deeper than that, however. For the outer demonic is not just shorthand for dehumanizing institutions and social systems. It represents the *actual inner spirit of these suprahuman entities*. The social demonic is the spirit exuded by a corporate structure that has turned its back on its divine vocation as a creature of God and has made its own goals the highest good. The demonic is not then merely the consequences that follow in the wake of self-idolizing institutions; it is also the spirit that insinuates itself into those whose compliance the institution requires in order to further its absolutizing schemes. Such systems cannot govern by force alone; indeed, force is always a counsel of last resort and a sign that a Power is losing its grip on people's minds. When a demonic institution is functioning normally, it does so by the enthusiastic and willing consent of those it is in the very act of oppressing, or at very least, with their terrified compliance. The policeman steps off the corner and into their heads. The Powers rule from within.

Conversely, the personal shadow or raw, unredeemed, and unintegrated darkness in the depths of the human soul is not confined to the individual either, because it is attracted to its collective expressions in society. It can even erupt into a frenzy of violence in the permissive context of a riot, revolution, or war. Feelings of inferiority can be played on by demagogues to produce monsters compensating for their low self-esteem and raining revenge on those whom they blame for having caused it. A megalomaniac like Hitler would get nowhere if he were not riding the cresting wave of resentment from millions of would-be megalomaniacs longing to be released from the restraints of truth and civility. Like the thousands of smaller sewage pipes draining from every house in a city into the central main, our inner demons feed the outer. Neither could exist without the other. Each mutually creates and perpetuates the other. Neither has pride of place. Together they form a united front of hostility to the humanizing purposes of God.

Within this united front, however, it may be helpful to make distinctions. I will propose that there are three types of demonic manifestations: outer personal possession, collective possession, and the inner personal demonic. By outer personal possession I mean the possession of an individual by something that is alien and extrinsic to the self. By collective possession I mean the possession of groups or even nations by a god or demon capable of bending them as one into the service of death. And by the inner personal demonic I mean the struggle to integrate a split-off or repressed aspect that is intrinsic to the personality, an aspect that is only made evil by its rejection.

Outer Personal Possession

The story of the Gerasene demoniac is the classic account of outer personal possession in the Bible (Mark 5:1–20 par.).[2] The story seethes with mythological motifs. The "duping of the devil" (by letting the demons destroy themselves in the swine) catches everyone's attention, but that motif is clustered with a whole set of other eerie touches: the harrowing "night sea journey" in which Jesus had silenced a storm as if it were a demon (Mark 4:39); Jesus' first entry into alien, Gentile territory (the Decapolis); the very name "Gerasa," which may be a fanciful allusion to the Hebrew *grs,* "to drive out, cast out, expel";

and the wild demoniac who dwells among tombs like a specter from the unconscious. We cannot speak with any assurance as to which of these elements was
original to the event, and which if any has been added. There was a time when
many would have dismissed all such additions as tampering; today we are far
more likely to see in them the very means by which a local affair was given universal significance and mythic depth. If the church has touched up the account
with dabs of Isa. 65:1-15, it was only to help the reader recall that God's intention to reach out to the Gentiles had been prophetically anticipated all along.[3]

We cannot be certain where this exorcism should actually be located. Various
manuscripts of the Gospels place it in the country of the Gerasenes, the Gadarenes, or the Gergesenes. The problem is that Gerasa was thirty miles southeast
of the Sea of Galilee, and Gadara was five! Neither fits well, even if their territo-
ries might be understood to extend to the sea.[4] Both cities lack the requisite
shore and cliff, so other texts, supported by Origen, proposed Gergesa, on the
basis of local tradition.[5] In the narrative proper no name appears, but only "the
city" and "the country" (Mark 5:14 par.). The one fixed point from which we
must proceed, then, is that the story was set on the southeastern shore of the
Sea of Galilee, in the Decapolis (Mark 5:20).[6] Later editors may have supplied
the name of specific locations on the basis of a rather sketchy knowledge of the
area.

The social location of the narrative is crucial, even if we cannot specify further. For this is Jesus' first entry into the Decapolis, ten proud Greek cities
founded or enlarged by Alexander the Great and his successors and settled with
Macedonian veterans. In that Semitic soil these free Greek city-states set about
sowing Greek culture. Gerasa boasted a temple to Zeus Olympus (to whom pigs
were sacrificed—were the pigs of our story being raised for that purpose?) and,
from 22-23 C.E. on, a temple dedicated to the cult of Caesar. Each of the cities
enjoyed various degrees of political autonomy. The Jewish ruler Alexander
Jannaeus (d. 76 B.C.E.) subjected or destroyed at least half the cities (Gerasa,
Gadara, Hippos, Scythopolis, Pella). Then in 63 B.C.E. Pompey brought them
under Roman control, restored some privileges, and placed them under the
oversight of the Syrian legate. Augustus awarded Gadara, Hippos, and
Scythopolis to Herod; when the Gadarenes failed in their petition against
Herod's cruelty they suffered even more cruelly still. At the beginning of the
Jewish War, Jewish rebels sacked most of the ten cities. Pity Gerasa: it was
sacked by both Romans *and* Jews. Gerasa alone had protected its Jewish
minority; the other cities, in mingled hatred and fear, butchered even those Jews
who had declared themselves pro-Roman.[7]

This then appears to be the pattern: the ten cities, fiercely jealous of their
right to mint their own coin and levy their own taxes, had watched their free-

doms be stifled, first by the Ptolemies, then by the Seleucids, then by the Jews, then by Herod. Their attitude toward Rome was ambivalent in the extreme. Pompey had delivered them from the yoke of the Jews, and Augustus, on Herod's death, had released them from rule by Herod's sons. Yet they were still subject to Roman control, tribute, and conscription.[8]

Gerasa is a case in point. Why, before besieging Jerusalem, did Vespasian dispatch Lucius Annius against Gerasa, unless it was considered hostile? Why were the gates closed against Annius, so that he had to carry the city by assault? Why did he "put to the sword a thousand of the youth" and sack and burn Gerasa and/or its surrounding villages[9]—unless old longings for independence and autonomy had reached a new pitch, fired by the example of near neighbors revolting against Rome? Apparently some of the Gerasenes misread the Jewish revolt as an indication of declining Roman power in the area, and gambled on Jewish success to secure their own much-desired freedom once more. The Romans at least saw the situation thus; they quartered a legion there during the Jewish War, and kept it there into the third century. And while the city flourished economically, the longings never died. All the dedicatory inscriptions of the period of the Emperor Hadrian's visit (129–130) have been partially erased, apparently prompted by anger at his renaming the city[10]—one more indication of its intense sense of independence.

This then was the social context of the demoniac. How is he related to it? The first impression is deceptive: not at all, he had been cast out. How then has he stayed alive? For he has not only avoided starvation but is possessed of a strength that is legendary. Someone must be feeding him. Luke depicts his malady as episodic: "For many a time it had seized him" (Luke 8:29). Perhaps he comes and goes from the nearest town. But note this odd feature: "No one could bind him anymore, even with a chain; for he had often been bound with fetters and chains, but the chains he wrenched apart, and the fetters he broke in pieces; and no one had the strength to subdue him" (Mark 5:3–4). René Girard is suspicious of these townspeople; it really *is* possible to fashion chains too powerful for anyone to break. They must be deliberately keeping him alive, and *they chain him in such a way that he can break free*. This must have been acted out like a ritual many times before. "The Gerasenes and their demons have for some time settled into some sort of cyclical pathology," Girard writes. In a sense they must have enjoyed and even needed this drama since they beg Jesus to leave immediately and not meddle further in their affairs.

Girard sees in this narrative evidence for the thesis he has been building through a series of brilliant volumes.[11] Human societies cannot face their own violence, he argues, nor can they permit endless retaliation against those who do express it. Therefore they devise scapegoats who will serve as lightning rods to draw away the volatile charge that would otherwise throw society into a paroxysm of internecine strife. The demoniac is a perfect case, argues Girard. The townspeople need him to act out their own violence. He bears their collective madness personally, freeing them from its symptoms. Unlike other accounts where the scapegoat is stoned, he does it for them: he bruises himself with stones. Yet he secretly lives out the freedom to be violent that they crave: he is the most liberated among them, shattering chains, parading naked, free from taxes and tribute and the military service due Rome. Yet he is the more miserable for it, and they insure that he remains so. They chain him and drive him from their midst, to dwell as an outcast among the dead. "The possessed imitates the Gerasenes who stone their victims, but the Gerasenes also imitate their possessed. It is a relationship of doubles and mirrors that exists between persecuted persecutors and this persecuting persecuted individual. The relationship is one of mimetic antagonism."[12] Franz-J. Leenhardt depicts the same reciprocity when he has the demons turn to the reader and say, "We are banished from society but are necessary for its functioning. Some scapegoats are necessary, as fate falls upon the weakest members of the group. But if you deprive these people who exile us of this possibility of projecting their madness upon us, they will all become madmen. We are necessary for their peace. Our impurity reassures them in the conviction of their purity."[13]

I believe we can consider the scapegoat motif established. But can we specify more precisely what is being laid on this miserable substitute? We can, because he himself tells us. "My name is Legion, for we are many." The Decapolis knew the legions. They were not "mobs" (as the TEV mistranslates it), but one of the most disciplined military formations the world has ever known. "My name is legion": can we not hear a whole region speaking in that voice? Has this man not taken on himself the actual situation of his people? He does what they would *like* to do: tear apart the chains and shatter the fetters of Roman authority. Here at least was a free man: "No one had the strength to subdue him." But he had also internalized their captivity and the utter futility of resistance: he gashes himself with stones. His great rage turns in only on himself. Here was the perfect scapegoat, a holy fool, an escape valve, a living parable of their seething discontent.[14] Tradition rightly calls him the Gerasene demoniac, for that is precisely his function—to be the demoniac of the Gerasenes. That is why he pleads that his demons not be sent "out of the country." They "belong" there. They are the spirit of the region, and the demoniac is their incarnation.[15]

He is "occupied," just as they are. Here mental illness becomes metaphor: the Decapolis was possessed by legions! But through the scapegoat, aggression against the Romans has been transferred to the demons. In Gerd Theissen's words, the demons "speak Latin, present themselves as a 'legion,' and like the Romans have only one wish: to be allowed to stay in the country."[16] Mythological language and bizarre pathology act as a screen to mask political unrest that cannot be safely expressed.

Paul Hollenbach cites evidence that mental illness is caused by, or at least aggravated by, class antagonisms resulting in economic exploitation, conflicts between traditions, colonial domination, and revolution. The natives will cope with these conflicts by strengthening their inhibitions against violence. This is achieved by creating a confining zone encircled by maleficent spirits that will attack them if they step out against the oppressor. Mental illness can also in such circumstances become an oblique protest against or escape from oppression and the pathological atmosphere that it creates.[17] The demoniac has reacted characteristically, then, by developing an oblique aggressive strategy in which his very madness permitted him to express hostility toward Rome in a politically cryptic manner. "His possession was at once both the result of oppression and an expression of his resistance to it."[18]

Classically, the scapegoat is driven off the edge of a cliff by the whole community hurling stones. All are thus responsible for his death, and hence none. (Those who stoned Stephen set upon him "as one man" [*homothumadon*], Acts 7:57, Phillips.) And because the scapegoat is someone that everyone agrees must die, and is also too weak to retaliate or too marginal to have powerful allies, he can be killed without fear of reprisal, and the threat of further violence is checked.[19]

That introduces the most curious aspect of our account: the substitutionary death of the pigs. *They* become the "scapepigs" in place of the man, who is healed. Jesus thus breaks the vicious circle of mimetic persecution. But—and this is astonishing—*there is no cliff on that part of the Sea of Galilee.* Nor is there a cliff in Nazareth over which the good townspeople might have hurled Jesus (Luke 4:28–30). "Steep bank" (RSV) is too mild. *Kremnas* means an "overhanging bank, cliff, edge." No doubt the cliff has grown in the imagination of tellers unfamiliar with the topography, but that misses the point: there *has* to be an "edge." The scapegoat motif absolutely requires it. But in this case the roles are reversed. It is not the scapegoat who is forced over the cliff, but a legion (upwards of six thousand made up the Roman unit) in two thousand pigs.

The crowd should stay behind and push the victim over. Here the crowd plunges and the victim is saved. . . . The demons are cast in the image of a human group. They are the *imago* of that group because they are its *imitatio.* . . . As there is one voice that at the end speaks for the Gerasenes, so there is one voice at the beginning

speaking for all the demons. And these two voices actually say the same thing . . .
there is no difference between asking Jesus not to cast out the demons, when you
are a demon, and asking him to leave the country, when you are a Gerasene."[20]

The demons are the spirituality of the people. The townspeople cannot rejoice
in this healing. It has proved too costly, and not only financially. Deprived of
their scapegoat, their violence has no valve. What further sacrifice would now
suffice to prevent its erupting *in the people*? Further, Jesus has sent the man
back among his own kindred, "clothed and in his right mind." We know from
family systems therapy what a threat this can mean to a sick system, which must
repossess its former victim or find a new victim if it is not to explode.

The townspeople remain remarkably calm, considering everything. They beg
Jesus to depart from their neighborhood, aborting any chance of coming to
insight about their own needs for healing. The Marcan story is prophetic:
having lost the scapegoat who had incarnated their hatred of the legions, the
region would literally be possessed, from 68 on, when Vespasian headquartered
a garrison there. History is itself mythic.

This demoniac was not, then, simply the victim of his own pathology, though
something in his own personal history must have predisposed him to this role.
Our individualistic culture has lost the sense that traditional societies all
retained: that personal aberrations are integrally connected with the breakdown
of right social relations in the community. The demoniac was his society's deviant. What do deviants tell us about their societies?[21]

Let me give two examples. When I was a pastor near Galveston, Texas, in the
early 1960s, the local press carried the story of Major Claude Eatherly, the navi-
gator of the plane that dropped the atom bomb on Hiroshima. He had been
involved in a series of petty crimes which he committed apparently for the sole
reason of getting himself arrested, and was now in the Galveston jail. The news-
paper dismissed him as suffering from a personal guilt complex. My own reaction was to want to go visit him and try to communicate to him God's
forgiveness. He was later committed, on the "expert" witness of psychiatrists,
to a mental institution on the grounds of "lunacy."

They did well, for he carried in his heart a bomb that could have exploded
and shattered all our sleep. He had been trying to make the nation face the
immorality of this act in which he had played a small but significant part. Failing that, he had sought, by increasingly bizarre behavior, to see that at least *he*
was punished, thereby forcing the guilty to punish him. In a letter to the German
philosopher Günther Anders, Eatherly wrote, "The truth is that society cannot
accept the fact of my guilt without at the same time recognizing its own far
deeper guilt." Anders responded, "One can only conclude: happy the times in
which the insane speak out this way, wretched the times in which only the

insane speak out this way." Bertrand Russell also swung to his defense: "The world was prepared to honor him for his part in the massacre, but, when he repented, it turned against him, seeing in his act of repentance its own condemnation."[22]

We had missed all this. We thought he was crazy. I never did get around to carrying the word of forgiveness to him. He probably would have been too magnanimous to accept it for himself alone anyway, *until his whole nation had repented with him.* His name was Legion, for we are many.

The second example is from a therapist who is working with a disturbed adolescent. He has delusions that he is a Vietnam veteran who was killed in the war and is living his second life. It is clear from the therapist's knowledge of his circumstances that his delusion expresses his family situation: he feels he has been "murdered" by his parents. But why did he choose to take on himself the guilt of the nation for the Vietnam War? Why did he identify with the soldiers we sent off to be killed (and to kill)? Curiously enough, he found another boy his age who had independently formed precisely the same delusion! Both are utterly preoccupied with death and are suicidal. They both "live among the tombs." How many other people are there who have taken on our collective guilt for the Vietnam War in this or similar ways? And what forms of mental illness are being spawned by the nuclear arms race? Is there any relationship between rising rates of teenage suicide and the dread sense that there will be no human future?

We have long known that to some degree mental illnesses are "faddish." Different cultures breed different styles of insanity, remarks George Rosen, and in the same culture psychopathologies differ at different periods. He cites as examples of "psychic epidemics" the dancing mania ("St. Vitus' dance") of 1374, possession and witch hunting in the fifteenth to eighteenth centuries, tarantism in Italy in 1695, the convulsions at the Lancashire cotton mills in 1877, the excesses of religious revivalism in the eighteenth and nineteenth centuries, the Sioux ghost dance of 1889, and the cargo cults of Melanesia. Some psychic epidemics have followed in the wake of military defeats or as a reaction to suppressed revolutions, as the abnormal expression of suppressed energies that had not been discharged.[23] Freud's Vienna produced hysterical neurotics plagued by conflicts between conscience and sexual desire. Jean Starobinski comments regarding hysteria that the definition and clinical description of it circulated in written and oral form and often played a role in creating the *best* cases of this disease. "One may speak then of a socio-genesis or word-genesis of the symptom."[24] Nowadays, hysteria is rather infrequent; instead, our boundaryless society induces disturbances in an individual's sense of belonging, meaning, and identity, leading to schizophrenia and the newly fashionable "borderline personality."[25] Soviet psychiatry is employed in thought-control and the punishment of dissent because Soviet psychiatrists apparently believe quite sincerely that people who marginalize themselves by criticizing the state are behaving abnormally, and may indeed be victims of "sluggish schizophrenia."[26] The state manufactures madness!

Outer personal possession thus reveals itself to be merely the personal pole of a collective malady afflicting an entire society. In outer personal possession one person bears the brunt of the collective demonism, which is thus allowed to remain unconscious and undetected by society at large. In the case of collective possession, however, all restraints are abandoned. The demon goes public.

Collective Possession

Our society has congratulated itself for having rid itself of demonic possession by having divested itself of the belief in demons. All it has really accomplished, however, is to rid itself of an earlier culture's characteristic expression of the demonic. In a highly individualistic society like ours it is rare to encounter single individuals who are possessed. Instead, the demonic has in our time taken the form of mass psychosis—what Rosen called "socially shared psychopathology."[27] Søren Kierkegaard prophetically announced this cultural shift:

> In contradistinction to the Middle Ages and those periods with all their discussions of possession, of particular men giving themselves to evil, I should like to write a book on *diabolical possession in modern times*, and show how mankind *en masse* gives itself up to evil, how nowadays it happens *en masse*. It is for this reason that people gather into flocks, in order that natural, animal hysteria should take hold of them, in order to feel themselves stimulated, inflamed and *beside themselves* . . . losing oneself in order to be volatilized into a higher potency, where being outside oneself one hardly knows what one is doing or saying, or who or what is speaking through one, while the blood courses faster, the eyes turn bright and staring, the passions and lust seething.[28]

Carl Jung also registered with deep disquiet the way his German patients, in the period after the First World War, during the years before Hitler came to power, were having disturbing, mythological dreams of violence and cruelty that seemed to go well beyond the limits of the personal unconscious.[29] Some deep and forgotten monster was stirring, soon to erupt on the world, incarnate not in a single wild demoniac among the tombs, but in a man capable of galvanizing an entire nation into diabolical possession. In such a society, those who are branded "insane" may in fact be *too* sensitive, *too* caring, *too* human to survive the collective evil given legitimacy by the inertia of decent and respectable people, Christians included.

How ironic: from the vantage point of a society sick unto death, we puzzle over what it was in an individual that caused him to become insane. As members of a society suicidally ravishing the environment and arming ourselves to oblivion, we are perplexed at the high rate of suicides. After almost a century of psychoanalytical introspection, in which far too often the therapeutic goal was adjusting people to a morbid society, we have become, in James Hillman's words, increasingly conscious of what we project outwards, and yet remain blind to what is projected onto us by the unconsciousness of the world. "Not only my pathology is projected onto the world; the world is inundating me with its unalleviated suffering." No amount of therapy can prevent the spread of that "epidemic psychic infection."[30]

The early church had already to some degree anticipated our situation. It regarded *everyone* prior to baptism as possessed, by virtue of nothing more than belonging to a world in rebellion against God. Baptism was far more than a rite of passage; it was an exorcism. No doubt some had been more deeply penetrated by the values and estrangement of that society than others; these might require a more concerted rite of exorcism.[31] Possession was thus seen not as an occasional aberration, but as a continuum on which all of us might possibly find ourselves.

Today even the inoculation of baptism has not prevented our being sucked up into mass possession. Why else are we paying our taxes to purchase ever more lethal weapons of mass suicide? Why else are we—to be sure, disquieted, disturbed, even perhaps outraged—yet still so supine, so compliant, so innocuous? Why, when it comes right down to putting our bodies on the line, do we draw back—unless we are in the grip of a Power that has us enthralled?

Our century has known some of the most bizarre and horrifying examples of collective possession in human history. Charles Manson, James Jones, Adolf Hitler—each tapped a deep longing in their followers to be cared for, to belong to a movement that gave their lives significance, to surrender themselves to the all-wise power of someone godlike. Indeed, the very essence of collective demonism is its explicit and avowed idolatry of the leader. Collective demonism is the abdication of human answerability to God and the investment of final judgment in a divinized mortal. And those who are thus possessed seldom know it until too late.

It is easy enough for us in retrospect to point to others who have given themselves up to collective madness, but are we able to discern our own complicity? "Unfortunately," it has been said with painful accuracy, "the United States has never learned to listen to itself as if it were the enemy speaking."[32] Martin Luther King, Jr.'s prophetic declaration in 1967 that the United States is the greatest purveyor of violence in the world is even truer now than when it was uttered—and now extends beyond the world to outer space.[33] But we do not feel possessed. We manifest no symptoms of Nazi enthusiasm. We do not herd into stadiums to be harangued by hypnotic speakers. We go about our lives largely oblivious to the demon, kissing our children before school, patting the dog, being polite to the bus driver. We are sane, civilized, perhaps a bit too given to violence and sadism on TV, but by common national consent still the most genial people on the face of the globe. We do not see that the demonic has been installed at the heart of national policy. The nation (administration, Congress, armed forces, CIA) carries out for us the dirty work required to maintain American political and economic dominance in the world. Most of us would rather not know the bloody tale of deeds performed on our behalf. We are content to be beneficiaries. In the same way people all around the globe are better informed about what is being done to South African blacks than the average white citizen of that country. As Ernest Becker put it, when evil is socialized, the public is relieved of guilt and rendered morally exempt in what is in fact a condition of group sadism.[34]

We will revert to this theme in greater detail when we deal with the angels of the nations (chap. 4). But now we must turn to the opposite end of the continuum, to the inner personal demonic.

The Inner Personal Demonic

By the inner personal demonic I mean a split-off or unintegrated aspect of the self which is not alien, but intrinsic to the personality, and which needs to be owned, embraced, loved, and transformed as part of the struggle for wholeness. This is not equivalent to the New Testament accounts of possession. Those seem to have been alien influences not integral to the self—elements introjected into the personality from the general pathology of society—what I am calling outer personal demons.

The biblical reference point for inner personal demons is not the stories of exorcisms, but Jesus' instruction concerning inner evil:

> Hear me, all of you, and understand: there is nothing outside a person which by going in can defile; but the things which come out are what defile. . . . For from within, out of the human heart, come evil thoughts, fornication, theft, murder, adultery, coveting, wickedness, deceit, licentiousness, envy, slander, pride, foolishness. All these evil things come from within, and these are what defile. (Mark 7:14–15, 21–23, *ILL*)

Jesus does not subscribe to the opinion that our emotions or habits can or should be cast out by exorcism. To attempt to cast out something essential to the self is like performing castration to deal with lust. Great harm is done by well-intended, self-appointed "exorcists," largely in neo-Pentecostal circles, by exorcising people who are not genuinely possessed (that is, are not possessed by outer personal or collective demons).

I once took a depressed friend to a charismatic prayer meeting where the leader offered to pray for her. In doing so he "cast out" her spirit of depression. In her case, however, as we learned somewhat later, her depression was being caused by frustration and repressed anger over the denial of opportunities for creative expression in the new community to which she had moved. To "cast it out" was merely to cast her depression's causes deeper into the unconscious, denying her the opportunity of gaining insight into her problem. And on top of everything else, it added an additional layer of guilt for not getting better.

It is imperative then that any person dealing with the demonic (that is to say, any morally sensitive human being) learn to discern between inner and outer demons. Inner demons are usually not intrinsically evil but are rendered grotesque from suppression, paralyzed from disuse, or wounded from rejection. They are the parts of us regarded as socially unacceptable. They rob us of our self-esteem. They undermine our ego's strategies for gaining respect by an outer show of competence or virtue. They are not worthy of fear, yet are a terror to the person who has not entered upon the death of the ego and rebirth to an honest life. Here the aid of psychotherapy can prove invaluable.

Traditional societies spoke of this distinction between inner personal and outer personal demons by contrasting "losing one's soul" and "being freed from a spirit." By "losing one's soul" they referred to the danger of being deprived of some essential aspect of personal identity that all the subpersonalities taken in their totality go together to create. To this they contrast being freed from a "spirit," the latter being understood as an alien invader that has seized the personality and holds it captive. It is therefore a loss to "lose one's soul," but a relief to lose a spirit.[35]

If the demonic manifests itself in such a variety of ways—collective, outer personal, and inner personal—then it follows that a variety of responses is in order. How, in each of these situations, are we to go about dealing with our demons?

Dealing with Our Demons

I am aware that I have been using the term "demonic" as if it were a normal part of our everyday discourse. I am, in fact, acutely aware that it is, for most people, scandalous, a stumbling block, generating resistance fueled both by the misuse of the notion in the past and misgivings about its compatibility with or pertinence to scientific understandings of the psyche in the present.

My friend and biblical colleague, Robert T. Fortna, was recently tutoring a Jamaican emigrant in a literacy program. The man had been dismissed as "backward" in school, beaten by his father, and ridiculed by his teachers as uneducable. Whenever Bob would press him to remember a word, he would begin to gesture as if pushing something away from his head. "The devil is trying to get at me," he would say, or, "They're after me." Bob was able to help him through these moments by showing him that he still knew the word, that "they" were not able to prevent his functioning. The man had apparently internalized the criticisms he had received lifelong for what may have been mild dyslexia and the illiteracy that resulted, and under pressure "heard" these voices crowding in to undermine his confidence. He was right to identify them as "demonic"; but by personifying them and projecting them outside he remained unable to identify their real source and root them out of his personality. And apart from that insight, exorcism could at best have provided only temporary relief. (An exorcist utilizing that insight, however, might be the best possible healer for such a person.)

Belief in demons has also been used as a means of evading sociopolitical insight and responsibility. At the end of World War II there was a great deal of discussion among theologians in Germany about the demonic. It was during one such session that Karl Barth suddenly broke in impatiently and said to his German friends, "Why all this talk about demons? Why not just admit we have been political idiots?"[36]

At another such meeting a German pastor commented, "You cannot understand what has happened in Germany unless you understand that we were possessed by demonic powers. I do not say this to excuse ourselves, because *we let ourselves be possessed.*"[37]

In a sense both statements are correct. The problem with both of them, however, is that they treat the demons as if they were disincarnate spiritual beings in the air, rather than *the actual spirituality of Nazism.* The demonic was inseparable from its political forms: the Hitler Youth, the SS, the Gestapo, the cooperation of the churches, the ideology of Aryan racial purity, and the revival of Norse mythology. The demonic was the interiority of the German state made into an idol. The demon was the Angel of Germany having turned its back on its vocation.

Priests in Brazil described to my wife and me how belief in possession merely reinforced the fatalism of people who believed that God had already planned everything. The church there is trying to teach people that they can make their own history, that they can be responsible, that they need not blame demons when their child's illness is worms caught because their family cannot afford to buy shoes for her. What is *really* demonic so often is the way religion and popular superstition conspire together to mystify the true causes of distress under a fog of demonology.

How then are we to understand the current wave of fascination with possession? We must return to the question of the social sources of the demonic. In modern secular society, the devil is forbidden. It is, as Peter Berger puts it, "naughty to believe in him." Faith, religion, God, have become, for many people, topics of acute embarrassment. It is in this social milieu that Berger sees demonology as a sign of the thirst for transcendence in a secular society which has deprived people of it. "The current occult wave (including its devil component) is to be understood as resulting from the repression of transcendence in modern consciousness." Secularity plays the role of censor, and, as Freud taught us, repressed contents manifest themselves often in bizarre forms. The current repressive triviality is enforced, like any other worldview, by its reality police: the teachers, psychiatrists, journalists, and other inquisitors of modern culture. "Their job is to make sure that no contraband items are smuggled across the frontiers. It is not surprising, then, that there continue to be people who rebel against this officially decreed boredom, that there continues to be a demand for contraband transcendence."[38]

There is a titillating quality, a thrilling flaunting of the Powers involved in entertaining their reality. The current fascination with the demonic (always depicted in completely personal terms, of course) has something pornographic about it, Berger remarks. Those who believe in it are deviants; those who yield to it become possessed. The dramatic agonies of the latter entertain us while at the same time serving as a warning: not too close, advance at your peril, hands off! After the horror of the occult TV show or movie, we gingerly turn off the lights, freed once more from the temptation to explore our own demonic depths. Thus secular consciousness succeeds in preserving its superficial limits. The scapegoat once more has done its job.

Berger's view is true as far as it goes, but there is something deeper than titillation. Behind the spreading terror of nuclear and ecological catastrophe is a pervasive sense that there is no one in control. The demonic has become the everyday policy of national leaders trapped in the momentum of a spirituality they can neither name nor discern, but which constrains them, against the best interests of humanity, toward rationalized suicide. The evil that grips us is simply too massive and intractable to face. Far easier to individualize it, concretize it, reduce its dimensions to the writhing flesh of a single victim. Perhaps someone can do something with an individual—incarcerate, medicate, isolate, exorcise—and relieve our sense of helplessness. We would gladly jettison a worldview that denies belief in *personal* demons rather than—paradoxically enough—admit that "the whole world is in the power of the evil one" (1 John 5:19).

Given the complex and problematic nature of the demonic, what function then does exorcism have? There is no simple answer to this question. Not only is a different response required for the inner personal demonic than for either outer personal possession or collective possession, but within each type we must discern, in each case, what is needed.

The Inner Personal Demonic

In the case of inner personal demons, as I have indicated, exorcism has no place at all. Exorcism is, as the medical people like to say, contraindicated. Inner personal demons must instead be handled the way the father treated the returning prodigal son in the parable: "His father saw him and had compassion, and ran and embraced and kissed him" (Luke 15:20).

Traditional Christian pietism has done little to help us embrace these inner demons. It has either denied their reality and projected the evil out on others, whom it has then "demonized" (communists, adulterers, homosexuals), or it has demonized the very emotions themselves, naming and "casting out" a Spirit of Anger, a Spirit of Envy, or a Spirit of Lust.[39] Neither solution acknowledges this evil as our own; indeed, as I noted in the introduction to this book, Christians have never dealt well with the inner darkness of the redeemed. The general tendency of spiritual direction over the past centuries has been to lead from strength: to try continually to increase one's commitment, obedience, faith, love. This high road to God has produced a kind of brittle and self-righteous sanctity whenever significant reserves of shadow simply remained repressed.

It has become our destiny today that the way to God should lead us first down into the depths, to encounter God in the darkness there—not in order to return purified to face God, but as the physicist Alfred Romer put it, because the darkness is where God is.[40]

This was forced on me with particular power by one of my dreams. I was standing before a bewitched nun who had fire in her third eye (in midforehead). I sensed evil in her, and said in the dream, "In the name of Jesus Christ I cast you out!" She merely leered at me with a malicious grin, and came at me . . . I woke screaming.

My first reaction on waking was that I had been assaulted by the demonic. The whole room seemed charged with evil. When I discussed the dream with my spiritual mentor, Elizabeth Howes, however, I began to feel differently. What is the third eye, she asked? The symbol of spiritual wisdom in the East. And what for me do nuns represent? In this case, repressed sexuality, I said. What is fire? Passion, libido, energy, eros, sexuality. What is *fire* doing in the third eye. That doesn't fit. No, she suggested, this is no outer demon. My own sexuality and spirituality were mixed up, unintegrated, in a way that was demonic. I needed that fire, and I needed the wisdom of the third eye, but they would have to be differentiated. I ought to get to know this nun, she felt.

So I made my nun in clay, wrote a series of dialogues with her, and finally dreamed the dream forward: letting myself back into a dreamlike state, I once again experienced her moving menacingly toward me. This time I said, "In the name of the Jesus I *do* know, I want to be reconciled with you." Over a period of time that has begun to happen.

How tragic, had my initial "exorcism" been successful. (At first, of course, I blamed myself for "lack of faith"!)

> Thou talk'st of Antichrist
> and Beast, and dost not see
> (If thou be not in God)
> that they are both in thee.[41]

The best "exorcism" of all is accepting love. It is finally love, love alone, that heals the demonic. "How should we be able to forget those ancient myths about dragons," wrote Rainer Maria Rilke, "who at the last minute turn into princesses that are only waiting to see us once beautiful and brave? Perhaps everything terrible is in its deepest being something helpless that wants help from us."[42]

Nevertheless, even here it is hazardous to hand down hard and fast advice. Sometimes we need to stand our ground and wrestle the inner spirit to grant its blessing, but at others flight is the only counsel of wisdom, if the power of evil threatens to inundate us. Everything depends on whether the spirit is inner or outer, whether it is a matter of healing one's own soul or being freed from an alien power.[43] At such times there is no substitute for the objectivity and experience of a spiritual guide who can help us determine whether what we face is "ours" or "outer."

Having said that, one must also say its opposite. Excessive fear of these dark shapes encroaching from our depths may stampede us into flight just when we need to summon all our courage to step forward with open hands to embrace them. There is that of God in every one of us which is sovereign over whatever aspects of demonic darkness we encounter. It is our fear itself which gives the demonic its power.

One of the turning points in my own spiritual development came through another nightmare. I was in a wooden frame house on the plains. Suddenly, out of the corner of my eye, I saw a shape at the open stairwell to the cellar. When I turned, it darted down the stairs. I rushed over and slammed the door. In panic I realized there was an outside cellar door, and it was open! I ran outside to shut it, just in time, for the figure was emerging. When it saw me it darted back. I shut the doors and secured them, only to realize that I had not locked the cellar door in the house! I burst back into the house—too late, he had already gotten out: an emaciated, pitiful, pale, pathetic young man whose eyes pleaded with me to let him out. All my fears melted in compassion and love.

Yes, perhaps everything terrible—or at least most of what is terrible in our own souls—is in its deepest being something helpless that wants help from us. To trust that, not only personally, but in our social world— to see the massive evils of our day as twisted and contorted "goods" that want to be redeemed— takes a certain kind of faith. But those outer evils will not loom quite so terrible if we have already begun to face our own demonic powers within.

Outer Personal Possession

Exorcism may be positively harmful in dealing with inner personal demons, but it continues to have a carefully circumscribed and limited use in genuine cases of outer personal possession. These seem to be relatively rare, and are most frequently the consequence of dabbling with the occult or deliberately playing host to alien spirits. Automatic writers, mediums, Satanists, and the manipulated manipulators of Ouija boards are often unable to disinvite the guest spirits that they have solicited. Some cases of possession begin with a child maintaining an imaginary friend far beyond the appropriate age, due to acute loneliness and lovelessness, only to experience the "friend" turning more and more malicious and even bringing in others worse than himself. At present little is known scientifically about the entire phenomenon, and M. Scott Peck's plea for an institute to document and study it has as yet borne no fruit.[44]

Our model for exorcism remains Jesus. In his encounters with the demonic there was no protracted struggle, no violence aimed at the exorcist, no magical words, crucifixes, holy water—not even the invocation of the divine name. Jesus is totally calm, totally in control. There is no question, as in certain healings (Mark 8:22–26; 6:1–6), whether Jesus will prevail. The demons are depicted as weak fractions of power unable to tolerate the presence of divine authority. The demonic attempts to make a part the whole, and cannot withstand the power of anyone who is related to that Whole in and through and for which all things exist. Nor is this because in Jesus the demons stood face to face with "Incarnate Deity"; apparently it was just as true for other exorcists as well: the disciples (Mark 6:13; Luke 10:17–20),[45] Jewish exorcists (Matt. 12:27; Luke 11:19), or even maverick loners who used Jesus' name as a magical talisman (Mark 9:38– 40 par.). Others shared this healing gift as well as Jesus. What made his exorcisms so distinct, and so frightening to those in authority, was their integration into his proclamation, in word and act, of the inbreaking of "the new order": "But if it is by the finger of God that I cast out demons, then the kingdom of God has come upon you" (Luke 11:20; see Matt. 12:28).

Exorcism in its New Testament context is the act of deliverance of a person or institution or society from its bondage to evil, and its restoration to the wholeness intrinsic to its creation. Exorcism is thus intercession for God's presence and power to liberate those who have become possessed by the powers of death. The demonic, by inference, is a will to power asserted against the created order. It is the psychic or spiritual power emanating from organizations or individuals or subaspects of individuals whose energies are bent on overpowering others.

It is important to stress the order of the above definitions. Demonic possession in all its depth cannot be known apart from the grace manifested by the dawn of God's reign. In the Gospels it is the presence of Jesus that precipitates demonic seizures.[46] This is because the demonic is not merely a cluster of pathological symptoms, but a radical rejection of God and a state of estrangement from God, from one's own higher self (the *imago Dei*), and from full social being. Because this atrophied form of existence has become normative in human societies, most people are unaware of what they have surrendered until they see it resplendent in a fully human being. The demoniacs saw it and wanted to be changed. The authorities saw it and killed its bearer. The human plenitude of Jesus was too scalding a reminder of what they had lost.

Exorcism is an act of considerable psychic violence, as Peck notes, and should be utilized only as a last resort, after every other avenue of help has been exhausted. Even for the most experienced exorcists, discernment can be a tricky business. The most generally accepted criteria and symptoms are far from providing infallible guidance. They are:

1. *The exorcist discerns when to exorcise by the power of the Holy Spirit.* No doubt the Spirit guides many thus, unerringly, to a proper diagnosis. But in circles where demonic power is regularly blamed for the slightest ill, the intuitive channels through which such divine inspiration could flow are blocked by an overinterpretation of all symptoms along demonic lines. Before long, exorcists are trying to cast out aspects of the personality that are intrinsic to the self, the loss of which would be equivalent not to being freed of an evil spirit but to losing one's soul.

The Roman Catholic church requires the rational elimination of every other possibility before turning to exorcism as a last resort. This excellent and today all-too-often ignored advice reduces the burden on the gift of discernment; in fact, it is not even initially required. Only after medical and psychiatric interventions have been exhausted does discernment come into play.[47] This caution is desirable not only because misapplied exorcisms heap guilt on the patient, but also because a demonized view of reality is itself unhealthy.

2. *The exorcist discerns an evil presence or personality that is alien to the*

individual being exorcised. The presence of demonic "personalities" in stricken people has been reliably documented, and it is hair-raising.[48] But here again we must discover whether the phenomenon in question is personal or collective, soul or spirit, an inner or outer demon. For it is axiomatic that every relatively independent portion of the psyche has the character of personality, and is personified the moment it is given an opportunity for independent expression. "Whenever an autonomous component of the psyche is projected," writes Jung, *"an invisible person comes into being.* In this way the spirits arise at an ordinary spiritualistic seance."[49] Unquestionably we experience the demonic; but if it arises from the personal unconscious it must be accepted, owned, loved, and integrated. Otherwise exorcism becomes the amputation of a part of the self, not a healing. Only if the "demon" is genuinely collective, outer, alien, should it be "cast out."

3. *The person possessed speaks in voices distinctly other than his or her own, or in foreign languages unknown to the victim.* Here again, since we know so little about the range of capacities of the vocal cords, it is exceedingly difficult to tell whether the "voice" emanating from a person is his or her own, cast in a different range and representing a subpersonality, or whether it is the voice of an alien "being" speaking through the person. The epic poet Lucan wrote about a Thessalian woman, Erichtho, whose voice was capable of emitting the sounds of dogs, wolves, screech owls, and the like. But she was not regarded as possessed so much as terrifying and talented, much as the girl Paul encountered in Acts 16:16–18.[50] Paul, to be sure, did interpret this as possession, and cast out the spirit of divination. The question in each case would be whether the person was in control of these powers, or controlled by them.

As to foreign languages, if the language is known (and hence recognizable) by others present, there is no way of excluding some kind of paranormal "borrowing" of such knowledge from those present. Outer personal demons do possess knowledge that goes beyond that of their victims, but it is usually of a fairly meager sort, and those involved in the exorcism would be better advised to silence the spirits altogether. In one case which a pastoral counselor shared with me, she had asked the demon its name and it had replied, "Dynamis," the Greek word for "Power." The patient was an uneducated woman who knew no Greek, but she may have heard the name during the time she belonged to a Satan cult, and recalled the word unconsciously (cryptomnesia). In all other respects, however, hers seems to have been a genuine case of possession, and the exorcism proved successful, so this may have been an authentic example of demonic knowledge.

On the other hand, if the language is unknown, there is no way of knowing whether it is a form of babbling, unless it is taped and submitted to linguistic study. So far as I know this had not been done on a rigorously scientific basis.[51] Speaking in tongues is by no means solely inspired by the Holy Spirit. It has been observed in Voodoo, Macumba, Satanism, and other ecstatic religions. Its presence in conjunction with other symptoms of possession is significant, but not sufficient of itself to indicate the need for exorcism.

4. *The person possessed utters blasphemies against God and everything sacred.* Often this appears in total contrast to the person's usual demeanor. The vast majority of documented medieval and postmedieval cases were of nuns. "Possession" seemed to be the socially channeled means by which they could unleash all their pent-up rebellion. Significantly, the "victim" of possession was not regarded as culpable and was not punished for anything that went on during a seizure. Repressed sexual feelings (both homosexual and heterosexual), unacknowledged ambivalence toward holy orders, and mental traumas related to molestation as children pepper the investigative reports of the priests who so objectively sought the causes of the frequent pseudo-possession of those credulous times. The nuns of Loudun blasphemed against the faith before credulous audiences day after day, yet the whole affair was a proven fraud.[52]

As to the content of the blasphemies, they boil down in medieval cases to a kind of homespun "unitarianism" with some psychic novelties thrown in.[53] One would have thought the Prince of Darkness could do better anti-theology than that! What usually comes out is simply an inversion of the values the person already holds. It is difficult to know whether the blasphemies are repressed feelings of the person or genuine diabolical tirades.

5. *The person possessed displays "impossible" physical contortions and undergoes convulsions.* This is certainly true in the case of the Gerasene demoniac, and may itself be the consequence of the desperate struggle within the split self for sovereignty over the body. But it is no infallible guide. The nuns of Loudun scrambled themselves into pretzels and were rocked by convulsions and fits of every kind, but did so under the effects of group hysteria, not genuine possession. And as for demons causing death to exorcists, that seems to have been the pure invention of pulp paperback hacks. Documented violence by demoniacs seems to be uniformly self-inflicted just as in the story of the Gerasene demoniac.

When my wife and I were in Chile a therapist described to us a patient who had what others called epilepsy or demon possession. The therapist discovered that his seizures began at the age of ten when his mother died. Since an epileptic was eligible for a pension for disability, he had a stake in manifesting symptoms. This pseudo-epilepsy was dramatically healed by hypnosis and gestalt therapy.[54] So once again, contortions and convulsions may attend demonic possession, but they are not adequate criteria for identifying a phenomenon as demonic.

There are, however, cases of physical alterations that are so bizarre and accompanied by such an overwhelming aura of evil that they simply cannot be dismissed as contrived. A medical doctor related to me how a woman's face became literally piglike, forming a snout, and her fingers arched and developed long claws. I frankly can draw on nothing in my experience that could enable me to render such an account believable. But my informant, and several psychotherapists who have related less dramatic cases to me, are persons whom I know well, and their veracity is unimpeachable. As an empiricist I can only maintain an open mind, which in these cases, despite my own training and predispositions (I do *not* want a world in which such things are possible), demands that I accord them the benefit of the doubt. Is it possible that these changes in physical appearances were delusions inspired in the mind of the healers by the demons? Or must we assume that these changes actually took place physically?

The sheer sensationalism of such a narrative is itself problematical, insofar as it tends to heighten credulity and belief in the power of the demonic. Including it will surely also subject me to charges of gullibility and irrationality. But if we are ever to understand this phenomenon scientifically, we must begin with the data, however alien it is to the middle range of paradigm-determined modern experience, with its heavy materialistic bias.

6. *Exorcism "works."* Sometimes this is the case, but so sometimes did leeching. The question is, is it "working" by repressing symptoms or by curing their cause? I know of a case where a man suffering from compulsory masturbation was "exorcised" by a Roman Catholic priest. It "worked": he became impotent. I would agree that compulsive behavior often is ascribable to the continuum of what is demonic, but exorcism was the wrong cure. Otherwise why would divine healing have left him impotent? The "demon," in my view, was a split-off aspect of his own sexuality. When it was exorcised, it was simply repressed, and with it, his capacity for sexual arousal. Here again everything depends on properly distinguishing between the personal and the collective, between soul and spirit, inner and outer.

7. *People believe they are possessed.* Some patients come for help because they believe themselves possessed; others, though manifesting all the signs of diabolic influence, resist the idea with all their might. In some cases of genuine possession the victim remains lucid and is aware of everything the "spirit" says and does. In others the patient becomes totally unconscious, remembering nothing that has happened.

In cases of pseudo-possession, however, the idea of possession seems to have been planted in a highly suggestible person. By group expectations, by TV, books, and movies, by subliminal cues and explicit norms, by the very questions the exorcist asks, people can be led to believe that they are dominated or possessed by evil powers. The exorcist can actually cause the "possession." The great chronicler of exorcism, T. K. Oesterreich, surely overstates his case, but he is correct about suggestible possession when he concludes, "The appearance of possession, particularly in its gravest forms, *is always in point of fact associated with belief in the devil.* It is this belief which by means of autosuggestion nourishes possession and maintains it."[55]

The idea of possession may offer an attractive alternative to taking personal responsibility for what is disturbing us. Credulity also enters the picture; the vast majority of those who are believed to be, or believe themselves to be, possessed, have generally been unschooled, usually illiterate, and believe heartily in spirits and demons.[56] More recently, however, as belief in demons has spread to the middle and upper classes, demonic possession or domination has spread as well. *But why was it not there before?* Are we not to suspect here that cultural cues have been transmitted for typical forms of behavior that have community credence and a communal cure? Why are the vast majority of victims women and the possessing spirits almost invariably masculine, regardless of the gender of the victim, in every society for which we have evidence?[57] Why is it that psychotics who speak with alien voices never curse God *unless they are religious*?[58] Why do the phenomena of possession appear only in spurts throughout human history, especially in periods of witchcraft? And why did outbreaks of possession not happen more often in major cultural centers (they seldom occurred in Paris or London, for example)? If the demons were maintaining a steady pressure of malevolence against humanity at all times and in all places, we would expect a pattern of perpetual assault. None exists.[59]

In any case the whole phenomenon is vastly overbilled and overindividualized. The Roman Catholic psychiatrist Jean Lhermitte scrutinized official church documents of possession and concluded that every one he examined was a case of pseudo-possession. He believes in demons and exorcism as a matter of dogma, not experience.[60] And J. de Tonquedec, S.J., looking back over nearly a half-century as the official exorcist for the archdiocese of Paris, was not convinced that he had come upon a single genuine case of possession, even though he had performed numerous exorcisms.[61] Morton Kelsey's conclusion after thirty years of healing ministry is the same.

There is a curious irony here, for the attempt to bring back belief in demons repudiates one of Christianity's greatest victories: the de-demonization of the world. Humanity has spent the better part of its life projecting the unknown dimensions of the self outward onto externalized and objectified spiritual beings. People lived out their unconscious by ritual and mythological dramas that effectively, but without insight, regulated the unknown and threatening parts of the world and of themselves. For many, such a world still functions adequately, and I have no desire to take it from them. But most moderns are in a state of limbo, no longer able to live out their unlived depths through the traditional religions, and not yet able to identify their projections and own them as an aspect of their own depths.

I am not enthusiastic about retrogressing to a world obsessed with the fear of demons and a conspiratorial, even paranoid tendency to find evil anywhere but within. In the vast majority of cases, I am convinced, we are up against inner personal demons. If you are persuaded that you are dealing with genuine outer personal possession, do not tackle it alone. Build a complete team, with help from your nearest competent Roman Catholic diocesan headquarters, and, if possible, a cooperative psychiatrist. We have let ourselves grow too unfamiliar with such things; corporate wisdom is required.

The whole aura of mystery and awe surrounding the topic merely serves to heighten the power of the demonic, however. Jesus' exorcisms are, by contrast, completely undramatic. He concedes the demons no power whatever. From his dimension of reality he sees them for what they are: the obsessions of minds caught in darkness. So he simply dismisses them, and they flee. They could not tolerate the blinding sun of his love. Likewise the early church freed people from the fear of demons, not so much by grim combat (for that merely reinforces belief in them), but by a triumphant satire of their impotence in the face of the risen Christ. Jesus and his first followers focused on the *new reality,* not on the darkness. Perhaps that explains why contemporary exorcists must sometimes wrestle for hours, days at a time, as if in mortal combat.[62]

Collective Possession

Finally, a word on the task of exorcising collective possession. Waving holy water and a crucifix over Buchenwald would scarcely have stopped the Nazi genocide of Jews, but think about it—what if the church in Germany *had* staged ritual acts of protest outside those gates? What if, in churches all over the land, pastors had read from their pulpits prayers exorcising the spirit of Satan and Wotan from the national psyche? It could not have happened, of course, because the prior understanding of collective possession and the church's task in unmasking the Powers was not in place. But the question is not idle, because it puts our situation in the United States in sharper perspective.

The march across the Selma bridge by black civil rights advocates was an act of exorcism. It exposed the demon of racism, stripping away the screen of legality and custom for the entire world to see.

Caesar Chavez's struggles to organize farm workers in California was an exorcism. It unmasked the pitiless system of bracero labor and won both dignity and a living wage for some of America's worst-treated workers.

Exorcism drives the devils first to reveal their names and then casts them out. Most do not come out without a struggle. When Phil and Dan Berrigan poured blood on the files of the Selective Service System, they were attempting to expose the demon of American messianic imperialism in Vietnam. They paid for it with stiff prison sentences as the war ground slowly to a halt.

The success of an attempted collective exorcism has no bearing on its efficacy. It is an act of obedience, performed in the name of the inbreaking new order. Its truth may not be acknowledged by the targeted Power or by the public at large, but the act is efficacious simply by virtue of its bearing witness to the truth in a climate of lies. That is why an exorcism outside Buchenwald would have been significant whether it "worked" or not. It would have named Satan's works and appealed to consciences. The rest is left to human freedom.

The paradigmatic collective exorcism in the New Testament is Jesus' cleansing of the temple (Mark 11:11, 15–19 par.). This act is depicted by the Synoptic Gospels as the climax of his ministry, the central focus of his journey to Jerusalem, and the final provocation of his arrest and execution: "And the chief priests heard it and sought a way to destroy him." Each account, even John's, uses the formulaic term for exorcism, *ekballō,* to describe his act of "driving out" those who did commerce in the temple.[63] The real purpose of his collective exorcism has apparently been suppressed, possibly, according to Eduard Schweizer, to render the story inoffensive in a time when the church still lived within the bounds of Judaism. A hint survives in Mark 14:58, however: "I will destroy this temple that is made with hands and . . . build another" (a saying now reinterpreted in terms of the resurrection). We know that some Jews repudiated the Herodian temple and expected an entirely new one based on Ezekiel 40—48, *1 Enoch* 90:28–29 and *Ps. Sol.* 17:32–33 (2C B.C.E.).[64] Exactly what Jesus had in mind we cannot say, but his act alone, however interpreted, stands in the line of the great symbolic acts of the prophets as a model for the exorcism of collective evil. The fact that the buyers and traders were back in their stalls soon after in no way invalidates the efficacy of his act; indeed, the destruction of the temple in 70 C.E. confirms it. But the point of collective exorcism is not in the first place reform, but revelation: the unveiling of unsuspected evil in high places.

Thus the exorcisms performed by the seventy disciples, according to Jesus, made Satan fall like lightning from heaven (Luke 10:18). Likewise in Rev. 12:7–12, Satan is thrown down from heaven, and "the accuser of our brethren, who accuses them day and night before our God" is conquered "by the blood of the Lamb and by the word of their [the Christian witnesses'] testimony, for they loved not their lives even unto death." Satan is stripped of invisibility ("heaven"); he is no longer able to coerce people unconsciously into conspiring with systems of evil and injustice. The task of the church in the face of collective possession is therefore consciousness-raising. Satan was not expelled from heaven "once upon a time"—that is the error of historicizing the myth. Satan is cast down every time people are liberated. Whenever people "love not their lives even unto death," they become free from Satan's final sanction, and Satan is cast down. Whenever people recognize that they are not powerless before injustice, but can change themselves and change things, Satan is cast down. The liberating witness of the martyrs does not end Satan's power; it drives him to desperation, "because he knows that his time is short" (Rev. 12:12). He redoubles his efforts to intimidate and silence his unmaskers, and with telling effect. In the laconic words of Rev. 13:7, the Roman Empire, Satan's incarnation, is "allowed to make war on the saints *and to conquer them.*"

None of this negates the value of the martyrs' witness. For through what they tell about what they see they make it possible for people to choose their own stories. Others can now decide whether theirs is to continue to be the story of how they have been conformed to or oppressed by a world alienated from life, or whether to take on a new story, which they are now, in the act of listening, freed to choose: the story of their liberation to fullness of life by dying to the alienating lies of the Powers. The work of the Holy Spirit involves unmasking the Powers and seeing that "the ruler of this world is judged" (John 16:11). As John Pairman Brown commented to me, if we simply state that Archbishop Oscar Romero was a Christian charismatic speaking in the Spirit, the true criteria of discerning the Spirit become infinitely clearer.

I have said that the success of a collective exorcism has no bearing on its efficacy, and that is true; but that does not mean that such acts have no effect. Mahatma Gandhi spoke about "non-attachment to results" as essential for the uphill struggle against entrenched evils. We must leave the outcome in the hands of God. Yet if we believe that God is the transformative power of justice in the world, we expect our invocation to make a difference.

The night before Richard Nixon's second inauguration as president, William Stringfellow preached to an ecumenical gathering of twelve hundred people in Rhode Island. He concluded by reading a prayer of exorcism, importuning God to free Nixon from demonic possession. The audience sat in stunned silence, then began to stand and applaud. It was their way of confirming the prayer, of saying yes to the exorcism. Their applause was intercession. Stringfellow had perceived, in a time of political frenzy, that our first responsibility toward those in the grip of evil is pastoral. I will not claim any connection between that act and the succession of events disclosed only a few weeks later that led from Watergate to Nixon's resignation from the presidency. The act was complete in itself.

Each year a group gathers in October at the White Sands Missile Range near

Alamogordo, New Mexico, at the blasphemously named "Trinity Site" where the first atomic bomb was tested on July 16, 1945. The group that met in 1984 was led in a rite of exorcism by Father Louie Vitale of the Franciscan School of Theology in Berkeley. The prayer called on "God who is stronger than sin and death" to "seize from Satan's power the weapons that now threaten our destruction . . . to deliver to perdition all nuclear weapons and their means of delivery . . . to deliver to perdition all the machines used to make and assemble nuclear weapons . . . to deliver to perdition the tragic pride that first made these weapons and the mutual suspicion that continues their manufacture." The exorcism ended with the sprinkling of holy water to the four points of the compass as Father Vitale prayed this blessing:

> Bless the sky that shelters us and forbid the missiles to fall upon us. Bless the earth that supports us and keep it safe and green. Bless all peoples and nations to the north from which comes our fall and winter chill. Bless all peoples and nations to the south which brings us warmth in spring and summer. Bless those who dwell in the east from which our sun rises daily. Bless those to the west where our solar star sets in glory. Bless all of us here, preserve our lives in peace, give our world a future and bring us to your eternal kingdom. We ask all of this through Christ our Lord. Amen[65]

"And he . . . gave them authority over the unclean spirits, to cast them out" (Matt. 10:1 par.). I am suggesting that symbolic acts of social protest gain a dimension of depth by being formulated as explicit rites of exorcism. One of the drawbacks of any act of protest is that the very specificity of the demand for change implies that a suitable response to the demand would satisfy the protesters. The ritual act of exorcism, on the other hand, unveils an entire system of death behind the specific wrong. It saves us from reformist naiveté and superficial utopianism by revealing the link between the immediate injustice and the entire network of injustices that the kingdom of death maintains at the willing behest of those who benefit from evil.

Exorcism speaks the archaic, subversive language of the unconscious. It is thus able to touch depths no political or economic analysis can reach, though they make their own indispensable contribution as well.

Exorcism is biblical. It avoids the invidious polarization that ideological language provokes, and places the scandal where it rightly belongs: our complicity with, obeisance to, and awed submission before the powers of darkness.

Exorcism is radical. It answers to the problem of ideological blindness. Our involvement in evil goes far beyond our conscious, volitional participation in evil. To a much greater extent than we are aware, we are possessed by the values and powers of an unjust order. It is not enough then simply to repent of the ways we have consciously chosen to collude with evil; we must be freed from our unconscious enthrallment as well. This is not an invitation for people to "blame it on the devil." It is rather the therapeutic insight that we only begin to heal when we take responsibility for what has been done to us. By acknowledging the possibility, in fact the probability, that we are to some degree still under the domination of the values of materialism, anticommunism, and imperialism, we do not absolve ourselves from responsibility but make our deliverance possible.

This understanding of the demonic has the capacity to reconcile the two contending views of the demonic mentioned at the beginning of this chapter—the one regarding evil as first of all institutional, social, and systemic, the other lodging it in the individual. If people are to a significant degree the network of relations in which they are embedded, then the person possessed must reflect to some extent the pathology of the culture, and the collective possession of the culture must feed on the unredeemed darkness of individuals. The demonic confronts us as a single realm, personal and collective, inner and outer, archetypal and institutional. It is the experience of the *unity* of the forces of fragmentation, and not religious obscurantism, that requires us to acknowledge the Prince of demons and his kingdom of death.

I am amazed, and a bit appalled, that I am speaking this way. It is not my native tongue.[66] I do not relish the misuse that a revival of demon-talk will predictably breed. It is my hope that the somewhat demythologized understanding of the demonic that I have proposed here will counteract the tendency to personify demons as little beings in the sky, and help us to identify the demonic as the psychic or spiritual power emanated by societies or institutions or individuals or subaspects of individuals whose energies are bent on overpowering others. I have long resisted this language. But I am constrained by the sheer evil that confronts us to question the utility of our more sanitized and neutral terms. Where are the resources to confront and combat these evils, if not in biblical tradition? Perhaps a careful, discerning, and corporately restrained use of the rite of exorcism can help us deal with collective and outer personal possession, while we struggle to name, own, and incorporate our inner personal demons as well.

3. The Angels of the Churches

The demonic in our time has a peculiar proclivity for institutional structures. It is as if the demons of the Bible grew up along with us and, while leaving some of their smaller cousins to continue harassing individuals, swelled to the gigantic proportions of our transnational corporations, military establishments, university systems, and governmental bureaucracies. The New Testament shows few signs of familiarity with such structures, but it does deal with two institutions, one quite small but growing, the other at its fullest massive extent: the church and the Roman Empire. What it has to say about them has, I believe, startling pertinence for the way we relate to any corporate entity.

My own introduction to the angels of the churches came in 1964 when I was teaching the Book of Revelation to a group of teenagers in the parish I was serving in Hitchcock, Texas. I had gotten no further than chapter 2 when I was arrested by the way the seven letters to the seven churches in Asia Minor were addressed. Unlike Paul's letters, which were sent to an entire congregation ("To the church of the Thessalonians"; "To the church of God which is at Corinth"), the letters in the Apocalypse of John are addressed to the *angels* of the churches in John's care ("To the angel of the church of Ephesus write"). I had never regarded angels seriously, and was not inclined to change. Angels had no place in my worldview. It had been an enormous enough effort to get the Trinity through the chain-mail mesh of the materialistic mindset of my training. I was not prepared to file for exemptions that would permit so large and seemingly redundant a host of spirits to enter a worldview so implacably hostile to all things spiritual. John was unnecessarily jeopardizing an already tenuous peace between my faith and the outlook of my times.

What Is an Angel?

Yet the question about these angels would not be dislodged. The easiest solution was to define these angels out of existence. *Aggelos* means "messenger," and can be applied to human as well as heavenly agents. Why trouble ourselves with the spirit world when John may simply be addressing the bishop or representative of these local congregations, as several scholars have suggested?[1] But I could not help noticing that elsewhere in the book John never alludes to any such leaders. He himself seems to be the spiritual guide of these seven churches. And everywhere else that the term "angel" appears in the Apocalypse, it unambiguously refers to *heavenly* messengers. Nothing in the letters indicates a shift in designation.[2] John receives these letters in a heavenly vision which is itself mediated by an angel (Rev. 1:1): God "made it known by sending his angel to his servant John." The symbolic logic seems to require angelic mediation for all communications in this book.[3]

Since contemporary Jewish and Christian literature spoke of guardian angels over nations, nature, and individual people,[4] John's usage would appear to be an extension of that usage to Christian communities, an analogy with Israel's belief that the congregation of Israel was under the special care of the archangel Michael. We have documentary evidence that at least some people in the early church thought this way. The *Ascension of Isaiah* refers to "the angel of the Christian church" (3:15), and Hermas designates Michael as "the one who has power over this people [the church] and governs them" (*Sim.* 8.3.3). In Rev. 12:7-9 Michael appears in some sense as the defender of the church, and Heb. 1:14 pictures angels watching over and serving the church.[5] The early theologians also interpreted the angels of Revelation 1—3 as spiritual guardians of the churches.[6] The attempt to interpret the angels of the letters as human beings was, I became convinced, prompted by embarrassment, not the data, and I was still left with my original question.

Why does John address each angel as a single entity, responsible for the church in its care, and yet pass with no warning in the body of the letters to exhorting the whole congregation or specific groups of individuals within the church? It would appear that the angel is not something separate from the congregation, but must somehow represent it as a totality. Through the angel, the community seems to step forth as a single collective entity or Gestalt. But the fact that the angel is actually addressed suggests that it is more than a mere personification of the church, but the actual spirituality of the congregation as a single entity. The angel would then exist in, with, and under the material expressions of the church's life as its interiority. As the corporate personality or felt sense of the whole, the angel of the church would have no separate existence apart from the people. But the converse would be equally true: the people would have no unity apart from the angel. Angel and people are the inner and outer aspects of one and the same reality. The people incarnate or embody the angelic spirit; the angel distills the invisible essence of their totality as a group. The angel and the congregation come into being together and, if such is their destiny, pass out of existence together. The one cannot exist without the other.

This way of understanding the angels of the churches finds additional confirmation in the way second person pronouns are used throughout the letters. In current English we have no way of distinguishing "you" singular from "you" plural, as does Greek. Most readers naturally assume that the "yous" in the letters are plurals, referring to all the people in the congregation. But the "yous" are almost all singular, and refer to the angel:

> But I have a few things against you [sing.]: you [sing.] have some there who hold the teaching of Balaam, who taught Balak to put a stumbling block before the sons of Israel, that they might eat food sacrificed to idols and practice immorality. So you [sing.] also have some who hold the teaching of the Nicolaitans. (Rev. 2:14–15)

> But I have this against you [sing.], that you [sing.] tolerate the woman Jezebel, who calls herself a prophetess and is teaching and beguiling my servants to practice immorality and to eat food sacrificed to idols. (Rev. 2:20)

> I know your [sing.] works; you [sing.] have the name of being alive, and you [sing.] are dead. (Rev. 3:1)

> For you [sing.] say, I am rich, I have prospered, and I need nothing; not knowing that you [sing.] are wretched, pitiable, poor, blind, and naked. (Rev. 3:17)[7]

It is the *angel* who is held accountable for the behavior of each of the congregations, and yet the congregation is virtually indistinguishable from the angel. They are the visible and invisible aspects of a single corporate reality.

Is the angel of the church then *real?* On the question of the metaphysical status of angels I have no direct knowledge. Even visions of angels (which people continue to have, though most are reluctant to discuss them for fear of being thought insane) do not settle the question of the nature of angelic reality, for visionary experience is open to the same ambiguities of interpretation (is it real or an illusion?). I am inclined to follow a more functionalist approach. What the ancients called the angel of a collective entity actually answers to an aspect of all corporate realities: they do have an inner spirit, though our culture has been trained to ignore it. To that degree their angels are real, whether they possess personal metaphysical reality apart from their function or not.[8] That function is manifested by their personality and their vocation.

The Personality and Vocation
of Angels

A great deal can be learned about the angels of the churches from the very structure of the seven letters. They begin, almost memolike:

To:

"To the angel of the church in _____ write."

From:

> "The words of" the one like a son of man (described with images drawn largely from 1:9–20).

Body:

> 1. "I know"—a descriptive section, itemizing what the one like a son of man sees in each church, both good and bad.
> 2. Exhortation—a prescriptive section, laced with imperatives challenging each church to fulfill its vocation.

Conclusion:

> 1. "He who has an ear, let him hear what the Spirit says to the churches."
> 2. "To the one who conquers I will give. . . ."

This carefully crafted structure is followed in each of the letters, with some variations in wording and order, so that the seven letters take on the texture of a single whole. Furthermore, the promises at the end of each letter are sprinkled with allusions that only become clear much later (see for example how the meaning of Rev. 2:28 only finally emerges in 22:16), so that the letters are integrally woven into the fabric of the total apocalypse. What is later to happen to nations and to history itself is therefore somehow related to what is going on in these churches.

And what is going on is far from ideal. These churches are riven by strife, factionalism, backbiting, and heresy. As human communities they have little to commend them. Except for Smyrna and Philadelphia they are anything but exemplary. Their sole excuse for existence is to proclaim that the one "who walks among the seven golden lampstands" (2:1) and finally out into the world has become the criterion and judge of human history (19:11–13). These churches endure, not because they have solved the problems of human crankiness and sin, but solely because God requires some group to declare, against the virtually universal defection of the race, that the world belongs to God and to the one who was "the beginning of God's creation" (3:14), the "first-born of the dead, and the ruler of kings on earth" (1:5).

Far from being perfect heavenly beings, these angels encompass every aspect of a church's current reality, good and bad alike. In the same way that I am at every moment simultaneously who I am and who I might become, the angel encompasses both what the church is and what it is called to be. The angel's present reality is described in the first part of the body of the letter: "I know your works," "I know your tribulation," "I know where you dwell." Before the prescription, diagnosis; before the injunction, analysis.

What it is called to become is revealed in the second part of the body, in the exhortations: "Repent and do the works you did at first"; "Do not fear what you are about to suffer . . . be faithful unto death"; "hold fast." The angel of a church is the coincidence of what the church is—its personality—and what it is called to become—its vocation.

The coexistence of these two aspects within a single image may be confusing, but this complexity is precisely what gives to this category its heuristic power. Sociological analyses of a congregation can lift up aspects of its personality, but can make no normative statement about what it should become. Theological analyses can speak about vocation, but tend to do so in global generalizations and categorical imperatives that make no allowance for the unique problems and possibilities of individual congregations.[9] The angel of the church provides us with an exceedingly rich category for congregational analysis, while at the same time providing us with a biblical image for reflecting theologically on the congregation's unique vocation. The angel gathers up into a single whole all the aspirations and grudges, hopes and vendettas, fidelity and unfaithfulness of a given community of believers, and lays it all before God for judgment, correction, and healing. How then can we perceive the angel?

Discerning the Angel of a Church

It is not easy for those of us who have been schooled in the Western outlook to discern the angel of a church. We are faced with two hurdles. First, our worldview is individualistic to an extreme; consequently, most of us regard a group of people as a mere aggregate of individuals, with no organic properties of its own. We do not perceive it as a Gestalt or whole, with its own history, character, and calling. Second, our way of seeing the world is materialistic, and denies that a group could have a spirit. Consequently we do not perceive the angel because we have been trained not to live as seeing the invisible.

If we wish to discern the angel of a church, then, we first need to *see what is there*. Once we have become acquainted with its personality we can ask about its vocation. If the congregation and its physical structures are the outward manifestation of the angelic spirit, then the inner reality should be made manifest by its outer concretions. So we can start from the visible, isolating the manifest characteristics of a church and asking what each reveals about its angel. The items that I will highlight are merely suggestive, certainly not exhaustive, and would serve as but starters for a full analysis of a church.

1. Architecture and ambiance are especially eloquent, since a congregation generally attempts to make an explicit statement about itself through its buildings. Even if a single wealthy member designed and imposed on the congregation a certain structure several generations back, that will still have a major

effect on the life that those buildings permit. One way or another, all the values, prestige needs, aesthetics, and class status of a congregation will be projected into brick, board, and stone.

Once I was leading Bible study in an exquisite mansion that had been turned into a retreat house. We were sitting in a circle on a twenty-five-thousand-dollar oriental rug, studying the "Rich Young Man." I began to notice an odd phenomenon. People simply could not believe that Jesus would say that the rich cannot enter the kingdom of heaven. They seemed puzzled, confused, irritated. Gradually I began to realize that it was the rug. The rug was saying, at a subliminal level so that no one was directly aware of it, "Not true." Since I was new to this business of angels, I did not have the presence of mind to stop right there and say, "Are you aware of what's happening? This rug is lying here denying that what Jesus said is true, and you're all agreeing with it!" I just gritted my teeth and tried harder. But nothing availed. The rug was stronger than I.

On Good Friday of 1982 my wife June and I entered a sparsely attended Catholic church on the main square of Cuzco, Peru. It was dead. What could the priest say that could counteract the thunderous statement made by a building erected on the site of a razed Inca temple, by virtual slave labor, adorned with gold leaf stolen from a high civilization by a group of Spanish thugs, and whose chapel had been converted into a curio shop?

Architecture, however, is not destiny. That same night we attended a different church, no doubt built under some of the same dubious circumstances, which was packed with young people and vibrant with commitment to the life of the common people. Its angel had been redeemed somehow, and the building was a vehicle for the liberating acts of God.

2. A great deal of what a church is and does is determined by the economic class and income of its members, their racial and ethnic background, level of education, age, and gender balance. These show in how the members talk, what they expect the church to do, where they live, where the church is located, and in the ideological and political preferences of the members. Class extends even to unwritten dress codes and behavioral norms. Congregations can to some degree transcend this determinism, but only if they are aware of its importance and are committed to higher values. Leadership is critical at this point; we all know clergy and lay persons who gradually conform to socioeconomic pressure, avoid every subject that might trigger controversy, and settle in as the kept chaplains of an unjust order.

3. Much is revealed by the power structure also. To a certain extent the way a congregation is organized is set by its denominational polity. Within that framework, however, there is tremendous latitude for leadership styles, theological orientations, and attitudes toward authority. Those of us who travel around

from church to church can tell after only a few minutes what patterns of authority have predominated over the past fifteen years, just by the way people defer to us, withdraw, or regard us as peers. It takes longer to discover where power is really located, or to establish the concentric circles that run from a sense of belonging and ownership near the center to marginalization and alienation on the outside. Pastoral leadership is significant but sometimes overstressed. If the congregation called the pastor, he or she may simply reflect the values the people already hold. Pastors can have a significant impact on the angel; all too often, unfortunately, that impact is the result of a dominating personality or an authoritarian style and not of a genuine angelic transformation.

Pastoral leadership can also be paralyzing. A prosperous church once asked a colleague of mine to lead its governing body in a five-evening exploration of ways to respond to its neighborhood, which was now populated by gays, blacks, Hispanics, and the elderly. For the second session she invited me to do Bible study with them focusing on the nature of their discipleship in that neighborhood. For the first hour I simply floundered. Everyone was perfectly nice. I encountered no overt resistance. Yet each question I asked seemed to be sucked down into a black hole. At the break I whispered to my colleague, "What's going on? Nothing is happening. Nothing!" "It's demons," she replied, half in jest. "You're right," I answered, shocked at our speaking this way. "But what are they?" After several weeks of investigation she discovered that the head minister had been there over twenty years and had a physical ailment that would become aggravated under stress. So over that period he had selected a governing board that "knew," without it ever having been said explicitly, that their job was to keep their minister from being upset. Into that situation we had unwarily come, with the ostensible task of helping the church launch out into controversial and risky new ministries to a community of gays, blacks, Hispanics, and the elderly. That task, which had been set by a new head of their session, was totally at odds with the session's unspoken job description, and at some deep level *they all knew it* and responded with passive resistance. They were doing exactly what they were "supposed" to do.

This put my colleague in a difficult position. She had been invited in as a change-agent, yet this new knowledge would demand upheaval far beyond what the church had anticipated, and would, if consciously faced, lead to a great deal of pain. Since the minister was due to retire in a year and a half, she decided she would simply have to leave the contours of the angel hidden in plain sight and let the session's renewal project abort itself.

Perhaps it was too strong to speak of the atmosphere in that session as demonic. What we had encountered was the angel—a particularly sentimental, shortsighted, and ingrown angel which, if not "converted" soon, would spell the death of that congregation. But even this defection from true vocation was a manifestation of deep caring; consequently, under new leadership, the church has blossomed into a fresh sense of mission—which illustrates how effective creative pastoral guidance can be when it is in tune with a church's higher calling.

4. One of the most telling indicators of the health of an angel is how the congregation handles conflict. There are some churches, like some marriages, where no one seems to be happy unless the members are at each other's throats. As a woman in one of our workshops commented, "I have belonged to this church for twenty-four years, and have watched how it ate a whole series of ministers. It simply crunched them up in its jaws. One had been a very successful minister of a church that just seemed to be holy ground. At our church he just got eaten up. Yet the church from which he came continued to be holy ground even after a succession of other clergy." Another, a member of a priestly order, remarked about one of the chapter houses, "There's pathology in the walls. You can be infected by it." In most cases the history of church conflicts goes back generations. A study by Speed Leas of the Alban Institute found that each year one out of one hundred churches in four major Protestant denominations (UCC, UPUSA, PCUS, Episcopal) dismisses its minister for reasons other than immoral or unethical conduct. The primary reason is congregational conflict that existed *before the pastor arrived*. What appeared to be a personnel issue was, in fact, often a case of a strife-torn angel. The pastor was made a scapegoat for deeper conflicts no one was willing to face.[10]

5. Again, within denominational rubrics there is ample latitude for high or low liturgies, the whole gamut of musical tastes, and various types of preaching. The educational program quickly reveals what premium is put on spiritual growth, as do the special groups that meet during the week (are they limited to social occasions and Boy Scouts, or do they reach deeper needs, like Alcoholics Anonymous, marriage enrichment, or singles and divorced groups?). The theology tends to be denominationally oriented, but not always recognizably so, and the role of the Bible stretches all the way from pretext to preeminence. It is in worship that the majority of the congregation experiences the angel; paradoxically, it is in worship that the angel most flagrantly goes unnoticed.

6. How does the congregation see itself? How do others see it? Does membership confer status, or does it indicate a high level of commitment to mission? Is the church inner- or outer-directed? Is it related to its neighborhood or the larger community? Is it self-engrossed, or engaged in struggles for social justice and global peace? Is it evangelistic or nurturing, or both? Is it on speaking terms with its angel, and fired by a sense of its divine vocation, or is it a country club,

or a haven against the chill of rapid social change? What is the place of spirituality, of prayer and meditation, of the inner journey? Is it easy to "get on board," to become drawn into the life of the group? What about its history, its traditions, its annual celebrations, its invariant money-raisers and teas? Who have been its heroes and its villains, and what are the skeletons in its closet?[11]

We Americans have so short a history that we seldom realize how far back these determinative stories can go. On the east coast of England are two small churches a few miles apart where, one thousand years before, the Danes invaded Britain. The bishop had tried repeatedly to merge the two congregations and appoint a single rector, but the people consistently refused. Finally he went to one of the churches and said, "You have told me many reasons why you don't want to merge with the other congregation, but none of them seems very convincing. Now tell me—what is your *real* reason?" One older member of the vestry finally replied, "Well, Bishop, if you really want to know, they didn't tell us the Danes were coming."

With a memory that long and that strong, their angels had little chance of merging, short of a major act of mutual forgiveness and perhaps a bit of light-hearted joking over the absurdity of it all.[12]

To this point we have largely been attempting to identify the personality of the church by edging in from the outside via its visible manifestations. The parts we have analyzed need not themselves be determinative, but they do tend to manifest the spirituality of the congregation. But now we would need to apprehend the invisible by moving beyond the outer manifestations of the angel and approaching the angel directly. Here on the fringe between seen and unseen are the sense of fellowship or friendliness, warmth or coldness, openness or closedness, and all the countless elements that build the mood, climate, or feeling of a place. Here one asks about color, not so much the ones used in the decor as those which the spirit exudes. If you drew the angel, what colors would choose you?

Finally, we must attempt to grasp the angel whole, to gain a felt sense of its spirit or energy as a totality. Even the most meticulous analysis sometimes overlooks the most important qualities. Whatever insight John may have brought to these letters, he claims for the final product an act of revelation. I am inclined to take him at his word, and to suggest that such revelation is available to us as well. It may be valuable simply to sit before the angel and invite it to introduce itself. This can be done by writing a dialogue with it, asking it questions, and allowing it to respond freely. We have unconsciously registered aspects of that angel that we may not be even close to being able to articulate; if we will let the angel do the talking, perhaps it will tell us about these things also. We might try doing an impressionistic image of it in pastels or clay. However we come at it, the task of learning to see the invisible will require the creative, active imagination.[13]

Origen had a quaint way of speaking about the invisible dimension of a church. "When the saints are assembled, there will be two churches, one of people and one of angels." For they "each have their own angel encamped beside them"; each angel will be with the person it has been "commissioned to guard and direct." Thus when he preached he was mindful that he was speaking "to people and at the same time to angels."[14] The profundity of this observation becomes clearest by contrasting it with the way we might describe a similar group. Our inclination might be to say just the reverse: whenever a group of people come together, there are two congregations, the manifest group, represented by the persona or mask we show each other, and the latent group, consisting of the sum total of the "shadow" each of us brings with us—the unredeemed anger, prejudice, fear, anxiety, feelings of rejection, and instinctual urges each of us tries so desperately to keep hidden from others. Normally only the manifest group is visible; but under certain circumstances of stress, friction, or conflict, that "other congregation" (the shadow element) can make its explosive and disastrous appearance. Schisms, riots, pogroms, lynchings, witch-hunts all have their origin in this shadow congregation.

That is more the way our society might put it. Perhaps Origen would have liked to have been able to learn that from us. But perhaps Origen could also teach us that there is still that other, higher congregation that can call out, not our basest selfish natures, but the higher self in each, and the higher vocation of the group. We may not wish to speak of "angels." But can we begin to perceive these higher operations and foster them? And do we really have any other name for them?[15] Our society has not, to my knowledge, learned to speak of such things.

Ministering to the Angel of a Church

The angel of a church becomes demonic when the congregation turns its back on the specific tasks set before it by God and makes some other goal its idol. A church with shrinking numbers may become obsessed with growth and the recovery of its former glory. A minister with a dominating personality may attempt to impose the program that worked so well at her or his last church. None of this may be evil in itself, but if it is done without consulting the angel, it can be disastrous. At times the angel behaves something like an alcoholic who knows what is right, knows that what he is doing is destructive and wrong, but is powerless to stop. The angel, it is important to stress, *is not an agent of change*. That role, the letters make clear, belongs to the "one like a human being," the Christ. The angel, because it can be nothing less than the sum total of all its parts, may be paralyzed by discordant factions in the church (the Nicolaitans, the followers of "Jezebel," Rev. 2:15, 20). It may be rendered impotent by the lack of commitment among its members ("lukewarm," 3:16). But no matter how far the congregation has deviated from the divine will, the knowledge of that will is still encoded in its "higher self," the angel. Indeed, it is precisely those institutions that have the highest task that are capable of becoming the most demonic.

Let me digress to remark that *every* collective entity that has continuity through time has an angel. General Motors has its own unique spirit that sets it apart from every other corporation.[16] Schools thrive on school spirit, and disintegrate without it. A staff of co-workers depends on high morale to keep motivated, an athletic team learns unselfishness by subordinating individual goals to the team spirit, and military units undergo combat simulations in order to weld the unit's fighting spirit. Political leaders hold rallies or preempt prime-time television in order to fire the public with patriotic rhetoric and build the national spirit. We are familiar with all this, but keep it on the fringes of our minds. Our worldview has no adequate categories for placing it at the center. We do not possess collective categories adequate for understanding how individuals could jettison their own values and be carried away by a "mob spirit." The idea of angelic spirits seemed too cumbersome for the modern mind; angels were always having to be multiplied to account for everything in the world. Now perhaps we are in a position to see why there were so many myriads of them: every corporate entity has one. They are simply the interiority or spirituality behind the visible façade of things.

And they can be extremely helpful in trying to comprehend institutions. A colleague commented, "When I was teaching in graduate school I didn't understand about the angel, so in trying to foster institutional change I attacked individuals. I thought they were evil people because they were doing evil things. That merely created such an unpleasant situation that I had to resign to get out of it. I didn't realize that I was up against the angel of the institution."

Corporate structures have a remarkable resilience through time. Change all the employees at General Motors and replace them with new ones the next day, and GM would probably go right on doing the same kinds of things it has always done, and in something of the same manner. Like a river which is never made up of the same water molecules from one moment to the next, yet remains the same river, or the human body, which changes all its cells over a period of seven years, institutions also undergo the perpetual turnover of their employees without *necessarily* changing their essential nature. Enlightened and humane corporate executives *can* make a difference in the tone, morale, and profitability of a business, but even the most sincere work under the severe constraints of the market, competition, and limited resources. The frequently heard complaints by executives that they feel relatively powerless simply attest to the sheer inertia that an institution achieves as it courses along its trajectory through time. There is an almost homeostatic quality, as if the angel acted like a gyroscope to resist rocking. Improvements can occasionally be brought about by removing obstructive personnel, but all too often, as we see in family systems therapy, someone else who had previously been cooperative suddenly assumes the vacated role of obstructionist *as if the system required it.* Real change must therefore affect not just the visible forms an institution takes, but somehow must alter the spirit, the core essence, of the entity as a whole.

How then does one address that spirit? In the case of the seven churches of the Apocalypse, the answer is clear: the angel must receive a message from the Human Being (son of man) through a prophetic intermediary. The angels are powerless to stay the fall of humanity, wrote Eusebius, "because of humanity's own free choice of evil."[17] The angel must be constrained to change by a higher power, one capable of transforming the choices of individuals in the congregation while fundamentally altering the group spirit or group culture as well. This higher power identifies itself in a variety of ways in the salutations of each letter:

> And to the angel of the church in Smyrna write: "The words of the first and the last, who died and came to life." (Rev. 2:8)

> And to the angel of the church in Philadelphia write: "The words of the holy one, the true one, who has the key of David, who opens and no one shall shut, who shuts and no one opens." (Rev. 3:7)

> And to the angel of the church in Laodicea write: "The words of the Amen, the faithful and true witness, the beginning of God's creation." (Rev. 3:14)

It is only the "one like a human being" who can bring the churches into line with the will of God. The churches believe that they have encapsulated Otherness in themselves, that they "know" God and God's will. They cannot be transformed, then, unless they encounter that Otherness as judgment and accounting: God must suddenly appear to the congregations as *outside* their ken. They must experience a jolt of recognition: we are out of phase with the will of God.

That Otherness that lays such a radical demand on these insignificant congregations must be revealed to them, however, in a way that is not wholly discontinuous with their history. Hence the role of the intermediary, John, who is a part of their sameness and yet has beheld the Otherness and can unmask the ways their existence is out of line with their vocation.

It is nevertheless strange that God should use a human being to deliver a message to an angel. One would have thought God would communicate directly with the angels. But such quandaries are the result of our separating "heaven" from everyday experience and casting it up into interstellar space. If, as I have suggested in *Naming the Powers,* we were to conceive of heaven as the transcendent possibilities latent in every emerging moment, then God *must* find a human being to carry the message. There is no other way to body it forth, to incarnate it. And John can carry the message to the angel of the church precisely because the angel is not somewhere off in Andromeda but is the living interiority of the actual congregation. John is the angel's angel! As messenger to the messengers, John recalls the churches to their task of declaring the sovereignty of Christ over the Powers, which is the burden of his vision from Revelation 4 on.[18]

In the final analysis only Christ as the Spirit of the whole church can change a church,[19] and only the renewed presence of that spirit can bring the churches into line with their supreme vocation. Only as changes in personnel, programs, and relationships take place in congruence with that vocation will genuine transformation take place. For that reason the single most important element in Revelation 1—3 is not the letters as such, but the primal vision that makes them possible: the vision of Christ as the Ultimate Human (1:9–20). Change requires all our strength and sagacity, but it also requires that we sit quite still until we have discerned the angel and have been caught up in a vision of what it could become if it were alive to the divine presence that "walks among the seven golden lampstands" (2:1). As we continue to rehearse this vision and to act confidently on the basis of it, our own demeanor will be experienced by others as invitation rather than demand. And lived visions are contagious.

This is in sharp contrast to the more usual attempt to change a church by direct assault. The very effort by a minister or a subgroup to impose change, however beneficial, constellates resistance in others, often those one might have expected to be allies. Well-intended intervention is regarded as manipulation or a power grab. The very attempt may in fact be quite egocentric, born of the need to see ourselves as "successful" clergy or "committed" laity. Only "the one like a human being" is able to change a church, and that one does so by means of indirection: by changing the angel of the church. This requires discerning the lineaments and characteristics of a church's angel. It means holding its present reality up before the one who is present in its midst for judgment or affirmation. It involves accepting and loving its present reality, however corrupt, just as one would any other sinner. Churches are like people: they do not change in order that they might be accepted; they must be accepted in order that they might change. If we accept and love the wounded angel, praying for a vision of its true potentiality (rather than imposing our own), and engaging with others in the struggle to discern the true nature of its calling, then the whole congregation may move toward it organically.

We must do everything we can to foster change, and we can do nothing. God calls us to transform the church, and yet only God can bring that transformation about. God sends us to proclaim the word, and we are utterly free of any responsibility to make the word effective. When we can live within that paradox without incredulity, we will discover that God is indeed the real sovereign of the world.

An Actual Case

I will conclude this chapter with a case study of an actual congregation, as an immediate test case of the utility of reviving and reinterpreting the notion of angels of churches.

Melinda is the pastor of two rural New England churches as different as joy and despair. One is alive, responsive, concerned. In the three years since her arrival, that church has tripled in attendance at worship. The other church greeted her with initial enthusiasm, but soon dropped back to the dismal worship attendance that had been the agony of the three previous pastors: sometimes as few as three to twelve people out of a membership of fifty-five. At first Melinda blamed herself, and tried all the harder. When people criticized her for not visiting as much as the former pastor, she tried to oblige, but soon learned that no upper limit of satisfaction existed.

One family that had been coming for two and a half years decided to join. Melinda spread the word that they were to be received as members the next Sunday, hoping that people would turn out to show support. Only three people came. The couple's best friend arrived twenty-five minutes late, after they had already joined. Melinda felt so deeply saddened by this that she pressed the session for an explanation. At heart, she discovered, they wanted the church simply to *be* there for weddings and funerals, but not for worship, or community, or celebration, or mutual vulnerability and healing.

Pushing her inquiry further, she found that the church was a microcosm of the community. The church had been founded a hundred years before, and hostilities between families went back several generations. The real power in the church was George, the wealthiest farmer in the valley, who exercised power behind the scenes and was not even at that time a church officer. When Melinda arrived she encouraged a more democratic style of church leadership than simply doing what George said. Gradually, new people rose to leadership whose enthusiasm Melinda hoped would strike a spark of life in the congregation. George was still as powerful as ever, but now he exercised power by criticism and by sowing dissatisfaction.

Nor had the new session members been able to change things, for one of the routines of the old guard was to elect new people who had become active and then to withdraw and leave them to fail. Then when the new people do fail, the old guard enjoys the satisfaction of having demonstrated that the church cannot function without them.

This was not a new pattern, however, Historically, whenever members got hurt they stayed away and joined the underminers. In their town the men form opinions and their wives spread them. Having a woman pastor only increased the women's hostility, since Melinda symbolizes what they will never be able to choose to be in themselves. The men oppress their wives in order to feel better about themselves, and the only outlet the women have is to dump their feeling onto Melinda. A high incidence of alcoholism and suicide in that part of rural New England is symptomatic of the emotional poverty of the members, who function at the level of sheer maintenance. And that reduced expectation of life is all they bring to the church as well: they only wish it to survive. They are not interested in growth, a fact that visitors quickly detect.

But there is a deeper, more sinister, though unconscious, reason these people want to keep their church, and to keep it precisely as they have it, in a condition of perpetual morbidity. The low self-esteem of the people in that town is transferred to the church. What appears at first glance to be a death-wish is really closer to a sickness-unto-death-wish. One way to deal with their own sense of failure is to structure situations where people better trained, more gifted and personally developed than they are forced to fail: their ministers. The three previous ministers were also subjected to the non-attendance torture. When the second blew up over the no-shows on Easter morning he was locked out of the church. When the third left, discouraged by the lack of response, two hundred people showed up to say goodbye. The sadism is unmistakable. The minister is to be a scapegoat, sacrificed on behalf of the community, so that people there can feel a bit less badly about themselves.

At one open meeting that Melinda called to deal with non-attendance, one man who seldom came asked what it felt like to lead worship with only three to six people present. She answered, "It feels like I am being stabbed in the heart." No one responded to her statement. Instead they defended their right not to come. What she had said merely confirmed them in the success of their mimetic ritual of sacrifice: she had gotten the "point." Killing the minister also serves to protect them against the pain of facing themselves, or the vulnerability that would be required for genuine community to emerge in their town. The vicarious death of the minister acts as a substitutionary atonement for them, relieving them of the terrible prospect of forgiving one another for feuds whose origins are lost to memory. Melinda summed it up, "I know that right now I am the projection of this community's shadow." Just knowing this helps, but the daily hemorrhaging of her own sense of self-esteem and competence throws the outcome into question. She may indeed become so disillusioned that she quits the parish ministry altogether, despite the success and acceptance she has experienced at the other church.

In the seminar where she shared all this, I asked her to make the angel of this church in clay. She made a heavy-bottomed bowl with a point, like an amphora, so that it could not stand by itself. The sides were filled with holes. The opening at the top was irregular, wide at places, narrow at others. She commented that the bottom was heavy, filled with a sense of failure so deep that it almost seems inherent. The holes are escape valves to release the intensity of the conflict in the bottom. These holes prevent it from exploding altogether, but also mean that it cannot contain the Holy Spirit. The pointed bottom requires Melinda to run around continually propping the church up.

What could possibly be the vocation of such a church? Does it have any reason or right to survive at all? Would the best solution be simply to help it die, to beseech the Human Being to remove its lampstand from its place (Rev. 2:5)? Such a strategy is not likely to work because the members seem determined to keep their church just the way it is. Can the angel then be redeemed? Can any healing take place when there is so little manifest desire for it?

In an ironic way, their very sadism betrays a misplaced longing for redemption. They want atonement, but they want it cheap, at another's expense. The clergy get impaled on this spike through their own desire for success. Their very efforts to make something of the church provide the congregation the very means by which to frustrate, demoralize, and finally crucify them. "It feels like I am being stabbed in the heart." Healing in such a setting would also probably require a kind of crucifixion, but this one consciously chosen. The first step would certainly require unmasking the angel. The unconscious, mimetic character of the church's life would have to be exposed, amidst much clamorous denial. As many people as possible would need to be involved in this unmasking—perhaps beginning with a study of Revelation 1–3 by the session, since they have a stake in discovering that they are but the latest to be granted position only to have effective power and support denied them. Melinda must expand the community of support willing to explore with her what is needed to redeem the angel, so that she cannot be isolated and undermined.

Second, she and this core of support need to find ways to break the vicious circle of gossip, sniping, and underground recriminations. One church has found it helpful to require of all church officers, and to try to persuade the whole congregation, that they refuse to listen to any third-party conversations, unless the informant has also spoken to the third party. Another strategy is to chase down every rumor or bit of gossip to its source, and to confront the originator face to face. This can be exhausting but finally creates a climate where it becomes too costly for people to continue backbiting, at least unguardedly. It is urgent that the members of the congregation be deprived of situations where it pays to sin. It is possible to maximize or minimize gains to be gotten from sin. Loving one's enemy means in part helping to redeem the enemy by making it less profitable for him or her to continue to do harm.

The leadership of the church needs to remove the old guard's incentive and capacity to dominate by negativity. That also means developing programs aimed at a different constituency that can be accomplished without the old guard attending.

These steps, though Herculean, are relatively minor compared to the even more central task of breaking the basic pattern of scapegoating and atonement. Melinda is a resourceful and dedicated pastor. Perhaps in the grace of God she will discover ways to help individuals, one by one, come to terms with their own self-rejection or, at very least, to stop displacing their own self-loathing onto the minister. Somewhere in the process, perhaps the congregation will catch sight of a whole new vision, and not so much solve the old problems as simply leave them behind, fired by a larger purpose. Then, like the man born blind whom Jesus healed, who though he had never possessed sight was able to begin a sighted life, this congregation and its angel might discover for the first time its real vocation under God. For even to such a congregation as this, as to the similarly flawed church in Laodicea, the promise still stands: "Behold, I stand at the door and knock; if any one hears my voice and opens the door, I will come in to him and eat with him, and he with me" (Rev. 3:20).

All of which is easily, perhaps even glibly, said. But one shudders to think of the cost of carrying out such a transformation. Perhaps it could only be achieved over decades, involving a series of clergy and laity. Each minister would need to balance staying on against the equally valid injunction to "shake off the dust from your feet as you leave that . . . town" (Matt. 10:14). But once we see what the issues really are, it is remarkable how God supplies us with staying power and renews our strength. Such an enormous outlay of energy would be scarcely worth it, except that these people, like so many people everywhere, think they have sight and are instead "wretched, pitiable, poor, blind, and naked" (Rev. 3:17). And to precisely such poor, once they discover themselves poor, belongs the kingdom of heaven.

Six months after our initial seminar together I received from Melinda this letter which I reproduce in part:

What a difficult fall. . . . I returned from the seminar wanting to deal creatively and effectively with the problems that had surfaced in _____. So I scheduled first a meeting with the pastor-parish relations committee. The meeting was carefully prepared for by the chairperson. . . . We decided no complaint would be heard if a name wasn't attached to it. The meeting date was announced a month beforehand with committee members listed in the bulletin. The congregation was urged to speak with a member of the committee if he/she had a concern, complaint, word of thanks, unmet need, etc. These were brought to the meeting. One by one we dealt with them. I was full of understanding, openness, lacking a defensive posture, yet was assertive. (I prepared well and was graced by the Spirit!!) The tables slowly turned at that meeting. One member (a "new" person in the church, yet born in that town) stated, "I come to church, look for my elders, and see none. Then I hear them spreading vicious rumors about the minister and anyone else trying to do something here." George, who was now on the committee, spoke rather defensively at this point, looked to me, and said, "Sis, we hired you to bring new people here. As far as I can see you've failed." To which I said, "George, I bring them in and you chase them away." "Examples, Sis, let me hear some examples." So I reeled them off. George heard the truth of my words and finally broke down and said something like, "We've always complained about our minister—no one's ever satisfied us—it's not you, Melinda. As a matter of fact, you're the only one who has been willing to deal with these problems, which are as old as the church. Perhaps it's *us* who are the problem, not you."

The beginning . . . much has happened since then. . . .

> Peace,
> Melinda

Yes, peace, indeed, or at least the aroma of it. That troubled angel is still a long way from being healed, but the process has at least finally begun.

But if transformation is possible in churches, is it an absurdity to hold out hope for the transformation of even larger collective entities? Can we hope for the transformation even of *nations*?

4. The Angels of the Nations

Nationalism is not, one could argue, an unmitigated evil. It provides a bonding force to unite highly diverse tribes and peoples. It furnishes a sense of collective identity capable of drawing people out of themselves and their family groupings into a larger whole. It is one of the sole forces capable of standing up against the economic onslaught of the transnational corporations. And it prevents the great empires from imposing their wills without resistance. More might be said on its behalf. But what makes nationalism so pernicious, so death-dealing, so blasphemous, is its seemingly irresistible tendency toward idolatry. In the name of this idol whole generations are maimed, slaughtered, exiled, and made idolaters. One hundred million lives have been offered on the altar of this Moloch thus far in the twentieth century,[1] and we are now watching in a kind of mesmerized horror as the two superpowers escalate the probability of destroying the planet—*in order to defend their nations.*

Only a god could command such madness, carried out with such lucid rationality by some of the brightest minds of each nation. And that is where the irony begins: modern people do not believe in gods.

We believe in the existence of idols, true enough—things falsely worshiped as gods. But our worldview and our theologies forbid us to believe in the real existence of gods. To be sure, we know that when people idolize the nation-state, this idolatry serves to make that state a god. But surely the state is *not* a god, in any sense of the word. We do not understand the real dynamics of idolatry—that when a nation is made a god *it becomes a god,* not just as the inner conviction of individuals, but as the actual spirituality of the nation itself. We do not comprehend what is unleashed when millions of people worship the state as absolute; we do not discern the spiritual reality such idolatry actually creates. And because we do not believe, as all ancient peoples believed, that there are gods *behind* the states, we have nowhere to *locate* the center to which all this false devotion flows. We believe that idolatry is something idolaters do, but we deny that they do it toward anything real. Thus we offer up countless new bodies to be sacrificed to the gods whose existence we deny, in order to make and keep the world safe for our nations and their interests.

Israel and the early Christians looked at the matter quite differently. Contrary to widespread misunderstanding, the ancient believers in Yahweh did not deny the existence of the gods. They merely—as we shall see later in this chapter and in the next—denied their ultimacy. They perceived that "every nation and tribe and tongue and people" (the Book of Revelation's comprehensive way of cataloguing the diverse forms of collective life before the rise of the modern nation-state[2]) was presided over by a spiritual Power. Rome had its *genius*, Athens its goddess Athena, Ammon its god Chemosh, Babylon its Marduk, Israel its Yahweh. Gods were abundant and filled a multitude of functions, but they were nowhere experienced more ubiquitously than as the gods of large collectivities.

It is a modern misconception that these gods were the focus of the *religion* of a people. Our distinction between church and state, and our very use of the word "religion," are anachronistic for the period prior to the rise of Christendom. Worship was not the private choice of people who just happened to belong to a certain nation or people; it was to a very large extent the collective invocation of the spirit *of* that nation or people. Worship of the gods of a nation was the spiritual expression of what it meant to *be* a nation, tribe, tongue, or people. The gods of the nations—later depotentiated by being demoted to angelic rank by Jews and Christians—were conceived of in a projected way as possessing a separate existence as heavenly, transcendent beings. On the hypothesis I am advancing in these volumes *they were the actual inner spirituality of the social entity itself.* I will argue in this chapter that the gods or angels of the nations have a discernible personality and vocation; that they too, though fallen, pernicious, and insatiable, are a part of the redemptive plan of God; and that our role in this redemptive activity is to acknowledge their existence, love them as creatures of God, unmask their idolatries, and stir up in them their heavenly vocation.

Such an undertaking will not easily command assent; it has been quite some time since the angels of nations have been a regular feature of religious language. I will not request credulity, but only patience in understanding the notion in its original setting. Then we can assess whether it offers any clues for comprehending the self-annihilating madness of the nations.

The Angel-Gods of the Nations

One of the earliest biblical references to the idea of angel-gods of the nations is Deut. 32:8–9. "When the Most High gave to the nations their inheritance, when he separated the sons of men, he fixed the bounds of the peoples according to the number of the sons of God. For the Lord's portion is his people, Jacob his allotted heritage."[3] Portrayed here are two levels of reality: heavenly and earthly. On earth, God separates humanity into its nations, traditionally fixed at seventy on the basis of Genesis 10. In heaven, God sets angels (called *bene elohim,* "sons of God" or "sons of gods") over each nation, to represent its interests and be accountable for its acts in the heavenly council, over which Yahweh alone presides. But Yahweh appoints no angel over Israel; Yahweh alone will watch over it. (Later tradition was to assign that task to the archangel Michael.)

Daniel 10 provides the Bible's fullest picture of these angels of the nations in action. The scene is ostensibly set in the third year of Cyrus, King of Persia. In actuality, however, the passage appears to have been composed between 167–65 B.C.E. in response to the attempt of Antiochus IV Epiphanes, the Seleucid ruler, to destroy the Jewish religion. According to the narrative, Daniel, a Babylonian Jew who has risen to a high post in the court of Nebuchadnezzar, and who now enjoys equal prominence under the conquering Persians, is moved by grief over the fate of the exiled Jews to fast and mourn for twenty-one days. On the twenty-first day an angel (I will call this angel the Messenger) appears to him in a dazzling vision, explaining that though Daniel's prayer had been heard on the first day of the fast, and the Messenger had been dispatched immediately, he had been withstood for twenty-one days by the "guardian angel" (*archōn,* LXX) of the kingdom of Persia. Finally, "Michael, one of the chief angels" (*archontōn*), came to help him, holding the guardian angel of Persia to a standoff while the Messenger slipped through to carry a message to Daniel (that message is the burden of Daniel 11–12). Then, the Messenger says, he has to return to "fight the guardian angel of Persia. After that the guardian angel of Greece will appear. There is no one to help me except Michael, Israel's guardian angel" (10:20–21, TEV).[4]

This is remarkable: the angel of the Persian empire, withstanding for twenty-one days the angel of God sent to Daniel! This is not the sentimentalized image of angels of Sunday school art. The angel of Persia at the very least does not want foreign angels entering Persian air space. It has a will all its own; it has a right to contend for the best interests of the Persian empire narrowly defined. It has a stake in censoring a message that foretells the destruction of the Persian empire and the emigration of a talented and productive captive people. We are not presented with perfect angelic beings as the idealized personifications of nations. On the contrary, the angels of the nations, like the angels of the churches in the last chapter, represent the actual spirituality and possibilities of actual entities.[5] The power of the angel-prince of Persia here reflects the political power of the Persian empire, before which puny Judah, its temple destroyed, its land desolate, and its people captive in Babylon, must have appeared insignificant. Even God could not easily muscle this empire into compliance—or, put less picturesquely, without the intercessions of Daniel, God could not intervene on Israel's behalf, since to do so would be to violate the Persian empire's freedom to resist the will of God.

Beneath the story of the Babylonian-Persian-Jewish "Daniel," however, lies another story altogether, like a buried portrait on a reused canvas. However, this picture is not older, but a representation of current events. The time is not 532 but 167 B.C.E. Antiochus IV Epiphanes, the Syrian ruler, has just proscribed the Jewish religion, declaring himself to be the "Manifest God." He has outlawed Sabbath observance and circumcision, had copies of the Torah burned, encouraged nude exercise in the gymnasia, after the Greek fashion, and sacrificed a pig on an altar built for Zeus in the Jerusalem temple, all for the purpose of forcibly Hellenizing the Jewish people. Against the background of those contemporary shocks, the author presents his hero as a stalwart Jew struggling to resist assimilation. Though he has served as a high official for first the Babylonian and then the Persian courts, and has been given the name of a Babylonian god (Belteshazzar, "May Bel protect his life"?), he has not compromised his faith in Yahweh. Daniel 10 finds him mounting a twenty-one-day fast out of grief for captive Israel, and continuing to fast right through the Feast of Passover. Since Antiochus has prohibited celebration of Passover, this may be a covert call to defiance, as if to say, You can prevent our eating the Passover feast, but you have no power to prohibit our fasting.[6]

One possibility for interpreting the meaning of this fast would be that the conflict between the Messenger and the guardian angel of Persia mirrors Daniel's own inner struggle to free his spirit from the last vestiges of internalized foreign ways. Daniel may then be made the model of the process demanded of Jews generally in the contest to save Judaism from enforced Hellenization. This interpretation founders on one point, however. The angel does not delay twenty-one days until Daniel has purged himself, nor is Daniel only *heard* after he has cleansed himself; "for *from the first day* that you set your mind to understand and humbled yourself before your God, *your words have been heard,* and I have come because of your words" (Dan. 10:12). Why then the delay?

Because the guardian angel of Persia blocked the Messenger. The scene answers to the question of theodicy. To the usual reaction to calamity, "How could God have allowed this?" the text poses a radically different and new one. God had no choice. The Powers are able to hold God's messenger at bay for twenty-one days and prevent the message from reaching Daniel. Israel normally factored only two elements into the equation of prayer—God and themselves. In that equation, if the petition requested of God was denied, only two alternatives existed: God had denied it, or the petitioners were at fault through sin or lack of faith. But here a third element is introduced into the equation: the

Powers. The angels of the nations have a will of their own, and are capable of resisting the will of God. God is perhaps omnipotent, but certainly not able to impose the divine will on recalcitrant Powers, due to God's own self-limitation: God will not violate the freedom of creatures.

This new element in prayer—the resistance of the Powers to God's will—marks a decisive break with the notion that God is the cause of all that happens. Here for the first time allowance is made for the mighty intermediate forces that have interposed themselves between God's will and the cries of the needy for justice. Prayer is often regarded as merely autotransformative: the one who prays creates in himself or herself a more receptive frame of mind. In many cases this may be a necessary component of effective prayer, but it is not the one stressed by the author of Daniel. The point here seems to be that Daniel's intercessions have made possible the intervention of God. Prayer changes us, but it also changes what is possible for God. Daniel's cry was heard on the first day; it opened an aperture for God to act in concert with human freedom. It inaugurated war in heaven. It opened a way through the impenetrable spirituality of foreign hegemony in order to declare a new and real divine possibility. And the message had the desired effect. Steeled by prophecies such as these, Jewish resistance mounted up against the policies of Antiochus, and in a shorter time than perhaps even the author himself envisaged, the temple was cleansed of pagan pollutions and Jewish traditions were restored (Hanukkah, December 165 B.C.E.).

War in heaven—every event on earth has its heavenly counterpart.[7] Thus when David was about to attack the Philistines, Yahweh counseled attack from the rear:

> And when you hear the sound of marching [the angelic army] in the tops of the balsam trees, then bestir yourself; for then the Lord has gone out before you to smite the army of the Philistines. (2 Sam. 5:24)

If we conceive of heaven not as a super-terrestrial realm in the sky, but think of it instead as the interiority of earthly existence in all its potentialities, the image of war in heaven can be understood as the struggle between two contending spiritualities or national spirits for supremacy. Everyone knows that it is the spirit of a nation that determines its capacity to fight. One need only look to recent history for examples. The Thieu government of South Vietnam had eight to ten times the firepower in the field as its opponents; yet the final battle to bring down the Thieu regime never had to be launched. Instead, its soldiers just laid down their weapons—they did not even carry them along for self-defense or looting—and retreated to the sea. The government had simply lost legitimacy. The same thing happened to the army of the Shah of Iran. In both cases the *spirit* of the nation—the felt sense of its cohesiveness, stability and power—had simply evaporated.[8]

Military superiority means nothing where there is no longer the will to fight. The angels of the nation fight from heaven "in the tops of the balsam trees"—what an apt image for the spirituality of a nation and its determination to defend itself or impose its will.

Medieval Christianity treated these angels of the nations as disincarnate spirits in the air. Modern materialism located reality in physical objects, and thus dismissed the notion of spirits as superstition. Neither view is adequate. What is required is to hold the spiritual and material together: to see the material as the means by which the spiritual is made manifest, and the spiritual as the interiority of every material or corporate thing. Spirit and matter are thus the inside and outside of every actual entity. Nothing exists without both. Neither matter nor spirit has priority in time or place. They are the inseparable but distinguishable components of everything in the world.

Some early Christian theologians believed that each nation had both a good and an evil angel (Origen). Others thought each nation had but one angel which was capable of both good and evil (on analogy to Revelation 1—3). Still others regarded the guardian angel of each nation as only capable of good, and blamed the people of the nation for choosing evil despite the best efforts of its angel. Eusebius represents the third view. "It was not the fault of their angels," he wrote, "but of the nations themselves, when they could not raise themselves to a sufficient degree to contemplate the invisible in spirit" (*Dem. Ev.* 4.7–8). In the flood of human evil, "the angels who had first been set in charge of the nations could do nothing for their subjects and were able to look after the rest of creation—being set up over those parts of the world and following absolutely the will of God, the Architect of all things, and yet unable to help stay the fall of humanity because of humanity's own free choice of evil" (*Hom. on Eph.*, 1). All peoples have received divine revelation, as Rom. 1:18–23 shows, argued Pseudo-Dionysius; it is no failure of the angels if the nations turned their backs on the divine truths they have received and continue to receive through the visible universe (*Hier. Coel.* 9.3).

A fourth possibility was that the nations were under evil powers: God "granted that certain angels who delight in evil should bear sway over the several nations—and to them was given power over individuals, yet only on this condition, if any one first had made himself subject to them by sinning" (Pseudo-Clementine *Recog.* 8.50). All seem to have agreed that the evil of nations is made possible only by the free choice of human beings.[9] Apart from that they did not concur, and their very disagreement suggests that they were trying to systematize what was in fact a widely fluctuating *experience* of the spirituality of nations under the Roman Empire. For our purposes what matters is that this spirituality really exists and that it is perceived to be both benevolent and demonic.

The angels of the nations, who have already exacted upwards of one hundred million human sacrifices in less than a single century, are not personifications. They are real. But their reality cannot be grasped if it is projected onto the sky. They are not "out there" or "up there" but within. They are the invisible spirituality that animates, sustains, and guides a nation. And we reckon with them whether we acknowledge their reality or not.

The Personality and Vocation
of Nation-Angels

As we saw in the last chapter, the angel of an entity must be seen under two aspects: what it *is,* and what it is *called to be.* What it is might be called its personality, what it is called to be, its vocation. A vast literature exists on the personality of nations, though it is generally fragmentary, anecdotal, and journalistic. One thinks of the travel sections in newspapers, with their thumbnail sketches of a Greek island or a village in Ecuador. Anthropological studies of tribes and subcultures have introduced a degree of precision into the attempt to characterize large populations, but the sheer complexity of an entire nation renders facile generalizations ludicrous and even serious efforts suspect. This is not to deny that every nation has a total Gestalt or personality that is in principle perceptible, but only to acknowledge the difficulties involved in seeking to encompass so much data. Those who have been considered most successful have combined a penetrating analytical eye with a keen intuition. One thinks of Alexis de Tocqueville's prescient observations on early America, or Count Hermann Keyserling's arch but insightful characterizations of nations and peoples, or James Michener's capacity to capture the spirit of a region through the medium of a novel.[10] I have nothing to add to such analyses. For our purposes it is sufficient merely to observe that there are in fact genuine differences between the various nations and peoples.[11] Many people assume that all other peoples are just like them, utterly failing to recognize the differences that climate, heat, light, moisture, quality of soil, availability and types of food, history, customs, religions, fears, guilts, and other factors play in making them different. Discerning the personalities of nations is fundamental to any understanding between peoples. Otherwise we talk past and judge each other by our own unique national values without recognizing their relativity.

It is in the realm of vocation, however, that the concept of the angels of nations makes its most signal contribution. The social sciences or fine-tuned intuition can discern the contours of a nation's personality, but only God can reveal a nation's vocation. Like the angels of churches, the angels of nations regularly abandon their vocations, falling into the utmost barbarism. Each considers itself superior to the others. People tend to laud the same egocentricity in nations that they find insufferable in their fellow human beings. Nations almost inevitably define their interests in terms of immediate short-term gains rather than considering the larger whole. For a nation to act in accord with the synergy of the planet would require subordinating personality to vocation, "is" to "ought." The angels of nations are not static, changeless entities, nor are their vocations irrevocably fixed in their foundation. God's will for the nations is continually being modified, in accordance with God's primary objectives, in order to encompass the nations' latest infidelities and achievements.[12] Nations, too, must repent. The somber refrain in the Book of Revelation, "They did not repent," even after the sun was allowed to scorch them and the kingdom of the Beast was thrown into darkness (Rev. 9:20, 21; 16:9, 11), does not mean that nations *cannot* repent, but merely reflects the common experience that they generally *choose* not to repent.

To repent means to recover vocation. To recover a sense of call requires acknowledging the sovereignty of the One who calls over the falsely exalted sovereignty of the nation. All the nations belong to God[13] and God is "King of the nations."[14] God rules over the nations[15] and judges them when they do injustice or forget God.[16] God seeks to guide the nations in the ways of truth,[17] so that finally all the nations might worship the Lord.[18] As the "messenger" from God, the angel holds the vision of what a nation might become. When the angel of a nation defaults on its task, it is judged along with the nation. When the angel turns its back on its vocation, it becomes demonic, and a threat to the peace of the world.

> God has taken his place in the divine council;
>   in the midst of the gods he holds judgment:
> "How long will you [the angel-gods of the nations] judge unjustly
>   and show partiality to the wicked?
> Give justice to the weak and the fatherless;
>   maintain the right of the afflicted and the destitute.
> Rescue the weak and the needy;
>   deliver them from the hand of the wicked." . . .
> I say, "You are gods,
>   sons of the Most High, all of you;
> nevertheless, you shall die like men,
>   and fall like any prince."
> Arise, O God, judge the earth;
>   for to thee belong all the nations!
>
>   (Ps. 82:1-4, 6-8)

God's revelation to Israel was to be extended to every nation. Israel was to be "a light to the nations," that God's "salvation may reach to the end of the earth" (Isa. 49:6; 42:6), and "nations shall come to your light" (Isa. 60:3).

Few have wrestled with the problem of Israel's vocation to the nations as profoundly as Martin Buber. In a little-known essay of 1941,[19] Buber acknowledges that every nation has a guiding spiritual characteristic, its genius, which it acknowledges as its "prince" or its "god."[20] That national spirit unfolds, matures, and withers. There is a life cycle for every nation. Every nation makes an idol of its supreme faculties, elevating its own self as absolute, and worshiping its own inner essence or spirit as a god. But to be limited to oneself is to be condemned to die. When the national spirit decays and disintegrates, and the nation turns its face to nothingness instead of participating in the whole, it is on the verge of death.

Only Israel is exempt from this law of the rise and fall of nations and their spirits, argues Buber. This is because Israel worships not a partial aspect of the divine, but the Divine itself: whole, undivided, spiritual being. Hence it has survived all the vicissitudes of history, arising as a new force after every downfall. Israel experiences the absolute as that which Israel itself is not and which it can never become, and reveres it as such. This separates its history from that of the nations. The nations have been ordained by Yahweh, but they do not know it. Israel, however, knows God's call, through revelation. But Israel, Buber confesses, has not yet embodied this reverence for the absolute in its actual national existence. It too has gone after other gods. It too has worshiped its own national self-interests, narrowly defined. It too has wanted to be a nation among the nations.

Israel's vocation is to be a light to the nations: to teach them to worship Yahweh as the absolute, and not to worship the absolutized faculties of their own nations. But it is not enough, says Buber, merely to negate the idolatry of the nations. Israel must also embody the meaning of true worship in its own national existence, and this it has never adequately done. "Up to now," he wrote prophetically—remember, this was 1941, before the holocaust—"our existence has only sufficed to shake the thrones of idols, not erect a throne to God. . . . We pretend to teach the absolute, but what we actually do is say, No, to the other nations, or rather we ourselves are such a negation and nothing more. That is why we have become a nightmare to the nations. *That is why every nation is bound to desire to get rid of us at the time it is in the act of setting itself up as the absolute.*"[21]

As Christianity took its gospel to the nations, it too largely failed to maintain the task of mediating the absoluteness of God to *this* world, and instead transferred the goal of redemption to another world in the beyond. This meant that the nations and their angel-gods were no longer the direct object of the church's evangelical task. And even though the church was occasionally able to exert a moderating influence on the nations during the Middle Ages, the practical consequence was that the nations and their guardian angels dropped out of the purview of redemptive concern altogether and became autonomous. The result was the secular state, which acknowledges no higher power than its own idolatrous aspirations, which subverts religion to the role of legitimating its claims, and which makes its own power the sole arbiter of morality. Whenever the state makes itself the highest value, then it is in an objective state of blasphemy. *This is the situation of the majority of the nations in the world today, our own included.*

The political and spiritual task of mediating the absoluteness of God to the nations has been largely abandoned by the churches. Yet it is unmistakably articulated in the New Testament. Christians are warned that they will be dragged before governors and kings for Jesus' sake, in order "to bear testimony before them and the Gentile nations" (Matt. 10:18).[22] Jesus' own coming was prophesied, according to Matthew, as a coming to "proclaim justice to the Gentile nations," "and in his name will the Gentile nations hope" (Matt. 12:18, 21). The gospel itself must "be preached throughout the whole world, as a testimony to all Gentile nations" (Matt. 24:14; also Mark 13:10). The very nations are called to repent, "that repentance and forgiveness of sins should be preached in his name to all Gentile nations" (Luke 24:47; see Rev. 14:6).

Alongside the motif of witness *to* the nations is the judgment *of* the nations. This point is emphasized in an unexpected way by Matthew's famous parable of the sheep and the goats (Matt. 25:31–46).

> When the Son of man comes in his glory, and all the angels with him [and if it is for judgment of the nations, these should probably be understood as including the angels of the nations] . . . Before him will be gathered all the nations [*ethnē*, a *neuter* noun], and he will separate them [*autous*, a *masculine* pronoun] one from another. (Matt. 25:31–32)

A pronoun, you will recall, is supposed to agree in number and gender with the noun it modifies. The shift here from neuter to masculine means that not the nations as such, but individual *persons,* will be separated and judged ("and he will separate *people* one from another"). But the people are gathered *by their nations:* they will be individually held accountable for what they have done collectively as *nations* to provide food, clothing, shelter, health care, and justice: "I was hungry and you [plural] gave me food, I was thirsty and you [pl.] gave me drink, I was a stranger and you [pl.] welcomed me, I was naked and you [pl.] clothed me, I was sick and you [pl.] visited me, I was in prison and you [pl.] came to me." Each individual is responsible for the way her or his own nation has responded to the needs of the most powerless for food, clothing, shelter, medical care, hospitality, and fair treatment. The parable is not then simply an appeal for private charity, but for national righteousness, on the order of Ps. 82:1–8.

It is true that people are not judged solely on the basis of what their nations have done, quite apart from their own responses; but it is not just a matter of solitary judgment either, for Christ is also Sovereign of the nations. Each one of us is responsible for the sins of our own nation, whether we condone them or not. No one is exempt, by virtue of her or his own goodness, from the judgment of the nation. It was not, after all, one of the "German Christians" who had collaborated with Hitler, but the leader of the Christian resistance who spent eight years in a Nazi jail, who after the war was the first to say, "We all are guilty" (Martin Niemöller).

This witness to and judgment of the nations will ultimately issue in the redemption of the nations. The nations are not, in the biblical view, historical accidents or human contrivances. They are an integral aspect of the divine creation. Gerhard von Rad points out that the creation stories of Genesis do not end with the creation of humanity in chapters one and two, but with the creation of the nations in chapter ten. Human beings, that is to say, cannot exist in isolation from their larger social and political units. In the same way, the story of the fall does not conclude with the story of the exclusion of Adam and Eve from the garden in Genesis 3; it concludes in Genesis 11 with the confusion of tongues at the tower of Babel and the scattering of the nations.[23] This "fall" of the nations is placed in parallelism with the "fall" of humanity. Their joint falls necessitate a divine-human drama of redemption played out on the stage of history, culminating in the salvation of both persons *and their nations.* "All nations shall come and worship thee, for thy judgments have been revealed" (Rev. 15:4). The redeemed nations will even enter the holy city, New Jerusalem, bringing with them "the glory and the honor of the nations" (Rev. 21:26), by which we are presumably to think of the distinctive gifts and achievements, arts and crafts, music and letters, science and deeds of mercy and justice that they have wrought in history.

One would have thought that the nations had been finished off once and for all at Armageddon (Rev. 16:16) or in the great War of the Lamb (Revelation 19—20). But the biblical view of the nations is more subtle than that. They are not demonized. They are not considered irremediably evil. Perhaps what we witness in the surrealistic violence of Revelation is their purgation from short-term views of their own self-interest and the destruction of the egoism of their collective personalities. In any case these smitten nations, trod upon in the wine press of the fury of the wrath of God the Almighty and devoured by vultures (19:15, 17), are integral to the Holy City. Even these shall be transformed at last by the tree of life, whose leaves Ezekiel had said were "for healing" (Ezek. 47:12)—to which the Seer of the Apocalypse has added, "of the nations" (Rev. 22:2). Our personal redemption cannot take place apart from the redemption of our social structures.[24]

That redemption, however, is eschatologically depicted, whereas the general tendency is to want to establish the Holy City by main force here and now. "Americans," William Stringfellow observes, "particularly persevere in belaboring the illusion that at least some institutions are benign and viable and within human direction or can be rendered so by discipline or reform or revolution or displacement." This "virtually incredible view" he finds both theologically false and empirically unwarranted. "It really asserts that the principalities are only somewhat or sometimes fallen and that the Fall is not an essential condition of disorientation, morally equivalent to the estate of death, affecting the whole of Creation in time."[25] The nations are, he believes to the contrary, incorrigible this side of the kingdom of God.

In the light of world history, this view can scarcely be regarded as too pessimistic. If anything, we are guilty of continually underestimating the capacity of the Powers to violate the public interest on behalf of private profits and the sheer lust for power. But the Powers are also no less the good creations of a good God than we are, and they are no more fallen than we. If we can experience redemption, so can they, though by virtue of their greater complexity, far less simply. In short, radical pessimism about the Powers needs to be balanced by a view of grace more radical still. But whether this redemption can take place in history is an open question, which only historical deeds themselves can answer. Perhaps the most we can say is that some nations can and have responded to demands for justice in specific situations; yet even these acts of justice have been contaminated by overzealousness, revenge, greed, and pride. Nations cannot escape the effects of the Fall—that is the ax at the root of all visions of gradual human progress toward utopia or the kingdom—but they can recover a sense of their divine vocation and manifest flashes of what will be when God is effectively sovereign over all creation.

Despite persecutions which cost his own father's life and almost his own, the early Christian theologian Origen (early 3C) believed that the angels of the nations could be converted. "If human beings can repent and pass from unbelief to faith, why should we hesitate to say the same of the Powers? For my part, I think that it has sometimes happened . . . some of the Powers were converted when Christ came, and that is why some towns and even whole nations accepted Christ more readily than others."[26] The "man of Macedonia" whom Paul saw in a vision beseeching him, " 'Come over to Macedonia and help us' " (Acts 16:9) was, Origen suggests plausibly, the angel of Macedonia, responsible for the collective well-being of that entire people, appealing to Paul for help.[27]

The nations are fallen, but they bear encoded within their very symbols, insignia, coins, and ideologies the memory that they are creatures, created in, through, and for the service of the truly Human (Col. 1:15–20). *Fallen* does not mean *evil;* human beings are also fallen, and yet are capable of natural goodness. The tendency of nations is toward absolutism, but they are capable of responding to the revelation of their proper vocation. Their angels can be enjoined, like the angels of the church in Ephesus, to "remember then from what you have fallen," and repent (Rev. 2:5).

Ministering to the Spirituality of a Nation

If we equate the angel of a nation with its spirituality, how then might we go about ministering to the angel of a nation? What advantages, what gains, lie in resuscitating this antiquated notion, so uncongenial to the modern temperament? I will suggest that it can help us to unmask a nation's apostasy more ruthlessly, discern its vocation more perceptively, and love it, despite its evils, more faithfully.

The very idea of a nation's divine vocation is likely to elicit shudders from any student of history. What empire has not pronounced itself divinely (or dialectically) ordained to impose its economic, political and military power, even its culture and religion, on the unfortunate objects of its kindness?[28] Seldom have the real imperial motives been explicitly acknowledged. And it is all done with a perfectly clear conscience. As the Spanish empire was collapsing, American entrepreneurs saw the possibilities of using the Philippine Islands as a door into the Asiatic market. Wishing to win over a group of clergy, President William McKinley told them how he arrived at the decision to seize the Philippines by force from Spain, crush the native revolutionaries, and bring Spain's colony under U.S. domination:

> I walked the floor of the White House night after night until midnight; and I am not ashamed to tell you gentlemen that I went down on my knees and prayed to Almighty God for light and guidance more than one night. And one night it came to me this way—that there was nothing left for us to do but to take them all, and to educate the Filipinos, and uplift and civilize and Christianize them [they were already largely Roman Catholic], and by God's grace do the very best we could by them, as our fellowmen for whom Christ also died; and then I went to bed and went to sleep and slept soundly.[29]

It is not easy to argue against sound sleep and a clear conscience! No doubt

McKinley sincerely believed that the United States had a special calling from God, a manifest destiny to be played out in the affairs of nations. But like Israel, that election has been continually confused with favoritism and a *carte blanche* to impose our will on the world, disguised as the will of God. In nations, no less than in persons, divine calling can lead to inflation, megalomania, and self-idolization. So why reintroduce the notion? Has not secularism done us a favor by stripping us of the very grounds of these pretensions?

Not at all. Secularism has simply insured that, in the absence of any divine constraints whatever, nations are free to behave as if they had complete autonomy, as if the nation were indeed absolute: as if it itself were God, deciding the fate of nations.

Secularism, however, has merely exacerbated a situation stretching back to the dawn of civilization. Andrew Bard Schmookler, in his epochal *The Parable of the Tribes,* offers a compelling theory to account for the systemic incapacity of nations to foster human values. Recent anthropologists have argued that primitive hunter-gatherer tribes were fundamentally in harmony with nature and lived a fairly symbiotic existence. The development of agriculture, however, made possible an unchecked increase of the human population in dense concentrations, which in turn necessitated the extension of hierarchical systems for their control. Population pressures led to the quest for ever more territory; this in turn led to warfare as a means of wresting territory from others and defending one's own.

Primitive humanity was not essentially warlike. This new and unnatural focus on militarism brought in its train conscription, slavery, repression of both native and conquered populations, and the inevitability and necessity of competition, conflict and enmity. The anarchy that existed between peoples led to the struggle to achieve power, measured as the ability to impose one's will upon others. Once "civilization" had thus begun its course, argues Schmookler, no one could any longer choose to opt out of the struggle for power without risking certain oppression. *"No one is free to choose peace, but anyone can impose upon all the necessity for power."*[30]

Unbidden by anyone, this reign of power came to dominate human life. A freedom unknown in nature was cruelly transmuted, through unchecked population increases made possible by agriculture, into an equally unnatural state of anarchy, with its terrors and its destructive war of all against all. No one chose this system of power; it was inadvertently stumbled upon as a response to the new challenges of agrarian life. Once it was in place, however, the struggle for power became beyond human ability to avoid or to stop. In an unnatural parody of natural selection, this struggle generated a selective process beyond human control which molded change inevitably in the direction of the maximization of power in human societies. Conscious, choosing human beings did not determine the outcome, nor did power-driven despots, but impersonal and ungoverned forces—what the Bible knows as principalities and powers. "That which chooses the chooser determines the choice."[31] The powerful get to speak, says Schmookler, because the unchosen structure of the system determines which messages will be heard. And the very nature of the power game makes it likely that unscrupulous and ruthless people motivated solely by the love of power will rise to national leadership.

Nations are thus swept along willy-nilly in a zero-sum game in which some-one must always be winning and someone always losing. Since a state of con-tinuous warfare is unnatural to our species, people must be coerced, cajoled, deceived, bullied and seduced into identifying their own self-interest with that of the powerful who oppress them. They must be ruled by laws, and the laws internalized. They must labor, and relinquish a just return on their work. They must learn to kill, and be willing even to be killed, for an abstract power-entity which dominates them. Even the ability of human beings to create new cultural forms to achieve their purposes, far from restoring to them the choice of their destiny, merely magnifies the impact of the selective process and speeds the evo-lution of civilization still further in the unchosen direction of power-maximization.

This brief summary scarcely even touches the key points of Schmookler's thesis. It is enough, however, to give some indication of why the nations find a state of idolatry not only congenial but virtually irresistible. They are in a game not of their choosing, where their subjects must be rendered pliable and willing to sacrifice themselves like pawns on a chessboard to preserve their king. To command such assent, against all the natural inclinations and urgings of the heart, requires that the nation establish itself as the highest value within the breast of each of its subjects. *As long as the power-system prevails, any other value placed higher will be a threat to the viability of the state.*

This is why the Roman empire could not tolerate the refusal of the early Christians to offer worship to the emperor (see on this matter The Powers, vol. 1: *Naming the Powers,* 110–16). This is why, in Revelation 18, the great multi-tude in heaven bursts out in crescendos of praise when it views the violent disin-tegration of the richest and most powerful empire of the time. This is why the American abolitionist and founder of the Oneida Community, John Humphrey Noyes, could write to William Lloyd Garrison,

> When I wish to form a conception of the government of the United States (using a personified representation), I picture to myself a bloated, swaggering libertine, trampling on the Bible—its own Constitution—its treaties to the Indians—the peti-tions of its citizens, with one hand whipping a negro tied to a liberty pole, and with

the other dashing an emaciated Indian to the ground. . . . The question urges itself upon me—"What Have I, as a Christian, to do with such a villain?"

My hope of the millennium begins where Dr. Beecher's expires—namely, AT THE OVERTHROW OF THIS NATION.[32]

I have quoted such an extreme view because it helps place in relief the most radical challenge of Revelation 18: its celebration of the fall of *the richest and most powerful empire of the time.* Are we then to entertain the terrible possibility that the salvation of humanity depends somehow on the decline, destruction or transformation of the United States as a sign of God's sovereignty over the nations? Rome, yes, but—America? Never! America the Righteous, America the Chosen, the Destined, the Apple of God's Eye? The very suggestion of such a thing will strike many Americans as subversive. And that reaction itself is an index of our idolatry. A godly people would react to the threat of God's judgment with fear, awe, consternation. They would *know* that no person and no nation is righteous before God. They would say, with Jefferson, "I tremble for my country when I remember that God is just." But Americans do not, on the whole, think that way. To the degree that they are religious at all, they actually believe that God is pleased, beholden to, partial to, and identified with our land.[33]

This is not to deny that, in many ways, our nation may be a more desirable place to live than some other countries. Nor do I wish to ignore the many positive contributions it has made to human society. My point is simply that these contributions in no way mitigate the objective state of idolatry that has been the price we have paid for nationhood. The power imperative has co-opted every nation. And the tragedy is that what enhances power has proven to be suicidal for the species. The nations have reached the brink of an abyss that no further gains in power can span; indeed, the very momentum of our technological developments of warfare threaten to push us over the edge by accident even if not by choice. In all their history the nations have not succeeded in realizing their vocations. The earthly city, as Augustine says in the preface to *The City of God,* has itself been ruled by its lust to rule. Will the last word on the nations be the terrifying pronouncement of judgment on the earthly city in Rev. 18:19— "In one hour she has been laid waste"?

Nothing in previous history prompts us to believe otherwise. One factor has recently emerged, however, that holds a thin margin of promise. The world has now shrunk to the communicative dimensions of a city. It may be, then, that the anarchy at the root of the power system may be checked at last by a growing recognition of world citizenship, matched eventually by some form of world government, or at least by enforceable mutual collaboration in the prevention of armed conflict. It has now become clear to increasing numbers of people that the natural system will select us out of existence unless we learn to live synergistically with nature and each other, by our nations. Each nation will now turn to its angel and ask what it must do to be saved, or it will perish. Either the nations will submit themselves to the judgment of God, or they will submit to a never-ending nuclear night.

Discernment is a form of judgment, but it is not indifferent or detached. The act of discerning the spirit of the nation—its angel—and naming it must be accompanied by an equally difficult, and far more demanding response: objective love. The great prophets' hearts broke under the burden of predicting cataclysm for their people. Is it only an old professor that I hear, or does Amos's voice crack in the midst of this lamentation:

> Fallen, no more to rise,
> is the virgin Israel?
> (Amos 5:2)

Or when Jesus weeps over Jerusalem, or reaches out to it like a mother hen to her brood (Luke 19:41–44; 13:34), what is this if not love pierced by grief over rejection by his people, now rendered desolate?

When people speak of loving their country, they mean, without having reflected on the matter, its spirit, its essence, what it stands for, its image in their minds and before the world. Naming this the angel makes it possible to distinguish the soul of the nation from the actions of any given administration, or leaders, or dominant class, race, or group. This distinction is crucial. It means we can censure, criticize, and oppose unjust policies without having to dissociate ourselves from our love and concern for the land, its history, traditions, and contributions to humanity. The angel makes it possible to relativize the psychic authority with which our leaders tend to become invested, and to recall people to the transcendent, spiritual vocation to which they are ordained and by which they—and their leaders—are judged.

A case in point is the difficulty many blacks have had identifying with or loving the United States. This is a crucial issue, since part of one's self-respect and identity is normally shaped by a sense of national feeling. As the black poet Langston Hughes put it,

> O, yes,
> I say it plain,
> America never was America to me,
> And yet I swear this oath—
> America will be!

Hughes could not stop with rejection of America. Something in him cried out for ownership, not from mere sentiment, but from fundamental justice. The land that had brought slaves from Africa and had been so glacially slow in making restitution ever since, that very land could never be freed or saved *from itself* unless the descendants of its slaves were finally liberated from the blot of racism.[34] What Hughes was demanding is that America fulfill its divine vocation. The angel or spirituality of America stands, as it were, before God; it bears the knowledge of that to which it is called. The angel of America is thus not identical with the present or past injustices of the nation. It always bears the divine judgment and calling to become what it is meant to be. "America will be!"—the poet can embrace the eschatological promise, and can therefore, in the interim, risk his loyalties and love on the angel.

In a seminar on this theme two white South Africans who had cast their lot with the liberation struggle of South African blacks discovered that the concept of the angel of South Africa made it possible for them to embrace their homeland in all its wild beauty as *theirs* for the very first time. They could detach the land from the apartheid government, transcend their collective guilt for all the injustices done, and celebrate South Africanness in anticipation of the day when justice *will* be done there.

Had we been more conversant with our American angel during the Vietnam War, we might have more clearly distinguished the policies of the incumbent war-making administrations from the angel of the nation. Instead, many fused the two, heaping hatred of "Amerika" and damning its very soul. Some who opposed that war have still never forgiven their country, and are eaten up with an unacknowledged and diffuse hatred for it that undermines their effectiveness in social change.[35]

Curiously enough, the Vietnamese themselves were able to maintain the distinction between America and its leaders. Visitors to Hanoi invariably reported that people there professed love for the American people despite the actions of its government. Recognition of the nation's angel might have made it possible for Americans to love it more profoundly and to intercede for it more resolutely during that time of national convulsion and violence.

People do not change national attitudes and policies simply because they are told they are wrong. They change because of love for their country.[36] Politicians have never forgotten this fact, and manipulate that love through misinformation and propaganda. Consequently many have come to abhor patriotism altogether. Yet in the deepest sense, we must instill again a love for our nation and its angel. Patriotism in some form or another is indispensable for the survival of any state, and if it is not informed by the divine will and judgment it will become captive to demagogues and jingoists. A chastened patriotism that views the interests of our nation within the context of the well-being of the whole family of nations is required in order to counter the shortsightedness of those who equate love for America with short-term economic gain or being "number one."

We cannot minister to the soul of America unless we love its soul. We cannot love its soul faithfully and truly, without sinking into idolatry, unless we have correctly discerned its true vocation under the God who holds the destiny of all the nations. And we cannot discern that calling unless we know the angel who bears the message of what the nation might become.[37]

In his penetrating analysis of national loyalty, Coleman B. Brown argues that if we regard God as the sovereign not only of persons but of nations and races, institutions and systems, then we must conclude that God wills the welfare of every nation as a part of the world God loves. Citing Dostoevski's statement that "all nations are immediate to God," Brown insists that there can be no prophetic word of historical judgment or hope for America if America does not have its own relationship to God. And if we believe that our nation stands under divine judgment for its evils, then we are also saying, by implication, that it has a vocation that it betrays by such acts.[38]

Many sense that our world today is emerging into a period of global citizenship. This is one of the greatest crises and possibilities in the history of our species. At least for the foreseeable future, however, we must exercise that global citizenship as national citizens. When the United States meddles militarily in Nicaragua, we cannot attempt to block, dissuade, or criticize that policy as world citizens; we must do so as U.S. citizens. That alone gives us any leverage we might have. Just as the emerging dialogue of world religions requires that we each engage, not syncretistically, but *as* Muslims, *as* Christians, *as* Jews or Buddhists, so the emerging world order requires citizens who each take responsibility for what their own nation is doing in the context of global solidarity. We will be judged by what we have done in our own nations (Matt. 25:32). We must be "international, transnational, but *not anti-national*."[39] The only cure for the evil of nationalism, paradoxically, is genuine love for one's nation as a creature of God.

The irony of Christianity is that it claims as Sovereign of all the nations a man who was executed by the state. By so doing it asserts that Human Being transcends all collectivities and absolutisms. The self-giving love and life-enhancing values demonstrated by Jesus have become the criteria by which the nations are to be judged. The church is planted on the earth as a harbinger of a single infolded humanity: "Here there cannot be Greek and Jew, circumcised and uncircumcised, barbarian, Scythian, slave, free," but the New Human is all and in all (Col. 3:11). The church is "a royal priesthood, a holy *nation*" (1 Pet. 2:9), pointing from within each nation beyond the nation to the God of all the nations.

The demonic spirit of nationalism has metastasized through the nations. It is a cancer that threatens to kill us all. But it is not enough to fight against each injustice piecemeal. The pattern of injustice perpetuated by the nations betrays a single spirit, a resolute momentum through time, a consolidated spirit of empire intent on gain at any cost. It is not just this policy or that which must be countered, but the very spirit of absolutism. It is not simply this leader or that administration which must be opposed, but the entire power system and the anarchic relationship between the nations that gives it rise. The weakness of the cross is the revelation in time—in precisely the time when the power system reigns supreme—that the ultimate system lies beyond the present power arrangements, and that it cannot be destroyed.

The human race was ill-prepared for the contest for power into which it was thrown ten thousand years ago, with the rise of agrarian civilization. It is even less prepared, by dint of experience, for shaping a world of concord. But it is at least prepared by virtue of creation. We were made for harmony and synergism. The image of God, so near to extinction under the suffocating terrors of civilization, still holds out the possibility of change. We will never build a utopia on earth—but will we take that one gigantic, necessary step out of the system of power into a system of human values? The whole creation is on tiptoe, waiting.

What is the Angel of America saying to us today? What is the vocation to which God is calling us as a people? I have attempted to discern, through active imagination, what the Angel might be trying to say. The result is so colored by my own feelings and views that I have frankly hesitated to share it at all. I do so only because I am convinced that each of us is responsible for trying to discern what God is saying to the nation through its collective spirituality or angel. Perhaps the subjectivity of the response is essential; it prevents us from claiming too much for our own visions of the national destiny. Here then is what I sense the Angel to be saying:

> I am a young and energetic servant of the living God. I bear a unique pattern and possibility which has already brought the world great blessings in freedom, and can do so more. But there are many whose vision has become clouded, who have lost the vision of America for the world, and now think only of the world for America. I hold this light, far higher than the lamp of Liberty, but indistinguishable from her: the vision of a nation free of poverty and hunger, a nation of opportunity, a nation where the creative novelty of the divine will is for the first time in human history celebrated and preferred, a nation which attracts other nations toward freedom rather than imposing it on them, a nation of persons liberated from the tyranny of convention, able to pursue their own creative ways. Learn to love this vision better.

Learn to love your nation's soul, and do not let its perversions of its destiny turn your heart away.

My light of hope is still raised over your shore, and more people than ever in history are fleeing to me, yet my hands are tied by the dark power created by your worship of things. Wealth is your real god, and all your gravest sins have been committed for it. You bought and sold slaves and killed my native peoples for wealth, you intervene in foreign lands for wealth, you sacrifice your own children in wars fought for control of world markets, and you demonize Communists because they challenge your system of wealth. Your idolatry is almost unlimited. You are now prepared to blow up the habitable planet for the sake of preserving your freedom to pursue wealth singlemindedly and unencumbered.

(I ask: "But why are you so powerless to stop this? Can't you do *anything*?")

I can only be what I am: the call to your own fulfillment as a nation. I can, no more than God, revoke your freedom to do evil. If you choose idols, I cannot stop you. I stand helpless while you do evil, and can only see that you are visited with the inevitable consequences of your acts.

I need help. I cannot get through to my people. They listen only to their idols. You must come to my aid, even as I have come to yours, now that you have become open to me.

5. The Gods

The angels of the nations, as we saw in the previous chapter, are only a special category of heavenly powers elsewhere called gods, angels, or spirits. The language of the Powers in the New Testament period is so imprecise that it is often impossible to maintain distinctions between these spiritual entities. Generally speaking, what pagans called gods, Jews and Christians called angels or demons, and everyone spoke of them interchangeably as spirits. In this chapter we will examine how early Jews and Christians regarded the gods and incorporated them into their understanding of the Powers. Then we will ponder the meaning of the gods for our existence today.

Briefly, I will argue that the old gods of paganism are still very much alive, and that denial of this fact only guarantees their repression. Hidden from consciousness, they strike from concealment and craze or cripple us without our having the slightest comprehension as to what has happened. The gods never died, remarks Jung; they merely became diseases.[1] To the degree that Christianity has conspired in suppressing the gods and denying them the cautious respect and serious attention they deserve, it has unwittingly contributed to disease.

Roman Catholic and Orthodox Christians have been far more cognizant of the reality of the gods than have Protestants, who mistook the prophets' critique of idolatry—the false worship of gods—for a denial of their existence altogether. A fresh reading of the biblical sources and new insights from depth psychology now make a complete reassessment of the gods imperative.

The Gods Are Real

Christianity has not been uniformly hostile to the gods. It is well known, for example, that Catholic veneration of the saints and the elaboration of various orders of angels was a means of absorbing the religious impulses of polytheism into Christian devotion. Some of the "saints" are the old pagan gods taken over wholesale, without even a change of name (for example, Brigid, the Irish goddess of fire, smithcraft, and poetry, became St. Brigid) and at least one order of angels (the Virtues) had served an earlier hitch as equally impersonal and impassive Roman gods. In many other respects Christianity melded elements of paganism directly into its life. To cite but two further instances, pagan philosophy was taken over as the intellectual basis of Christian apologetics,[2] and the orgiastic Roman Saturnalia was absorbed and neutralized by the celebration of a mass for Christ's birth.

On the whole, however, the pagan gods were ruthlessly suppressed. Christian theology was filtered through the monistic philosophies of Greece and Europe until it came in time to represent the belief that the gods never had any existence whatever. But "monotheism," if it is not purely a modern construct, could not have meant that to the ancient Hebrews, who regarded the gods of their neighbors as very real indeed.

The Israelites found three different solutions for dealing with the gods of the surrounding peoples: *syncretism, suppression,* and *subordination.*[3] *Syncretism* involved taking over alien beliefs, myths, and practices. Baal could be renamed Yahweh; Canaanite mythological conceptions and expressions could be adopted, such as Baal's victory over Chaos or the concept of an assembly of gods presided over by a high god. Syncretism was unavoidable and advantageous; it made possible a degree of accommodation with the Canaanite inhabitants. But it involved dangers as well: the loss of the distinctive qualities of Israel's religious experience.

Consequently, others tended to champion the *suppression* of Baalism, stressing the uniqueness of Yahweh's covenant with Israel and of Israel's calling in history. Exclusion of Canaanite elements preserved the uniqueness of Israel's perception of Yahweh as the one God, but often within a narrowly nationalistic focus that was slow to acknowledge the universality of Yahweh's dominion and hence of Yahweh's objectivity in regard to Israel's fate among the nations. What reflection failed to grasp, repeated captivities taught. In time Israel came to perceive Yahweh as God of the nations and the universe who transcended the parochialism of both early Israel and its neighbors.

More characteristic of Israel's handling of the gods is *subordination.* Pure monotheistic thought is extremely rare in the Hebrew Scriptures. Second Isaiah alone denies the very existence of other gods.[4] Even in Jeremiah, where Yahweh's sole reality is declared,[5] the prophet nevertheless pictures Yahweh as presiding over a heavenly council made up of the *bene elohim,* the "sons of God," who do Yahweh's bidding.[6] Yahweh is supreme over this host of subordinate powers, which include the gods of all the nations. The first commandment itself assumes this henotheistic belief. It does not deny the existence of other gods, but only their primacy: "You shall have no other gods before me" (Exod. 20:3). Other gods may be real, but they are of a different order of potency altogether: "Who is like thee, O Lord, among the gods?" (Exod. 15:11). By being made Yahweh's cabinet and chiefs of staff, the gods of the surrounding peoples were acknowledged to be real *in their own domain of influence,* but not ultimate. They possessed a certain degree of autonomy but were subject to Yahweh. "Ascribe to the Lord, O sons of gods (*elim*), ascribe to the Lord glory and strength" (Ps. 29:1, RSV margin). Those prophets and saints who saw Yahweh in vision were admitted to the divine throne room and took their places (temporarily) among the gods: "I give thee thanks, O Lord, with my whole heart; before the gods (*elohim*) I sing thy praise" (Ps. 138:1). "God has taken his place in the divine council; in the midst of the gods he holds judgment" (Ps. 82:1). "All gods bow down before him" (Ps. 97:7). In short, the gods of the peoples were, for the Hebrews, real, and Yahweh is their sovereign. "For the Lord is a great God, and a great King above all gods" (Ps. 95:3).[7]

There is nothing unique in the Israelite conception of God presiding over a heavenly council made up of lesser gods. The same view is recorded in Canaan, Babylon, Egypt, and Greece. It is reflected, for example, in this prayer to the Babylonian moon-god Sin (c. 7C B.C.E.): "Bowed down in thy presence are the great gods; the decisions of the land are laid before thee; when the great gods inquire of thee thou dost give counsel. They sit (in) their assembly (and) debate under thee. . . ."[8]

This subordinationist conception did not, surprisingly, throw Israel open to the risk of encouraging the worship of other gods beside Yahweh. As Yehezkel Kaufmann points out, the gods were of a different order altogether. They were, even for the surrounding peoples, not the ultimate powers of the universe, but rather part of a realm that preceded them and which they did not create. They were as dependent on this prior realm as humans. They too must obey its decrees and laws. They may create the world and humanity, but they do so with preexisting stuff, and they do not comprise, singly or together, a divine will which governs and is the cause of all being. They themselves are generated out of the primordial substance, and therefore they are subject to sexual conditions, and engage in procreation. Since matter transcends them, they need food and drink. In subordinating such gods to Yahweh the Israelites were merely acknowledging the reality of a limited aspect of nature; they never even bothered to give them names.

Yahweh was of a different order entirely. Yahweh created the world, including the gods; Yahweh is subject to no law or necessity. Nothing is prior to Yahweh, all is created at Yahweh's word. Humanity was created for relationship with Yahweh in Yahweh's image; the gods have nothing to do with it.[9] Idolatry in Israel was thus not caused by including the gods in the heavenly council, but by foreign political alliances that established the cult of other gods in the king's house and even occasionally in the Jerusalem temple.

This "henotheistic" or "mono-Yahwist"[10] solution (which provided for belief in one high god served by lesser gods) offered the opportunity to subordinate and thus depotentiate the gods of the nations. Pagan deities were absorbed into the heavenly council and given the status of messengers or servants of Yahweh. Those gods who obeyed their Sovereign's will were members in good standing (Pss. 103:21; 148:1–6). Those gods who failed to do justice among their people were judged and sentenced to die like mortals (Ps. 82:1–7; Isa. 24:21).[11]

As we have seen already (chap. 4), the pagan gods were appointed by God over other nations and peoples to guide them into justice and serve as their ambassadors in the heavenly council. "When the Most High gave to the nations their inheritance, when he separated the sons of men, he fixed the bounds of the peoples according to the number of the sons of God" (Deut. 32:8). Israel alone would be God's special portion (v. 9), and Israel was therefore forbidden to worship the gods appointed over the nations. "Nor must you raise your eyes to the heavens and look up to the sun, the moon, and the stars, all the host of heaven, and be led on to bow down to them and worship them; *the Lord your God assigned these for the worship of the various peoples under heaven*" (Deut. 4:19 NEB, italics mine).[12] These gods should have lifted the eyes of the pagans to contemplate in nature and history the workings of the Lord Most High, but the peoples instead fell to worshiping their own national gods as ultimate—an act that had immediate and devastating political consequences as well. Nevertheless, Israelites were not to speak evil of gods (Exod. 22:28 LXX), for Yahweh has ordained them for the nations.[13] As a hedge against the worship of the gods of the nations, it occurred to later Jewish writers to designate them simply as angels.[14]

Philo represents the high-water mark of Jewish openness toward the existence of the gods. By identifying the Greek gods (*daimones*) as angels (not "demons"), he made possible a positive evaluation of Greek culture by means of allegory. "It is Moses' custom to give the name of angels (*aggelous*) to those whom other philosophers call *daimonas,* souls that is which fly and hover in the air. And let no one suppose that what is here said is a myth. . . . So if you realize that souls (*psychas*) and *daimonas* and angels are but different names for the same one underlying object, you will cast from you that most grievous burden, the fear of *daimones*."[15] These *daimones* must not be confused with the "demons" of the Gospels, which were petty, localized entities and uniformly evil. By contrast, in Greek thought the *daimones* were regarded as supernatural powers not specifically personified but which exercised an influence in human affairs. They were bearers of both good and ill; they maintained a profound ambivalence right into the New Testament period, despite attempts to rationalize them.[16]

Philo provides a valuable glimpse into the intersection between the Greek and Jewish worlds when he writes:

> The common usage . . . is to give the name of *daimōn* to bad and good *daimonas* alike. . . . And so, too, you also will not go wrong if you reckon as angels, not only those who are worthy of the name, who are as ambassadors backwards and forwards between men and God and are rendered sacred and inviolate by reason of that glorious and blameless ministry, but also those who are unholy and unworthy of the title. (*De gig.* 16)

This is advice, however, that most Jewish and Christian writers after him ignored. Those Powers whom the Greeks called *daimones* or gods were neatly divided into two camps, good and evil. The first were called "angels," the second, "demons." The holy *daimones* of the Greeks now entered their unhappy and violent servitude as the "demons" of the Christian church, and responded to this denigration with all the virulence at their command.

The seeds for the demonization of the pagan gods, and hence their *de facto* expulsion from the heavenly council, lay already in Deut. 32:17—"they sacrificed to demons (*shedim*) which were no gods." But that line is followed by several others that affirm the reality of the gods: "To gods they had never known, to new gods that had come in of late, whom your fathers had never dreaded." The process of demonizing the gods gained impetus from Ps. 106:37 and from the LXX translation of Ps. 96:5. The Hebrew text of the latter had rendered a nice pun by saying that "all the gods (*elohim*) of the peoples are worthless (*elilim*)," not implying their nonexistence but rather their impotence.[17] The LXX chose to translate *elilim* by *daimonia,* which in the context can only have been intended pejoratively. *1 Enoch* and *Jubilees,* like the LXX also from the early second century B.C.E., witness to the increasing polemical utility Jews were finding in this demonic interpretation.[18] Paul takes this idea straight over into his epistles. "What pagans sacrifice they offer to demons and not to God" (1 Cor. 10:20).

Paul, however, did not endorse the monistic philosophies of most of his later interpreters, and did not therefore choose the easy solution of denying that gods exist altogether. His converts in Corinth apparently were tempted in that direction, however. Their logic seems to have run thus: If there is only one God, there are no other gods; if there are no gods, there can be no scruples about eating food sacrificed to idols.[19] But Paul regarded this "solution" to the problem of polytheism as too simplistic (though it later came to be the dominant view among Christians, and continues to be today). For the Corinthian solution had created friction in the church and jeopardized the faith of those whose previous experience of the gods had been more like possession, and who therefore knew them to be "real." So Paul made a concession for their sakes: there are indeed many gods and many lords, but Christians are under the one God and one Lord, Jesus Christ (1 Cor. 8:5-6). He is clearly avoiding metaphysics here; he is not interested in the ontological existence of gods, but in the existential fact that whatever is worshiped is indeed, for that person, a god.[20] Some in that church had been so liberated from their former beliefs (or had been such disbelievers, even in gods) that gods no longer held any spells for them. These may eat food sacrificed to idols because they are freed from their power. But they should abstain from eating sacrificed meats in a temple banquet (8:10-13) or even at someone's private home (10:27-29) if doing so would tempt a fellow Christian who did not share this inner freedom to do the same.

After further reflection Paul hedges the last opinion. They should not eat in a temple at all, and for quite a different reason: by so doing they participate in partnership with the demons (1 Cor. 10:20).[21] Despite their disbelief in the god, by their act they bring themselves into union with it. For the "weaker" brethren this might activate old patterns and deep stirrings over which they had no power. And yet Paul had asserted, however briefly, that the Christian is *in principle* free to eat in a pagan temple (1 Cor. 8:9). He could argue thus, not because he believed that the gods were non-existent, but because, as he says of the elements in Gal. 4:9, they were merely "weak and beggarly." This comes home with striking force in 1 Cor. 10:22. He is not afraid that the Christian will be overwhelmed by the numinous power of idols, but by the wrath of God. "Shall we provoke the Lord to jealousy? Are we stronger than"—not *they*, but—"he?" The gods conjure no fear in Paul, only God.

This equation, gods=demons, was the new formula by which paganism would be eradicated by the church. For the early apologists, "all the gods of the Greek and Roman mythology were supernatural and real, only malignant, beings," writes F. C. Conybeare.[22] Demonization of the gods, however, really represented a new departure. Israel, as we saw before, had dealt with the gods by means of syncretism, suppression, and subordination, often all three together. If, however, the gods are demons, there is really no further place for them in the heavenly council. They are merely "idols." The use of this term by the translators of the LXX was itself an act of derision, for Greeks did not use *eidolon* for gods. It meant "phantom, unsubstantial form, reflected image, fantasy." It had previously been used of ghosts, specters, or underworldly beings. Its use for the higher gods cast aspersions on their reality. The term was a weapon in the attack on the mythological foundations of the pagan worldview.[23]

The apocryphal Epistle of Jeremy (c. 316-306 B.C.E.) is typical of this Jewish polemic against idols. They are carved holding daggers or axes, says the author, yet are unable to deliver themselves from robbers. Their eyes are coated with dust stirred up by the feet of their worshipers, yet they cannot even wipe their own eyes. Bats, swallows, birds, even cats perch on their heads, and they are unable to prevent the predictable results. If they fall, someone has to right them, and if the temple burns, their priests escape but they themselves are consumed.[24]

All this makes for very clever rhetoric, but it misses the mark. Among the masses of people, the gods may well have been regarded as identical with their representations. And such gods indeed "spoke," for they embodied the projections of their worshipers, projections which themselves arose out of the deep, collective unconscious of the people and the very structure of the psyche.[25] In the Roman period, however, more sophisticated devotees were aware of the difference between the symbol and its referent. The pagan Maximus Tyrius (2C c.e.) knew perfectly well how to use images as genuine symbols:

> It is because we are not able to apprehend His [the god's] being that we lean upon words, and names, and animal forms, and representations of gold and ivory and silver, and plants and rivers, and mountain tops and groves. . . . It is like the case of lovers to whose sight the representations of their beloved give most pleasure, and pleasure, too, is given by a lyre of his, a javelin, a chair, a walk and, in short, everything which awakens the memory of the loved one.[26]

The weakness of the attack on idols is clear the moment we apply it to the Christian church, with its crosses, crucifixes, statues of Mary and the saints, depictions of God, Christ, the angels, and apostles in stained glass, and so forth. The Jews forbade all images, and were immune to the reversal of their argument against themselves, but Christians were not. As symbols, how do any of these differ from the images of paganism? Yet for a practicing Christian, such an argument has no force whatever. For the believer knows, or at least has faith, that there is a reality which the symbol expresses. And here is where the polemic against idols hit raw nerves. The pagan gods were too local, too identified with the devotion of certain *cities*. They were not prepared for a cosmopolis. And they were too fragmentary; there were too many, too vaguely specialized in their benefits, too various for a world converging on itself and needing a centralizing coherence.

In a living religion the image signifies the divine reality itself. It is a material expression of the being it evokes. It participates in the reality and conveys it. As the neo-Platonist Iamblichus (c. 330 c.e.) put it, "idols are divine and filled with the divine presence."[27] The image is like a hole dug in sand beside the sea, into which the whole sea presses. The sea is in the hole, but not the whole sea. The image is thus not empty, an "idol," except for a person for whom it evokes no reality. The images of any religion are "idols" to unbelievers or other-believers. For a devotee of Apollo or Artemis, the cross would have been an idol: empty, vain, nothing—or worse: repulsive, disgusting, hideous. In short, an idol is in the eye of the beholder, and the charge of idolatry is always polemical, always born of a counterdevotion. It is an evaluation, not a description. It is a lethal instrument of ideological warfare.

Paganism's susceptibility to this attack lay in its own decline. For all too many people, the gods no longer spoke with any frequency; finally they scarcely spoke at all. Even the artisans who fashioned the images recognized this. They were honest workers. They began to portray the gods as no longer young, but aging.[28]

Where once the common workers in a city could appeal, through strikes and protests, to the gods and to their immediate representatives, the liturgy-funding aristocracy, now their appeals were brutally repressed without effecting change. They could no longer invoke the higher authority of the gods of the city to censure the tyranny of rulers; the rulers were now sent from Rome, and the gods would not help.[29]

It was not simply religious credibility that the gods had lost, but their capacity to cement society and to legitimate, correct, and chastise its rulers. Already weakened, the gods were delivered yet another blow by the withering criticism of philosophical rationalism. One last desperate pagan revival swept the second-century empire. When it ebbed, Christianity had already secured the future.

Yet for all that it is not the case that the Greek gods represented a chaotic welter of contradictory or vying forces. On the contrary, the very term *theos* ("god") expressed what had been felt to be the *unity* of the religious world despite its multiplicity. "The Greek concept of God," writes Hermann Kleinknecht, "is essentially polytheistic, not in the sense of many individual gods, but in that of an ordered totality of gods, of a world of gods, which . . . forms an integrated nexus."[30]

Indeed, what polytheism provided, in its hierarchies of gods, their polar oppositions, and continual warfares and intrigues, was a mythological depiction of what we might today call fields of forces in both the psyche and the everyday world. "The Greek gods are simply basic forms of reality."[31]

Seen in that light, polytheism represents a piecemeal approach to divine unity. The Greeks apprehended the world as primordially many, but in the process of many cumulative experiences the gods acquired a consequent unity. Hence the movement of Greek religion toward *unity in multiplicity,* which it could only accomplish partially by its death and resurrection in Christianity. Israel, on the other hand, experienced God as primordially one, but in the process of unfolding the many potential forms God acquired a consequent multiplicity, which the primordial character absorbed into its own unity. Thus the movement of Israelite religion toward *multiplicity in unity,* evidenced by the proliferation of angels and the emergence of Satan and demons in apocalyptic Judaism. These momentous and ancient opposite movements of convergence finally collapsed upon each other in Christianity. The synthesis that was the result, though it might appear unintelligible to some, was in fact gemlike and dazzling in its simplicity and power: the holy Trinity.

But what had become of the gods? They had not simply been eclipsed by the rational elegance of the world they had helped to structure. The archetypal images no longer communicated the archetypes spontaneously. But the archetypes did not die. They went underground, partly as a consequence of their loss of numinosity as the traditional symbols were emptied of their power, and partly because they were hounded there by the uncompromising rhetoric of the Christian apologists and the suppressions of Christian emperors. Now they were "demons"—so they became demonic in the extreme. The gods were powerful archetypal images in the unconscious or invariant structures in nature or human society. Hence their demonization could lead only to a massive rebound in the form of obsession with the demonic.[32]

By the year 1200, a monk like Caesarius could write his *Dialogus Miraculorum,* depicting a world infested with demons, where not even the crucifix was protection enough, where every forbidden human impulse was ascribed to ravenous exterior powers, where the common folk had no hope of overcoming their wiles, where only saints could expect to prevail against them, and then only through the greatest suffering.[33] The gods extracted a fierce revenge, almost eclipsing belief in the one God and terrifying a whole civilization from their impregnable stronghold in the core of the psyche, the bosom of nature, and the collective pathologies of society.

The Rehabilitation of the Gods

The gods, like stars, have been put out of heaven, leaving no light for exploring the darkness. They have become part of the darkness themselves. The gods once named the shapes that came to meet us in the gloom; without them we are pummeled and maddened by forces we have never named and cannot tame. What else was mythology but a map of these dim regions where the elemental forces of the universe mingle without distinction? We need the gods back to guide us through this night of history and of our own souls.

The gods never died, they only became diseases, as Jung put it: "Zeus no longer rules Olympus but rather the solar plexus, and produces curious specimens for the doctor's consulting room, or disorders the brains of politicians and journalists who unwittingly let loose psychic epidemics on the world."[34] The great archetypal powers of the soul have always behaved demonically whenever they were not channeled and propitiated as divinities. In a conjectural emendation to a missing section of Euripides' *The Bacchae,* the god Dionysus is depicted as crying out against the people of Thebes:

> Behold me, a god great and powerful, Dionysus, immortal son of Zeus and Semele!
> I come to the city of Seven Gates, to Thebes, whose men and women mocked me, denied my divinity, and refused to receive my holy rites. Now they clearly see the result of impious folly. The royal house is overthrown; the city's streets are full of guilty fear, as every Theban repents too late for blindness and blasphemy . . . for no god can see his worship scorned, and hear his name profaned, and not pursue vengeance to the utmost limit; that moral men may know that the gods are greater than they.[35]

This sense of being held fast by some overwhelmingly powerful, higher being is common to all religions. Jung chose the term "archetypes" as a more phenomenologically neutral way of speaking about what religions have called gods, spirits, angels, and demons. The archetypes are the numinous, structural elements of the psyche that preform our experience in certain typical ways. They are not inherited or eternal ideas but inherited *possibilities* of ideas, not a predetermined content but only a form. Like the axial system of a crystal, which does not determine the concrete shape of the individual crystal or its infinite variety of sizes or combinations with other crystals, but only its stereometric structure, so also the archetypes in themselves are empty and purely formal. They are predispositions to set reactions in universal situations. They are possibilities of representation which are provided by the very structure of the brain over the immense course of its evolution.[36] All human beings have mothers, fathers, grandparents, and experience hunger, sexual desire, fear, fury, and so forth. Endless repetition has engraved these experiences into our psychic constitution or collective memory, so that there are as many archetypes as there are typical situations in life.[37]

These archetypes possess a certain autonomy and specific energy which enable them to attract those contents best suited to themselves out of the conscious mind. Thus the archetypal image is at once both universal (insofar as it reflects a fundamental structure of human experience) and specific to the person and the culture which lends its symbols. The gods want to be known; they reveal themselves in the diaphanous imagery of dreams, to the end that their exile might be ended—or, to put it in the more neutral language of the archetypes, that the libido (energy) committed to maintaining their autonomy might be integrated into the larger self by making the unconscious contents conscious.[38]

From this phenomenological point of view, the "god" archetype is the fullest expression of life-energy in the psyche and therefore has the greatest degree of energy attached to it. It is through this symbol that the individual may experience his or her relationship to the total life process. This function is so important that feeling accords it the highest value. Anything psychically powerful is invariably called "god," says Jung, and cannot but carry conviction and evoke faith. When the god-image is no longer vital, however, the intensity of libido-energy that is constellated is no longer channeled toward consciousness by the symbol, and the energy turns within, with the result that the individual is subject to the delusion that a superhuman power belongs to one's own or another's person.[39] The psychic danger of so much of the new religiousness today is its blithe conviction that we are divine, with no apparent awareness of the psychic inflation which that involves or the arduous task involved in encountering the divine image within us. Such spirituality is less a solution to our dis-ease than a symptom of it.

The collapse of the god-archetype for so many in our time has meant that the central thrust of life-energies in the self has been bereft of symbols of expression, and so has unconsciously been projected on more or less suitable human personalities—messianic figures in politics, movies, sports, entertainment, and therapy. The most catastrophic recoil of the gods in our time was Nazism, with its volcanic revival of the cult of the Norse god Wotan, and its hysterical adulation of Adolf Hitler. To the degree that the Christian God had died in the psyche of the German people, as Nietzsche had prophesied, to that degree vast sums of psychic energy were set loose to craze certain individuals with a lust for power and to inspire others to follow them blindly.[40]

But that is only an extreme case. All of us, from time to time, come under the spell of the gods, for they are images of personal and collective processes that are formative of life. On the one hand, they are personal insofar as they are to some degree the unconscious distillate of instinctual demands, the patterns of instinctual behavior.[41] They are, in terms of the general thesis of this work, the "within" or spirituality of the physical instincts. The gods, we might say, are, at the personal level, a psychic representation of our organism's cravings for life. No wonder the gods of the Greeks were lusty, furious, greedy, lascivious, erotic; they are the voices of the self's instinctual homeostatic processes. They provide feedback to the psychophysical system about compensatory needs that the ego is neglecting.[42]

On the other hand, at the social level, aspects of the inner drama can be played out collectively, through myths, which function as the "dreams of a people." These myths are both guides and protectors through the bewildering maze of the unconscious, providing social support and sanction for an otherwise perilous and lonely journey. Myths can help us to sort out the bizarre eruptions from the depths, to identify their myriad voices and actors, to lend dignity to the humiliations of the ego by naming the assailant a god, and to promise a blessing to those who wrestle through the night.[43]

When I speak of the gods as the "within" of instinctuality or as the collective spirituality of a society (including the gods or angels of nations and other corporate entities), I do not intend to reduce them to mere personifications of bodily or social processes. I could have said as easily that the instincts or social entities are the clothing of the gods. Gods, angels, and spirits on the one hand, and instincts and institutions on the other, are the inner and outer aspects of a single phenomenon that has both spiritual and material components, and is far more rich and complex than anything materialism has been able to say about the instincts or society. In the materialistic perspective gods are "only" the instincts, purely chemical and neurological reactions of the body. In that view the gods are rendered mere allegories of mechanical processes, and can fruitfully be dropped from the race's fund of resources. Or they are "only" naive projections of the regularities and requirements of the physical or social order.

I am suggesting, on the contrary, that the gods are the "mentality" and "communicability" of the instincts or of institutions, their capacity to "speak" and thus provide information to an organism or a society. They are not rendered less real by being located, whether at Olympus or in the psyche. They are not a postulate or a hypothesis, but an experience. They are known through revelation, today just as in all times, in the dreams and visions of everyday people. They are not mere projections of subjective states. They are the very structures by which personality and society are formed. They are as real as anything in the world. Without them we would not exist.

After this book was completed I came upon Curtis Bennett's *God As Form: Essays in Greek Theology*, the best study of Greek religion that I have found. The gods, he argues, are necessary psychic forms for very real pressures and powers. They are the discrete categories, given shape by the imagination, for the powers which we encounter in the processes and events of the natural, social, and inner psychological environment. These forms are in the mind, but they are not simply human shapes assigned to immanent powers and energies. These forms, rather, are themselves precipitated by the pressures, energies and processes of the body and its world. As such they are indispensable images, because they alone historically carry the dramatic intuition of the relationship of a given individual to the unwilled and ungovernable processes of nature. We cannot relinquish the gods without relinquishing that intuition and hardening the delusion that individuals are self-determining. On the contrary, urges Bennett, human existence is beyond the control of any of its individual expressions. The psyche is not self-determining; it is rather expressive of the powers that determine its history. The gods are not just projections. They are environmental powers as well as elsewhere determined elements in the individual psyche and its destiny. "Instead of being projections from the psyche of its hoped-for magic powers, the Greek gods denote the projection into the psyche in recognizable form and accent of all that determines its history; they are the mode of its realization of its own form, its own elements, and their place in the natural environment" (38–39). "As our dreams will forever show, we can not live without psychic projection, in the naturalistic sense, for realizing the elements of our own nature as independent of our authority" (35). For the same reason the anthropomorphic aspect of deity is essential: it is the way to see the power defined as it impinges on the individual mind. The image enables us to see what cannot be seen physically, *as if* it were seen physically.

Bennett also relates the gods to the instincts. "Instinct and capacity for the individual are realized in as-if human forms of enduring existence." They express the pressure of that instinct for self-expression in the individual of his or her non-individual endowment. There are, he remarks, no "instincts" or "needs" or "drives" any more than there "are" gods; all are processes rendered as psychic entities. The gods speak within, and one recognizes the experience precisely because it is not unique but generic, an external form. The human ego is only local, but the gods bespeak power, instincts, forms of action that automatically recall their manifold manifestations elsewhere, as immortal forms, gods. They therefore must "speak" as a "voice" communicating the extra-individual pressure or capacity of self-realization to the individual psyche.[44]

The gods live. Monotheism is constitutionally incapable of acknowledging this fact. Biblical henotheism has affirmed it all along. "Who among the sons of gods is like the Lord, a God feared in the council of the holy ones?" (Ps. 89:6-7). Even when we had suppressed the memory that Yahweh had a heavenly council, we continued in our worship and eucharists to chant, "Holy, holy, holy is the Lord of *hosts*"—those hosts who were none other than the gods themselves. But now that the gods have returned—are we equal to their epiphany?

Relating to the Gods

One of the gods who has been playing special havoc with the psyches of moderns, though she is seldom given credit, is Aphrodite. She is the goddess of love, goddess of the holiness of the sexual act. Sexuality always has something daimonic, something uncanny, even sinister about it, some quality of numinosity, of the unintelligible, the superhuman. There are occasions when it uses us, compels us, drives us, even when our physical needs would appear to have been satisfied. There is more than biological urge involved here, something at the other end of the spectrum, more like a lure toward self-transcendence and individuation. For that reason intercourse often symbolizes in dreams the conjunction of opposites in a new increment of wholeness. The ecstasy of sexual union is "heavenly," insofar as it expresses the transcendent sanctity of the sexual act. More than this woman or this man is present. At that moment one communes with gods.

It is important to note, as Curtis Bennett points out, that Aphrodite is neither sex personified nor an abstraction of sex. She is the form by which the psyche realizes that it is in the domain of sex. She is not the idealization of woman as a sex object, or a wish-fulfilment projected on a female form. For when she appears to Helen, enticing her to Paris, she nevertheless appears as a woman. She is rather the form presented to the psyche of the sexual need of one human being for another.[45]

Pagan worship sometimes externalized and literalized this psychic experience, enacting it with sacred "prostitutes" of both sexes. But the term of odium is ours; in their own context theirs was regarded as a "service to the gods." Our culture no longer builds shrines to the gods of sex, yet who has not known of couples enmeshed in furtive affairs that are invested by their participants with all the numinous qualities of powers divine? Now, as modern society has broken free of so much of its Puritan and Victorian restraint, pinups and pornography have become antimadonnas,[46] and sexual freedom is the new evangel. And Aphrodite is behind it all.

Christians are so accustomed to diatribes against her dangers—they are real, and we will get to them—that it seems only fair to point out that she can also bring blessings. She showers joy and a taste of eternity on people otherwise trapped in humdrum lives. And she can be a trickster used by God. Let me illustrate.

As a child, this man now in his midthirties had stuttered. His feet turned in. And his father had already had massive heart attacks. His older brothers would get into fights and then, when their father intervened, turn on him, terrifying this youngest child that they would cause his father's death. At night he would pray, O God, please make me better tomorrow, so that I won't be a burden to Dad.

Puberty hit this child who had to be good to save his father's life like a tornado. Powers reared up in him over which he had no control. Aphrodite—he himself used that word—ruled him like an autonomous force. He lived in terror that people would discover that he really was not good, that he was an evil boy swept away by sex. Nor had Aphrodite released him since.

Now he was thirty-five, telling his story. He felt no redemption in it. He could not embrace his demon. He could not even bring it into the presence of God. He was sure that having shared all this, no one could accept him. Yet he had been driven to say it all. One person responded, "Isn't it just the opposite of what you think? Wasn't this the only power in your world strong enough to shatter the tyranny of the 'good'? Wasn't Aphrodite the seducer who lured you out

of the Castle of Phony Goodness? Wasn't she the thin margin between saintli-
ness of a bogus sort, and your real humanity? And isn't this the reason why,
when you shared all these things, one of us struck you incredulous by saying
that she saw Christ in you right then? It is only because of Aphrodite that that
sublime humanness shines through. She was God's grace to you. She had to be
autonomous. Your world allowed no space for her otherwise. You need to love
her for what she has done for you. That doesn't mean it's easy—you now have
ahead the long hard task of integrating your sexuality at last. But you can do
so now because you need no longer dread it as an external power beyond your
control. You can honor it as a part of yourself that almost destroyed you trying
to save you from becoming nothing more than an automaton of the good." He
was thunderstruck. "I can't believe you are saying that to me," he murmured,
then said it again. He seemed to become lighter as we watched. The burden of
a lifetime was falling from him. His problem was far from solved—it had only
finally been adequately identified—but for the first time he felt he had a fighting
chance to overcome it.

What the poet Rilke declared of the god Orpheus is true here of Aphrodite
as well: "And she obeys, even as she oversteps the bounds."[47]

Aphrodite, however, has many faces. All the gods are ambivalent. She is content to incarnate herself in anyone and can be served by sexual alliances of every
sort, wholly apart from any concern for morality, appropriateness, or the consequences. She is no monogamist. In American society, where people tend to
vaunt themselves on their sexual freedom, what many experience is in fact
sexual possession. They are *not free not to* engage in compulsive sexual fanta-
sies, masturbation, or affairs, and are often unaware of the extent of their bondage until, by some means, they are liberated. The danger echoes still in Helen's
plaint in the *Odyssey,* "It is Aphrodite who deceived me and brought me out
of my village."[48] Jung points to Aphrodite's work: "When, for instance, a highly
esteemed professor in his seventies abandons his family and runs off with a
young red-headed actress, we know that the gods have claimed another
victim."[49] And she has other aspects as well: her love of war (Ares was her husband), of orgies, of prostitution. She is far from archetypal femininity; hers is
a masculinized image of sex as power, rebellion, lust, and conquest. We have
to bridle her, bring her powers into the service of relationship, or else she may
consume us.

Aphrodite is alive and well and inspiring a profitable sex industry grossing
billions. Ares/Mars is alive and well and devouring more money, material, scientific creativity, and human flesh for past, present, and future wars than all the
gods combined. Dionysus is alive and well and staging a major revival in
voodoo, Macumba, the charismatic movement, the drug culture, the rock scene,

and generally mocking to derision the rigid etiquette and emotional sterility of the traditional religions. Christians have been afraid to admit the existence of gods for fear people would succumb to worshiping them. That danger is great, but no greater than the opposite danger of denying their existence and being unconsciously tyrannized by them. The only sane course would appear to be to acknowledge their reality, learn their characteristics, raise to consciousness their ineluctable workings in our depths, and subject them to the sovereignty of the God of gods.

Besides the reality factor, there is the simple fact that Yahweh cannot symbolize all the ways in which we encounter the divine. There is no way of speaking of Yahweh as Cupid or Eros, for example, or as involved in the positive aspects of sexuality. Apart from the Song of Songs, one looks in vain for anything in Jewish or Christian sources that celebrates sexual intercourse.[50] Little of the trickster quality of Hermes adheres to Yahweh; most of it was displaced on Satan, but humorlessly, with the result that the wonderful subterfuges by which we are beguiled into coming to terms with the darker aspects of ourselves are blamed on Satan and "righteously" resisted. And perhaps if we could perceive that much of the love for order and tradition that conventional Christianity ascribes to God is really more characteristic of Kronos/Saturn, then congregations might not absolutize familiar ways of doing things as much as they do.

I am aware that this openness toward the gods was not an option for the early church, picking its way through a world dense with idols. But our situation is fundamentally different. Ours is not a god-sotted world; it is god-bereft. The flames of secularism have destroyed much that is of value, but they have also incinerated great heaps of religious rubbish. Perhaps we are freer now to sort through the ashes to recover the finer metals refined in the fire. Furthermore, I believe that depth psychology now provides us for the first time with cognitive tools for relating to the gods without lapsing into their worship, and that these are already filtering down into a general cultural awareness. In short, I believe that Christianity can at last open itself to receive gifts from the other religions of the world.

And why should this not be the case? We believe that Jesus fulfilled the Law and the Prophets; why should he not also have fulfilled the myths of the pagans? I am not proposing syncretism, but merely the incorporation of the gods among the Powers where they belong, just as Ephraem Syrus said they should be.[51] As such they are part of God's good creation, bearing all the marks of the Fall, yet still part of the divine economy and necessary for our development and redemption. Such a hermeneutical strategy simply carries on the ancient Israelite practice of conscripting the gods into the heavenly council. The gods are divested of ultimacy both by subordinating them to God and by ordering their myth within the foundational myth of the Judeo-Christian tradition. This "hierarchical principle of preference among values," as Paul Ricoeur puts it, makes it possible for us to remain deeply rooted in our primary myth and still appropriate values drawn from any other complementary mythic source.[52]

I am not the least bit interested in reviving polytheism. People today are lost enough without being thrown into a wilderness of vying spiritual powers, none of which possesses ultimacy though all alike claim it. The great revelation given Israel to give the nations, that there is one God beyond the gods, is the single greatest treasure the world possesses. Monotheism is an abasement of that gift. It snaps the tension between multiplicity and unity, declares for unity alone, and teaches unbridled intolerance toward all other opinions. And it also has induced a simplistic notion of the self as indivisible and one, denying us the very guides whose aid we must enlist to find our way through the bewildering labyrinth of personal development and collective life.[53] The henotheistic or mono-Yahwist view of the Bible, on the other hand, acknowledges the rich multiplicity of Powers in the soul and in the world, yet encompasses them all within an integrative principle of coherence.

Perhaps the time has come to recast the henotheistic metaphor of God as a king presiding over his court into a new, less patriarchal, hierarchical and antiquarian image. Not all forms of coordination require central control, after all. An ecosystem, for example, has a most intricate coordination of synergistic actions, yet there is no central power. A market economy can likewise rely on Adam Smith's "invisible hand" to weave together the pursuits of individual economic agents into a coherent fabric of exchange.[54] In each case the control is in the total system, not some key point in it, much as the self cannot be located in any central point in the body, but pervades the whole. The picture of God as King requires a controller outside the system or atop its hierarchical apex, directing the whole. It is only in direct contests of power that a directing authority is required at the center. It may be that the very power-system of civilized society has entrapped us into conceiving God as a despot anxious to maintain ascendancy, demanding unquestioning obedience, and served by a heavenly army (the original meaning of "Lord of *hosts*"). For the very epitome of centralized control is the military organization, with its pyramid of power and centralized chain of command. What the ancients designated by "King," we are free to reconceive as the System of the systems, the Soul of the cosmos, the Mother of all, the Life of life, the I AM still and forever, the Eternal.

However we choose to speak of God, we should be clear that God is not merely the sum of all the gods, or the complex of opposites, but the dynamism that thrusts toward their synthesis. Along each loop of the spiral of life we encounter the gods arrayed in polar opposition. On each revolution we confront them again, over and over—the same archetypal patterns, the same neurotic complexes, the same cultural or political compulsions. Each god is ambivalent, possessing its own component of good and evil. Our capacity to be faithful in these encounters and to transform that bit of evil and encompass that bit of good adds incrementally to the total available energy and being of the self and the world. As the spiral widens in its gyre, life is enhanced.

The problem of false worship of the gods stems from the fact that as the "within" of instinctuality or the collective compulsions of society, they encounter us with such almighty power that we not only fail to resist but are awed into submission. We worship what enslaves us, forging our own chains. This lies at the heart of Paul's critique of the gods. He could not take the easy route of denying the gods' existence, as the Corinthians were doing. He knew their power to *enslave*. "Indeed, there are many gods and many lords—yet for us there is one God. . . ." How then, he cries in another place, "can you turn back again to the weak and beggarly elements, whose slaves you want to be once more?"[55] Such idolatry mislocates the reverence due to the Creator and lodges it in a Power that is only a subaspect of creation.[56] Whenever this happens, the god does become demonic, just as the Apologists said—but without their realizing that the demonic quality does not inhere in the gods but in the way we *relate* to the gods. When we worship them we abdicate our lives to them, thus destroying the creative tension that the ego must maintain with and against them in order to wrest from them their blessings for the self.

How then can we relate to the gods without inundation? Much depends on *ego* and *altar*. The archetypes should be honored, but honored at a distance, as a fire that can consume, as a force that both blesses with its presence and inflicts itself as curse. The ego (the conscious aspect of the self) must therefore not only participate in living forward the pattern provided by the archetype, says Murray Stein; it must at the same time monitor the process as a cautious and interested observer. Without this dual consciousness, the participatory 'I' is simply a puppet of the archetype, and the pattern simply repeats itself rather than providing the key for release. Yielding to the archetype can be pathological. If the mythology lives us, instead of our living it, we can fall into a state of inflation, possession, bondage, one-sidedness, and stereotypy.[57] All the more soul-wise cultures have shown an acute sense of the "perils of the soul" and of the dangerousness and general unreliability of the gods, Jung remarks. Hence one ought to avoid at all costs identification or union with the god, for as psychosis and certain contemporary events demonstrate, the consequences are terrifying.[58]

Thus forewarned, the ego's next task is to find the god's blessing—to read, in the disgusting compulsiveness of our neurotic behavior or the crippling effects of our diseases, some divine rune that unravels its meaning. Our mistaken quest for perfection ill-prepares us to find the healing value in the very inferior and unacceptable aspects of ourselves that we have so long tried to flee, deny, crush, amputate, or disown. But it is just there that the God of gods waits to be discovered, in the integration of autonomous parts of ourselves into the total selfhood to which we are called.

Such integration will require sacrifice. We must therefore have an *altar.* But what is the proper gift? The ego is desperately trying to hold its own, over-matched by a god—and we are told that the ego must itself be sacrificed. That it must abandon control, so that the entire Gestalt of the self can absorb, digest, and integrate this new thing. But that can only be done on faith that something or someone is in charge, greater and better than the ego. It demands trust that there is a higher will in this encounter, working to augment life. Here both the ego and the gods must bow, and be ordered under an organic principle that tran-scends them both. The "altar" frees us to honor the gods without worshiping them, to keep our distance and yet relate to them. This is the religious task of the ego: to worship only the God of gods, weaver of life's purposes.

Honor the gods; worship God. Something of the same formula animated the anti-iconoclasts in the great controversy over icons. The seventh Ecumenical Council at Nicaea in 787 adopted the distinction between reverence (*proskynesis*) and the true worship of faith (*latreia*). The first could be offered as a form of veneration before icons of Christ, Mary, and saints. This was no different in kind from the *proskynesis* performed in the East before bishops or the emperor and empress. But *latreia,* true worship, was appropriate only to God.[59]

Psalm 29 goes one step further. *We* are to order the gods to worship Yahweh!

> Ascribe to the Lord, O sons of gods,
>   ascribe to the Lord glory and strength.
> Ascribe to the Lord the glory of his name;
>   worship the Lord in holy array.
>   (Ps. 29:1-2, RSV marginal reading)

This is finally the only way to keep the gods in their place—to remind them of their fealty to their sovereign. (And here, too, despite every attempt to recast the image, the metaphor of kingship *means* something so central to the life of faith that one wonders if we will ever be able to dispense with it.) The gods too are creatures. When we do not command the gods to worship thus, we forget ourselves and worship them. When that happens, they are potentiated as autono-mous powers. They become disobedient to the divine will, possessing us with all the irresistible force of a neurotic complex or a political obsession. It is *our* task to keep them in their seats in the heavenly council, ours to signal their praise to Yahweh. What a glorious picture of the role of choice, of our own role in helping to determine the good or evil of the gods!

The gods live. They are real but not ultimate, transcendent but not absolute, suprahuman but not superior to humans, more powerful than we yet subject to our responses, worthy of honor yet never to be worshiped, manifestations of the divine yet never to be identified with godhead. If we do not acknowledge them they compel us from concealment. If we demonize them we lose their blessing. If we worship them we risk possession by what is fragmentary and lose our relatedness to the whole.

Perhaps it will be the case that in the twisting and surprising turns of our development it may be our fate to have as our dancing partner for a few spins one of the great gods. But it is still the Fiddler that calls the tunes. The trick is staying in the dance—do not, oh do not let the god escort you off the floor and out into the dark. Stay in close earshot to the music, keep moving with the beat, and the Fiddler will see you through.

6. The Elements of the Universe

We now turn to a unique class of entities that were generally ascribed divinity in the Greco-Roman world, the "elements of the universe" (*stoicheia tou kosmou*). These differ from every other category of Powers so far discussed. Whereas Satan, the demons, and the gods manifest themselves primarily in the human psyche, and the angels of the churches and nations are encountered as the interiority of corporate systems, the elements of the world encompass us about at every level of existence. They are the ubiquitous building blocks of reality. They form the basic stuff of matter—earth, air, fire, water. They constitute the irreducible principles and practices of mathematics, science, art, and religion. Because they are so invariant, so essential, so unvarying and universal, the ancients accorded to them divinity. This did not mean that they were beings, but only that they were suprahuman. They determined life. They set the bounds. They possessed an ultimacy that could not be mocked. Therefore they were honored with the respect due to gods.

That is an attitude we today have left far behind. No self-respecting modern person would admit to worshiping matter. We do not treat first principles as gods, or accord reverence to invariant laws and ritual practices. Our "table of elements" may have grown from the ancient four (earth, air, fire, and water) to upwards of 104, but we no longer consider them divine.

In our own search for the most elemental and fundamental particles of the physical universe, we have ironically pushed through matter and out the other side. The "particles" proved not to be there, after all, but only processes of energy in dynamic fields of forces. But even that surprise has not induced reverence. We have de-divinized nature. We live in terror of extermination by the fusion of nature's most fundamental elements, but we see nothing godlike in this power.

So here we are, contemplating the harrowing possibility of our destruction by the elements of the world. And rather than acting to defuse this threat, we are daily adding to our arsenals new megatons of annihilating powers. The procedures for making such weapons are now available in popular magazines. Com-

128

puter malfunctions continue to signal false alerts of nuclear attacks. Several dozens of military personnel stationed in armed missile silos have experienced severe psychological problems. Quite apart from deliberate decisions that our leaders might take, we live in perpetual threat of the accidental initiation of humanity's last war.

Any objective observer arriving on this planet would declare us certifiably insane. Prior to our adoption of the even more destabilizing policy of a nuclear first strike, the arms race was correctly identified by the acronym MAD (Mutual Assured Destruction). This situation registers unavoidably in the psyche of everyone, even those who refuse to think about it, creating responses from hedonism to despair. We are the abject slaves of a technology that has unleashed some bright genie from its restraining bonds, and now with no trace of compunction it seems destined to end our human journey toward consciousness with a paroxysm of excessive light—a death-bringing light, the light of a thousand suns. It is as if our quest for lucidity must end in a demonic parody of our one-sidedness.

We are in bondage to the elements of nature, and no one can see any longer how we can become free. And we are utterly without categories for understanding what could have reduced us to such a state.

What is an "element"? Why has physics provided us the skill to release the power of the elements but not the wisdom to constrain it? How is it possible for humanity in its entirety to be taken hostage by inert, inanimate matter? How is it that this Power that we stalked now stalks us? That the myth of Frankenstein's monster should have become our living nightmare?

These are not questions for which I have much by way of answers. I write them each in utter astonishment, defenseless against them. The New Testament, so far as I can tell, offers us no solution to the nuclear crisis. No one knows whether this genie can ever be put back into its bottle. Even disarmament by the superpowers, or by the nations generally, would not remove the threat of nuclear blackmail of cities or even nations by terrorists, nor guarantee that some country would not in desperation resort to treaty violation and nuclear attack. We must struggle for as much disarmament as can be achieved, hoping against hope that the human race will learn to live with this dread capability without using it.

Robert Oppenheimer, scientific director of the Manhattan Project, which produced the first nuclear device, quoted this line from the Bhagavad Gita as the first bomb was tested: "I am become Death, the shatterer of worlds." Our failure to control the production and proliferation of nuclear arms while it was still perhaps possible means that his self-imposed judgment has become true of us all: We are become Death.

It may at least serve the interests of truth and perhaps of survival if we were able to understand how this bondage to the elements has come about. And for that wisdom the New Testament does provide help, if we are patient enough to let it speak in its own idiom and time and place.

The Elements as Basic Principles of the Universe

In *Naming the Powers* I presented evidence for defining *stoicheion* or "element" as that which is the primary and irreducible component of a thing, the most basic constituent of any substance or entity.[1] This usage of "elements" corresponds precisely to its use in English. We are accustomed to speaking of the periodic table of basic substances as the "chemical elements"; these still function as the fundamental constituents of molecular chemistry, but they are no longer considered the ultimate constituents of matter. The ancient Greek dream of discovering some principle of matter to which all forms of physical existence might be reduced has now been transferred to the field of nuclear physics and the search for the ultimate or "elementary" particle. But the word "element" has a place in virtually every field—in anatomy, of the ultimate units of a tissue, such as a cell; in mechanics, of the individual parts comprising a machine; in philosophy, science, art, or music, of the basic principles that undergird the field or discipline. And we can tell immediately by the context whether someone is referring to the elements of a military unit, or the elements of the Lord's Supper, or the elements of a storm, or the elements of a problem.

In the New Testament "elements" is used in Col. 2:8 to denote the first or fundamental principles of the physical universe. Its use in conjunction with "philosophy" and as a synonym for "human tradition" suggests that Paul is warning his readers against the tendency of all Greek philosophy to account for the origin of everything by positing one or a few elemental substances as their source. "See to it that no one takes you captive," Paul warns, "through hollow and deceptive philosophy, which depends on human traditions and the basic principles of this world (*stoicheia tou kosmou*) rather than on Christ" (NIV). In 2 Pet. 3:10 and 12, on the other hand, we find "elements" meaning not so much the basic principles as the basic stuff, matter: on the day of judgment, heaven and earth will be burned up, and "the elements will be dissolved with fire."

On analogy from this usage, "elements" can be used to refer to anything basic. In the arena of religion it denotes the fundamentals of religious belief (Heb. 5:12), or the basic principles of religious life, such as the law (Gal. 4:3), or more broadly, all the rites, festivals, dietary regulations, observances, doctrines, and beliefs common to Jewish and pagan religion alike (Gal. 4:9; Col. 2:20): the "elements" of religion.

The characteristic that all these "elements" have in common is their being the irreducible and basic principles or entities of a particular class of phenomena. But they also have this in common: they are powerful, indispensable, and ubiquitous. Like gravity (itself the "basic principle" or *stoicheion* governing the attraction of matter) they are boundaries that cannot be transgressed with impunity. They are the very conditions of existence. We cooperate with them or we are "judged" by them. We might usefully speak of them as "invariances" and "physical determinants."

"Invariances" is increasingly used by natural scientists in place of "laws" to refer to those unchanging conditions and requirements according to which the more changing phenomena of nature and society operate. They are not "iron laws" so much as statistical probabilities, but they are probabilities of a very high order of predictability. Gravity, which I just mentioned, operates invariantly, though like other invariances it can be transcended by *stoicheia* or invariances operating at a higher level (as gravity can actually be used for flight by the principles of aerodynamics as employed in aviation).

Every field of knowledge has for its concrete footings some such basic principles or *stoicheia*. Take mathematics. Euclid articulated the basic theorems of geometry in a book he called *The Stoicheia of Mathematics*. Today there is a multitude of mathematical systems, each of them possessing its own *stoicheia* or basic axioms. In the field of biology the *stoicheia* that seem to be the basic principles by which life evolves have been identified by the majority of scientists as random mutation and adaptive selection. In physical chemistry the most fundamental principles or *stoicheia* are the laws of thermodynamics, which articulate the process by which energy is expended. In astrophysics the *stoicheion* is the velocity of light as a fixed universal constant of nature having the same value for all observers regardless of their state of motion with respect to the source of light.

Other *stoicheia* would include the "axioms" of logic, the "rules" of chance, the "laws" of society, the "letters" of the alphabet, the "notes" of the scale, the "numbers" of arithmetic, the laws, beliefs, and rituals of religions. These are the irreducible components or basic principles upon which whole realms of knowledge are established. But they are not simply human projections of regularity and order on the universe. Consider that most subjective of spheres, aesthetics. For the Greeks, the *stoicheion* of art was the "golden mean," a rectangle that measures to the ratio of .618034 to 1. Thousands of objects even today randomly approximate it: index cards, playing cards, stationery, boxes.

Apparently people sense, without knowing why, that rectangles of roughly the proportion of three by five or five by eight inches are pleasing to the eye. They are also, it seems, pleasing to nature, for the proportion .618034 to 1 is the mathematical basis for the shape of sunflowers and snail shells, the curl of surf and the chambered nautilus, spiral galaxies and pineapple scales, elephants' tusks and lions' claws. Even the cochlea of the inner ear is shaped in a logarithmic spiral of the proportion .618034 to 1.[2]

The *stoicheia* are not then merely constructs of human thought (though they are, of course, also that). They are given within nature, patterned into organisms and objectified in science, symbols, images, art, rules, and religions. These function in nature and society the way electrostatic bonds function in molecules: they operate to hold the shape or maintain the stability of physical, biological, and cultural systems.[3]

No wonder then that so many modern scholars and translators have mistakenly assumed that the elements were "spirits." For though they are not beings as such, they certainly are real. Insofar as they are fundamental principles or cultural symbols or derived axioms or psychological archetypes or social or religious laws and beliefs, they are invisible. Yet for all that they are not simply human inventions. Numbering is possible for us only because the universe is numerable. Social laws and religious taboos may vary from place to place in content, but the presence of such laws and taboos is ubiquitous. Societies could not survive without them, and none do exist without them. These *stoicheia* then are the very building blocks of physical, social, and spiritual reality. They antedate us, they transcend us, they outlast us. To a degree far beyond awareness, they determine and shape us. We are compassed about by superhuman powers, and we come into a world already organized for their idolization.

Ralph Wendell Burhoe specifically associates the notion of invariances with the rise of belief in gods. "In the history of human thought, among the earliest and most comprehensive systems of abstractions of invariance were those of primitive myths and theologies, which *gave the name of gods to the sources of the invariant and powerful forces or laws which man had to obey* if he was successfully to adapt to life."[4] It is the physicists, Burhoe argues, who have today

become the best revealers of the elusive but sovereign entities and forces, not immediately apparent to common sense, that do in fact far transcend human powers, that did create life and human life and do ordain human destiny. I suggest that it is to such real, superhuman, and ultimately insuperable powers and conditions of the cosmos—however primitively envisaged—to which the gods or supernatural powers of prior cultures referred rather than to nonexistent beings. "Supernatural" refers not to their unreality but rather to both the hiddenness of their reality from our common-sense view and also to their prior reality as a more ultimate source and ground of the more apparent or "natural" phenomena.[5]

The *stoicheia* manifest themselves not only as invariances but also as physical determinants. The latter are elemental forces characterized not so much by their law-like behavior as by their sheer power to constrain life. Everyone is aware of the more tangible influences of the elements on life. We must have food, clothing, and shelter in order to survive. Hurricanes, tornadoes, and typhoons devastate whole cities. Floods and drought destroy crops, and thousands starve. Earthquakes, volcanoes, and dustbowls spur mass migrations of refugees. These are the more dramatic instances of our interaction with the elements, when we are most keenly aware of the fragility of our lives before such awesome powers. Most of the time, however, the elements are so benign, so supportive, so symbiotically integrated into all the processes of life, that we scarcely realize their presence until something goes wrong.

We have only an inkling of the magnitude of the dominance of these "elements" over our lives. Light and color, for example, are now known to enter the brains and cells of mammals directly, and not only through the visual system, with consequences for bodily adaptations to changes of seasons, sexual activity, menstrual cycles, and so forth.[6] The air itself affects us, not simply by being "there" to be breathed or polluted, but by the degree of negative or positive ions it contains at any given place and time. (Atmospheric ions are electric charges in air molecules.) The famous "ill winds" that blow seasonally in certain places—the Khamsin, the Mistral, the Santa Ana, the Foehn—do in fact bring with them a higher incidence of crimes of violence, admissions to mental hospitals, and certain illnesses, though once these claims were regarded as superstition.[7] These winds are now known to contain unusually high concentrations of positively charged ions. Smog also evidences high levels of positive ions, and laboratory studies have shown that positive ions can reduce resistance to infectious diseases and even retard the growth of certain plants. Negatively charged ions, on the other hand, speed up tissue growth, remove the "stuffy" feeling in rooms, and aid in healing, especially in recovery from burns. While research on these matters is still in its infancy, enough is known to explain why adepts of the contemplative life have gravitated toward waterfalls, mountain tops, deserts, and shores, for these are places where negative ions tend to preponderate.[8]

The frequency of sunspots—or perhaps more exactly, variations in the sun's magnetic field—also affects human life in ways only now beginning to be perceived. Their incidence correlates with temperature averages, glacial activity, the winter-severity index and carbon-14 abundance in tree rings. All of these phenomena seem to result from fluctuations in the rotation of the sun. The consequences for human life are subtle but far-ranging. During one period of prolonged sunspot inactivity, for example, the ice pack off the coast of south-

western Greenland failed to thaw year after year. Because their boats could not
be freed, the Norse colony there could not secure food, and all perished.[9] Were
they not victims of the "elements of the universe"?

Since we are surrounded by so great a cloud of invisible determinants, it is
not surprising that peoples of every culture would have attempted to identify the
unseen factors that seemed to be constraining their behavior. In the world of the
New Testament, and even more so in the period of the early church, many
people ascribed to the heavenly bodies the power to predestine their lives.[10]
Others blamed physical diseases on harmful influences from the spirits of the
dead, or Satan, or demons, or unplacated gods. Because these "influences"
were so often destructive of human life, it is not surprising that they were
regarded as malevolent spiritual beings intent on our undoing, when in fact
people were often simply crosswise with unknown invariances or determinants
in the natural order.

The extent to which human existence is imperceptibly bounded and constrained by the elements of the universe is so extensive that the real margin of
human freedom is actually quite small in comparison to the degree that we are
determined by these Powers. Yet most of us have been so deeply inculcated with
the belief in free will that we ignore or suppress awareness of the ways we have
been "cribbed, cabined, and confined." We scarcely even attempt to integrate
the flood of data pouring in on us from the physical and social sciences that
reveal our vassalage to the elements of the world.

That, however, would be but a minor case of self-deception, a thin cardboard
of conceit propped against our sense of insignificance in the world, were the
deception not coupled with outright slavery. There is nothing evil about living
within constraints; indeed, one mark of maturity is the capacity to accept them
and work creatively within them. Paul however speaks unequivocally of those
who are "slaves to the elements of the universe" (Gal. 4:3, au. trans.), to beings
that by nature are not gods (4:8), "weak and beggarly elements whose slaves
you want to be once more" (4:9, au. trans.). If the "elements of the universe"
are merely the invariances and physical determinants that make human life possible we are unavoidably subordinate to them. But how do we become their
slaves?

Idolatry of the Elements

We become slaves of the elements by granting them an ultimacy they do not
possess. Clement of Alexandria flails the Greek philosophers for positing godhead in matter. "Some philosophers," he writes, "left us the elements
(*stoicheia*) as first principles (*archas*) of all things." But these thinkers were
really atheists, he says, "since with a foolish show of wisdom they worshiped

matter," and missed entirely "the great original, the maker of all things, and creator of the 'first principles' (*archōn*) themselves, God without beginning (*anarchon*). . . ."[11] Apparently it was to some such situation that Col. 2:8 was addressed, with its warning against "secondhand, empty, rational philosophy based on the principles (*stoicheia*) of this world instead of on Christ" (JB). Put broadly, whenever one's life is oriented around a subsystem rather than the whole, the result is slavery and the forfeiture of life. The Colossians were in danger of mistaking the basic elements of things for the ultimate reality.

That, however, is still too broad. How could the elements attract such energy to themselves that people would become enthralled by them? When the ancients declared the four physical elements to be gods, they were in effect projecting into them the image of the quaternity, one of the oldest symbols of individuation, wholeness, and the world-creating deity. The very choice of but *four* elements was itself entirely arbitrary unless the choice was determined by the archetype of four-foldness.[12] But this would mean then that an unconscious psychic content is being invested in matter.[13] This is the whole point of paganism and nature worship: that gods dwell in created things. But the gods, as we saw in the last chapter, are integrally related to the archetypes of the collective unconscious. Gods in matter—this cannot refer to the "within" of matter, which has a quite limited freedom and, so far as we know, little capacity for mentation or self-transcending initiatives. The gods are in matter only if we put them there, by projection. "In the darkness of anything external to me I find, without recognizing it as such, an interior or psychic life that is my own," writes Jung.[14]

A central element in Christianity's appeal over against senescent paganism was precisely its capacity to break the spell of nature and its gods, to distance itself from the onslaught of sense impressions and to establish a new and independent relationship with the physical universe. This liberation was heady, but was still guided by something of the old religious piety and ethic long after science and religion parted company. First Christianity and then the Enlightenment drove the gods out of matter, freeing scientists to manipulate physical substances with impunity. We congratulate ourselves for having risen beyond superstition; but the gods are still within us. Consequently we simply project them *unconsciously* into matter, with no awareness of having done so.

As a result, remarks Jung, the very attention we have lavished on natural objects, and the very success of our increasingly deep descent into the abyss of nature, have left us at their mercy. "The more successful the penetration and advance of the new scientific spirit proved to be, the more the latter—as is usually the case with the victor—became the prisoner of the world it had conquered."[15] What began by appearing to be an incarnation of Logos as rational science soon revealed itself rather as the mythological descent of Anthropos or

Nous into the dark embrace of Physis. Having first been deprived of its gods, the world had now lost its soul to the gods of the underworld.[16]

But modern scientists, and the culture they carried with them, were not prepared for this dark embrace. The very fact that human beings are able to conceive of subatomic particles means that we somehow participate in and with the forces of nature. John Davy has commented very profoundly on this issue. Since Descartes introduced the attitude of detached observation, he says, scientists have not seen themselves as participants in nature, and the scientist's own personal life has seemed to have little relevance to his or her science. "To undergo a scientific discipline, it is in no way necessary to follow a moral discipline," apart from not falsifying results.[17] The scientist's "opus" or work was conducted *ex opere operato*—"done by the act itself"; that is, like the Catholic priest performing the sacrament, the scientist's own character had no bearing on the efficacy of the act. As Morris Berman puts it, for modern science, What can I know? and How shall I live? were totally unrelated questions.[18]

In a Heisenbergian universe, however, where every observer is a part of what is being observed, *we as human beings become part of what we behold,* says Davy. Scientists knew that the atom was a Pandora's box of unimaginable powers, but plunged ahead anyway with little concern for their readiness to cope with such forces. Yet all their predecessors had warned of the dangers. At the very fountainhead of Western science, the Neopythagoreans had declared that the nether regions of inanimate matter are ruled by evil. In Yoga a pupil was not permitted to study the disciplines of science before mastering Yama, the disciplines of the spirit: the overcoming of violence, theft, covetousness, lying, incontinence.[19] Likewise the immediate precursors of modern science, the alchemists, were wise enough to know that in plumbing the darkness they would be exposed to powers greater than their own. Therefore they admonished: "Fall on your knees before you undertake this operation." "Know that thou canst not have this science unless thou shalt purify thy mind before God, that is, wipe away all corruption from thy heart." The same text lists fourteen virtues which must be first mastered in order to "purge the horrible darkness of our mind."[20]

Because we did not face all that within, and were even to a large degree unconscious of it, we have introduced our own darkness into our relationship with subatomic matter. *And we have found there precisely what we brought.* The initial assault on the atom was made, as we all know, for the sole purpose of violence and death. The peaceful use of atomic power was to have been a sort of atonement, but even here we have encountered unanticipated nightmares that have brought new starts of nuclear plants in the United States to a complete halt.

The atom has become our shadow. We have invested it with our darkness, and it now rears up like an independent force, intent on our extermination. We brought to the elements of the world a request: give us the power of massive, unimaginable death. And our request has been granted. We are become death.

This only comes at the culmination of a long process, however, in which we gave the kiss of death to one aspect of nature after another. The ideology of this death-contagion was materialism, and its methodology, reductionism. We could have brought to subatomic physics a sense of awe at the unimaginable infinitude of God the Creator, transposed into an evolutionary key. Instead scientists dusted off the ancient materialistic dogma of Democritus and projected it onto the universe. "Death is nothing to us," wrote a follower of Democritus; "for the body, when it has been resolved into its elements, has no feeling, and that which has no feeling is nothing to us."[21] The implications are unmistakable. We are made up of atoms and molecules. When we die, we will cease to exist, but out atoms will not. Hence atoms and molecules are more real, more ultimate than we are.

We need to be very clear that the decision to orient modern science in terms of the atheistic materialism of Democritus was a matter of preference, not a necessity imposed by the data. Most scientists prior to one hundred years ago were theists; many were clergy; some wrote more theological treatises than scientific works. But the moment the decision was made to seek for the ultimate principles of nature in nature's irreducible components, the choice had been made for materialism, whether one was a theist or not. Paul's prescience in Col. 2:8 is remarkable; he somehow understood something that our age, with all its feats of knowledge and technology, has been unable to grasp: that the fascination with first things—the elements of the universe—would inevitably lead to idolatry and to a subtle but insidious slavery to matter. The moment we declared these principles ultimate, we elevated them in value above ourselves. Having projected ultimacy onto matter, we could only bow before it. For whatever is ascribed ultimacy functions as a god, whether its devotees would describe it thus or not. And the preferential selection of matter as the ultimate reality of the universe, as its fundamental constituent and determining factor, meant that the entire spiritual dimension of reality was ruled illusory from the outset.

When a worldview ceases to have cogency—when it is out of phase with the data and experiences of everyday life—then a culture is faced with more than simply an intellectual problem, but an epidemic sickness of soul. In our time the sickness brought on by the failure of the materialistic worldview is expressed in the pervasive sense of alienation structured into our lives by the subject-object split. If everything is an object, exterior, alien, distinct, not-I, then, as Berman remarks, I am ultimately an object too, an alienated "thing" in a world of other, equally meaningless things. Materialism teaches us that in order to know nature we must treat it mechanistically; but then I, as a part of nature, must be treated as a mechanism as well. What resulted from the shift from a participative worldview to mechanism was not merely a new science, but a new personality to go with it: a human being with a death-oriented view of nature. This new being was not one with all things but rather a ravisher of things, a "consumer" (literally, "one who uses things up wastefully or destructively"). For if nature is dead, there are no limits set on exploiting it for profit.[22]

Typically, many people who are discovering the aridity of the mechanistic worldview are turning to meditation, dieting, fasting, and holistic healing—mechanistically. They want the benefits of meditation without divine Presence. They want to possess healing energies without a relationship with the Healer. Such an attitude, like sex without love, is entirely characteristic of our age. Place their meditation manuals beside their sex manuals and you will see what I mean: everything is technique, physiological responses, benefits, good feelings. As in casual sex, the focus is egocentric; not relatedness, but one's own pleasure or well-being is the goal. The whole thing reeks of the technological mindset. Even the revolt against technologism is made through technique.

This process of dehumanization is parallel to Marx's theory of fetishism, except that instead of personifying capital and reducing labor to a "thing," the materialist absolutizes matter and reduces people to things. Matter, like the "invisible hand" of capital, is treated as a *deus ex machina* capable of spawning its own evolution wholly without design or purpose. And since this meaningless process has produced us, our lives can have no intrinsic purpose. (We can, of course, create purposes of our own, though those purposes would be a matter of indifference to the universe.) We are mere epiphenomena of matter, and our lives in astronomical time are too short to pause over.

One can locate this death-kiss in every current field of knowledge. Mathematics, by which we could have "thought God's thoughts after him," as the astronomer Johann Kepler was fond of saying, has become for many a rage for statistical quantification. We have still not recovered from the attitude of the nineteenth-century physicist, Lord Kelvin, who remarked, "When you can measure what you are speaking about and express it in numbers, you know something about it; but when you cannot express it in numbers, your knowledge is of a meager and unsatisfactory kind."[23]

Number has assumed such god-like powers in the modern world because number is the most primitive of all devices for ordering the cosmos. If we could set aside the contemporary bias that number is an arbitrary convention, and recognize that it is more on the order of a revelation or discovery, then we could understand that number itself is every bit as archetypal as images or gods. Indeed, the whole of Israel's struggle for identity and integrity centered on its tumultuous attempt to live out the practical consequences of the revelation that

God is "one." And the whole of Christian reflection about God was condensed into the apprehension that God is "three-in-one." One of the weaknesses of polytheism was its lack of such fundamental clarity about the numerical value of ultimate reality.[24]

In this light then the rage for quantification and the attempt to reduce all reality to number can be seen for what it is: a religious instinct made fanatical and demonic by its severance from its divine ground and its total isolation in matter.

Logical positivism actually tried to bring something of the same attitude into philosophy, with the demand that every meaningful statement be empirically verifiable. The enterprise has largely been abandoned; but how could an entire generation or more of some of our best philosophical minds ignore the fact that many of our most important and meaningful statements are beyond empirical verification, such as, for example, the statement "I love you"? Why could they not see that the assertion that unverifiable statements are meaningless is itself an unverifiable statement? What drove them to ignore Leibnitz's salient distinction between accurate knowledge and adequate knowledge?[25] More was at stake here than the asserted value of the philosophical issues themselves. Behind it was the conviction, raised to a virtual wager with the universe, that everything is capable of empirical proof by the tools of scientific and logical analysis. Perhaps the effort was necessary in order to establish the limits of analysis; no doubt it contributed to greater rigor in the use of language. But the scalpel, misapplied, can kill. The analytical imperative was itself the offspring of the materialistic view of the universe.

It is sobering to observe how one *stoicheion* after another was conscripted into service to the materialists' faith. Random mutation and natural selection were quickly caricatured as "survival of the fittest" and turned to the needs of industrial capitalism as an ideological justification for the crushing of the weak by the strong. This "social Darwinism" was also used to legitimate various schemes of eugenics, from the Nazi attempt to "cleanse" Germany by wholesale genocide of Jews, gypsies, and homosexuals to the more "harmless" schemes for producing "superior" men and women through genetic engineering. (The criteria for selecting the superior race or genes is of course no longer left to nature but to a power-elite.)

The laws of thermodynamics might appear benign enough in their own field, but their application by Henry Adams to a vision of the winding-down of our solar system left many around the turn of the century with a worldview of unrelieved gloom and purposelessness.[26] And Einstein's theory of relativity, which found its Archimedean point in the absolute speed of light, was twisted by the popular imagination into a pseudo-scientific justification for regarding everything as relative and nothing as absolute—especially ethical judgments.

Every people has known how powerful chance is as a *stoicheion*. It was even worshiped as a god by the Romans. Now it has found a modern exponent in the Nobel laureate biologist Jacques Monod. In *Chance and Necessity* he writes, "Chance alone is at the source of every innovation, of every creation in the realm of life . . . at the very root of the towering edifice of evolution."[27] Well, yes, chance is certainly the basic principle operative in random events, but must one regard it as ultimate and take such a religious attitude toward it? Monod's tone of mixed rapture and dogmatism is scarcely distinguishable from Roman hymns to Fortuna!

The kiss of death: whatever we love we kill, because we insist on investing it with an ultimacy it cannot bear. In each case the *stoicheion* involved is itself benign or neutral. It is simply the basic principle or fundamental constituent of a given field of knowledge. *We* bring to it the orientation that determines how it affects our lives. We are not just observers of the elements of the world. We are participants with them, and we become part of what we behold. If we bring to them a refusal to acknowledge our and their unity with God and all created things, or if we bring the desire to kill, or if we bring our own unconscious shadow projected into matter, we will discover over and over again that *the elements become for us what we have become for them*.[28]

I have resisted speaking of the elements as "beings" with their own wills, but I should point out that there is a long esoteric tradition that regards them as such. I have not been able to document the rise of belief in these "elementals," as they are called. No ancient source that I have found treats them as animate; Philo explicitly states that "the elements themselves are lifeless matter incapable of movement of itself and laid by the Artificer as a substratum for every kind of shape and quality" (*Vit. cont.* 4). Jews and Christians continued to assert that angels were appointed *over* the elements. In the Middle Ages, however, the "elementals," under the influence of Northern European beliefs in gnomes, fairies, elves, and dwarves, came to be conceived of as nature's little blue-collar workers, building matter according to specifications out of the appropriate materials. Their task, according to popular folklore, was to take the angelic pattern and work it into the stuff of rocks, trees, and so forth. Their manifestations as fairies or other forms, according to the best sources I have found, were considered a mere convention adapted to our limitations.[29] They are, according to one esoteric, more like "balls of light" and take on human-like forms by drawing on our own unconscious images. "Such things do exist but are *within* physical matter and because of this you cannot see them," he writes. But "each of these elements exists also within your own being"; they "interpenetrate your physical life. You see matter as solid mass and find it difficult to believe there can be another life within this apparent solidity. You forget that matter is really only loosely knit and can be interpenetrated by other forms of matter, vibrating at different rates." This, he continues, is what makes it possible for us to "see" the elementals in visionary form, and to know about their work.[30] Unlike the angels of nature, the elementals can become outright hostile to humans who violate nature: "they react to violence." But, according to the same source, elementals are created by thought from elemental essences. *We* create them by impure and violent thoughts or by feelings of fear and depression. "Sometimes people say that they have had undesirable spirits near them—and it is difficult for us to explain that these undesirable spirits are nothing but creations of their own thoughts."[31]

I find it fascinating that the "elementals" should be described as hostile toward us when we behave violently toward them. And if they are indeed thought-forms clothed in the available archetypal images of the psyche, then they are not "beings" in their own right. At the same time, however, they are not inventions of our own overactive fantasy-life either. They are *images mirroring to us our actual relationship to the elements.* But we scarcely need to meet an elf on a woodland path to learn what the elements would tell us about our strip mining, our untreated sewage, our chemical dumps. We have only to do a current missile count. The "elementals" have become incarnate as the destructive fury of our nuclear arsenals.

Long before our misuse of the elements assumed present proportions, Hildegard of Bigen (1098–1179) warned; "I heard a mighty voice crying from the elements of the world: 'We cannot move and complete our accustomed rounds as we should do according to the precepts of our Creator. For humankind, because of its corruptions, spins us about like the sails of a windmill. And so now we stink from pestilence and from hunger after justice.' " Hildegard prophesies, "As often as the elements of the world are violated by ill-treatment, God will cleanse them through the sufferings and hardships of humankind. . . . All of creation God gives to humankind to use. But if this privilege is misused, God's justice permits creation to punish humanity." Or as our wise contemporary, Gregory Bateson, put it, "The systems are . . . punishing of any species unwise enough to quarrel with its ecology. Call the systemic forces 'God' if you will."[32]

In our downward quest of the "ultimate" particle we made matter ultimate and ourselves at once its exploiters and its slaves. Bondage to the elements is the spiritual problem of modern science. "The physicists have known sin" (Oppenheimer). Indeed, one sign of that bondage is that science has not even considered that it possesses a spirituality. That too is a consequence of materialism, and of its methodology, reductionism. Reduction (without the "ism") is an indispensable tool for bracketing out the dense underbrush of phenomena and focusing on just one thing at a time. It is a component of any analytic procedure, and is one of the keys to the success of modern science. Reductionism, on the other hand, is the tendency to "explain" phenomena at higher levels as if they were "nothing more" than the sum of their most fundamental parts. Descartes's statement became the motto of all reductionism: "If anyone could know perfectly what are the small parts composing all bodies, he would know perfectly the whole of nature."[33] This attitude was applied to evolution as well. Once we erred by ascribing to animals faculties found only in humans; today behaviorism denies to humans faculties not found in animals. In Arthur Koestler's sardonic phrase, we have substituted for the anthropomorphic view of the rat, a rato-morphic view of humans.[34]

Recently a powerful attack has been launched against reductionism by a handful of scientists themselves.[35] They point out, first of all, that the search for ultimate particles has proved a will-o'-the-wisp; there are none, but only energy patterns and processes. An elementary particle is by definition supposed to be a simple, irreducible building block in some more complex structure. We go on speaking of subatomic particles as "elementary" when they are nothing of the sort. Two hundred or so nuclear particles are now recognized as existing. Quarks, it was briefly claimed, were to be the end of the story, but more than thirty different quarks have already been discovered, with gluons to hold them together. As Geoffrey Chew has pointed out, we are only able to detect particles because they interact with the observer, but in order to do so they must have some internal structure. This means that we can in principle never get to some object that has no internal structure, for a true elementary particle could not be subject to any forces that would allow us to detect its existence (if we find it by its weight, for example, then it must contain something within it producing a gravitational field). Werner Heisenberg called for an end to the concept of the elementary particle in 1975, but old habits are not so quickly changed, especially when they are invested with the aura of a religious quest.[36]

Second, even when we focus just on atoms and molecules, we take with us knowledge of the larger complexes in which we find them, and surreptitiously *include* that knowledge in a bogus "reconstruction" from the bottom up. But there is in fact no way to know in advance what, for example, sodium and chlorine atoms will do when combined. If we had not *begun* with sodium chloride and analyzed it into its discrete parts, we would never have been able to guess that the combination of these parts would taste good sprinkled on meat. In short, when atoms are organized in particular ways, they reveal aspects of their nature not predictable in isolation.[37]

In the third place, reality is not granular, like sandstone, with everything made up of the same little pieces. It is complex, and at each level of complexity we encounter new sets of invariances. Every entity is a whole in reference to the parts composing it, and a part of a larger whole. As the "elements" (the irreducible constituent parts and their invariant ways of behaving) of a lower level are gathered up into a higher level of complexity, new modes of explanation become necessary. The principles of physics and chemistry are employed at the higher level of mechanics, for example, and are operative in the atoms and molecules of a machine, but they cannot explain why the machine runs. For that we require the principles of engineering. Psychological principles (*stoicheia*) are operative in the love between two people; but love cannot be "reduced" to oedipal longings, the search for a parent, or vestigial dependency—*even where these are operative*. There is what Nobel laureate Roger Sperry called an emergent causation, which exercises downward control of the whole over the parts, without interfering with the rules and forces of entities at lower levels.[38]

This is clear even at the lower levels of complexity. The fact that two atoms of hydrogen and one atom of oxygen can be combined to produce water is a possibility inherent, not in hydrogen or oxygen as such, but only in their relation to the total system of reality. That is why worship of the lower elements—which is what reductionism essentially is—fails even as an explanation of phenomena. Not that which is *lowest* in the chain of being, but that which is the *source* of all possible transformations and brings them about—that alone deserves the name "ultimate." The observation of Clement of Alexandria is so unerring that it bears repeating: "The great original, the maker of all things, and creator of the 'first principles' themselves, God without beginning, they know not, but offer adoration to these 'weak and beggarly elements'!"[39] The whole history of modern science demonstrates time and again the tendency of scientists to absolutize one immanent aspect of creation after another. Science, it now appears, cannot dispense with God after all. It needs God, not as an "explanation," but as a grounding presupposition of reality that transcends every theorem, principle, or created component. Acknowledging God is the sole check against idolizing the elements.

Analysis and synthesis belong together in any approach to a phenomenon. It was only one-sided analysis, with its rejection of synthesis in its fascination with the part, that became reductionistic. E. E. Waddington has recently proposed a way beyond the reductionist problem by locating a different starting point: not objects but events. Events are four-dimensional happenings, that is, space-time processes. All knowledge is derived from experiences of events. Scientific objects—atoms, electrons, and so forth—are not basic but derivative; they are intellectual constructs invented to assist us in understanding events. There are no fundamental objects to which something must be added to make them "go" (energy, organization, systemic properties); they are all already "going," in actual events, in actual entities, and can be studied either from the angle of their constitutive properties (analysis) or their systemic relations (synthesis), or both.[40]

It is tragic that so much of modern science was unreflectively formulated along materialist and reductionist philosophical lines. There is a wonderful irony in the fact that it is not through the abandonment of science, but through pushing through it to its ultimate implications, that materialism is being refuted by science itself. If we are to move beyond materialism and reductionism to a more positive relationship with the elements, we must find a way of honoring their ubiquitous power without being overwhelmed by their numinosity. We must, I believe, learn to regard them as theophanies.

The Elements as Theophanies

To summarize: in granting ultimacy to what is most elemental, modern scientists have projected ultimate value into matter. Since matter, not the person, soul, or God, was regarded as ultimate, human life was rendered insignificant and without fundamental meaning. This inevitably led to our being dehumanized by the very sciences we ourselves fashioned and pursued. The act of penetrating the darkness of the subatomic world was mimetic of plunging into the unconscious. But because scientists had not in fact examined their own personal depths, or entered upon a spiritual path to cleanse their souls from at least the more gross forms of violence, power-lust, and hatred, they introduced their own darkness into their relationship with the elements of the world. And they found in them precisely what they brought, but now on a scale of infinite magnitude: unmitigated violence, uncontrollable power, and an almost fatalistic momentum toward planetary destruction. We as human beings always become part of what we behold. The elements have returned the favor. They have become for us what we became for them.

The moment scientists opted to make the basic constituents of things ultimate, heedless of Paul's advice, they were inexorably driven to adopt the philosophy of materialism and the methodology of reductionism. Thus they were "made captive through hollow and deceptive philosophy, which depends on human traditions and the basic principles of this world rather than on Christ" (Col. 2:8, NIV). Within the terms of the materialist/reductionist paradigm there is no hope whatever, since that is precisely what forged the chains that now bind us. Is there any hope at all?

We must reckon with the possibility that the descent into the abyss may now be irreversible. For the person of faith, God will still be God even if we utterly destroy life on this globe. But that in no way relieves the inexpressible grief that overwhelms any sensitive person who contemplates the loss of his or her family, children, friends, the loss of all that humanity has done and might still accomplish, the loss of all the children yet to be, and the irreversible destruction of countless species of flora and fauna. That prospect must be faced entire if we are to do the impossible thing that alone might bring survival: disarm our nuclear forces.

That *must* be attempted, but even if it could be successfully achieved, the elements would still threaten. We must also change the way we relate to them, therefore. It seems to me that the safe path into the future lies in *regarding the elements as theophanies: revealers of God.*

They are, after all, created in and through and for Christ, along with everything else in creation (Col. 1:15-20). They exist solely for the service of the whole. They are essentially benign, not evil; it is primarily our idolatry or evil that turns them to destruction. They are essential as the basis for all that exists. We could not live for a moment without them. Sirach hymns their significance:

> The works of the Lord have existed from the beginning
>   (*archēs*) by his creation,
> and when he made them he determined their divisions.
> He arranged his works in an eternal order, and their
>   dominion (*archas*) for all generations;
> they neither hunger nor grow weary,
>   and they do not cease from their labors.
> They do not crowd one another aside,
>   and they will never disobey his word.
> After this the Lord looked upon the earth,
>   and filled it with his good things.
>
>   (Ecclus. 16:26–29)

From the last verse we discover that these "works" that God made in the beginning are "heavenly," that is, transcendent powers.[41] They antedate life and operate invariantly ("they will never disobey his word"). They maintain themselves harmoniously ("they do not crowd one another aside") in their ceaseless maintenance of the universe. So indispensable is their work, in fact, that they alone of all the heavenly powers are not permitted to celebrate the Sabbath (*Jubilees* 2)!

The elements are good. Matter is good. It is our relationship to them that makes them evil. Yet having idolized them, we must be redeemed from them (Col. 2:20; Gal. 4:3, 9). How might they function if we saw them with redeemed eyes?

Paul himself stresses in Colossians that the "first principles" themselves only exist in and through and for Christ (1:16). By virtue of being "the firstborn of all creation," Christ has priority over every element, cause, or principle in nature (1:15). His preeminence over all things (1:18) means that Christ, and nothing else, is the first principle of the whole creation, "the head of all rule (*archēs*) and authority (*exousias*)" (Col. 2:10). Fritjof Capra points out that mystics and the new physicists share the realization that no phenomenon can be fully explained, since the properties of any single part are determined not by some fundamental law or ultimate particle, but by the properties of all the other parts. "Being well aware of the essential interrelationship of the universe, they realize that to explain something means, ultimately, to show how it is connected to everything else."[42] Since this cannot be done intellectually, the mystics attempted to obtain a direct intuitive experience of the unity of all things. What Paul is asserting in Colossians is precisely the primary intuition of the oneness of reality that is revealed in the cosmic Christ. "For in him the whole fulness of deity dwells bodily" (2:9). "He is before all things, and in him all things hold together" (1:17).

Such assertions are meaningful only if they are grasped at the imaginal or symbolic level. One can only give oneself over to the image, experiencing in a direct, unmediated way what it means that the whole (rationally inexplicable) universe is comprehended in Humanness. If the crucified and rejected Christ has become the cornerstone of reality, then the dehumanization of people by their subordination to matter as "ultimate" is a crime against being. The fully human life does not depend on philosophical speculation or scientific research into the invariant principles or physical elements that shape and determine reality anyway. Nor can science provide the sense of harmonious unity at the heart of things that human beings need in order to live trustfully in the universe. One needs merely to see through and behind phenomena to the unity of all things in the human form of One who is the head of every head, the ruler of every rule, the system of the systems, the principle of coherence. Through this One we are enabled to live through the flux and change of life with the knowledge of the absolute love that encompasses us. Cradled in such love, we are freed from the old principles by which an alienated reality sought to rectify itself (Col. 2:20). We do not need to hedge ourselves about by rules and regulations, human precepts and doctrines, as if to please an omnipotent Tyrant (Gal. 4:3, 9). We do not have to mortify ourselves at the close of the day in terms of every do and don't we have violated. Encompassed by such love, we can yield to the inner unfolding of our beings in the daily conversation of our own emergent self with its Creator, who alone knows its mystery: the secret of the "white stone, with a new name written on the stone which no one knows except [the one] who receives it" (Rev. 2:17).

What if we were to look a second time at those *stoicheia* which in our time have been the focus of idolatry, turning to them this time full of the knowledge that Christ is the principle of coherence in the universe, the one "in whom all things hold together" (*synestēken*, the source of our word "system"—Col. 1:17)? In the world of subatomic events, having abandoned the quest for the "ultimate particle," we might then discern a theophany in the short-range bond between neutrons and protons, a bond millions of times stronger than any other bond in nature. This is not animism or anything of the sort. Such energy or bonding is not "God," not if we intend by that to speak of the reality of God in its totality. Yet wherever such energy is manifest it is possible, for those whose eyes are ready, to see a revelation of God as the principle of "concrescence" (the growing together or union of separate things). This is merely the recognition, at the physical level, of what faith has always proclaimed. The words of the old spiritual put it in all simplicity: the whole world is in God's hands.

Such an attitude would free us from the "dark embrace of Physis" (matter) by seeing the elements as neither ultimate nor insignificant, but as revelatory. If the heavens can tell the glory of God, why not the atoms? And if the atoms reveal God, they must not at the same time be idolized, or enlisted in our schemes of destruction. I would think that a physicist with this theophany before his or her eyes would find it difficult to design nuclear weapons.

We could make similar observations about the other *stoicheia* as well. George Riggan, who introduced me to this idea,[43] sees a miraculous theophany in the stability and infinite variability of DNA. This *stoicheion* makes up the genetic code that guides our creation, keeps the body receiving nutrition, and preserves its unique shape and qualities.

To be sure, much of what we experience as evil in the world comes through the genes in the form of genetic defects, deformities, retardation, and illnesses. No theological "explanation" can ever mitigate the suffering involved. God too must suffer in the suffering of these creatures. Nature is not an unambiguous theophany. The elements are only able to mirror God brokenly. Genetic risk is the price creation pays for the infinite proliferation of species that grace the earth. Without such risk, life as we know it would not have been possible at all. DNA enables us to exist, systemically. As such it can declare the glory of God.

Ralph Wendell Burhoe, formerly the executive secretary of the American Academy of Arts and Sciences and a campaigner for dialogue between science and religion, sees a theophany in the principle of natural selection. For like the biblical God, says Burhoe, natural selection judges from the future those experiments in nature and human society that promote the highest value: survival of the species and its further mutation toward its highest potentialities. The psalmists have long concurred in the judgment that the creation shows God's handiwork (Ps. 19:1); in that sense biology does give us, in Riggan's phrase, a preliminary vision of God (Rom. 1:18–32). But when Burhoe goes on to reinterpret God as natural selection and to make it the ultimate principle of reality,[44] he crosses the line from theophany to idolatry. For what Burhoe calls "God," the New Testament knows as a *stoicheion:* the basic principle operative in a field of knowledge (here, biology). Far from being the ultimate principle of the universe, the principle of natural selection is but a special case of the second law of thermodynamics and applies only to closed systems. When Burhoe extends natural selection to human societies and argues that civilizations are "selected out" by their responses to the challenges before them, this comes dangerously close to a might-makes-right type of social Darwinism, where the mere perpetuation of the Roman or Assyrian Empires is identified as the will of God. And when he speaks of the species' mutation toward its highest potentialities, he is smuggling in values that he himself has "selected out" from the religious traditions that have stood the test of time (survivability), without explaining why he rejects other values that have proven equally durable (religious intolerance, male supremacy, divine vengeance, holy wars).

Yet despite these objections (he is usually more discreet) Burhoe has seen something important and neglected: the very biological processes that the sciences are uncovering are themselves revelatory of the glory of the God who made them and works through them. Only as we hold fast to the first commandment, though, can we see the theophany without being bedazzled into false worship: "You shall have no other gods before me."

And what of mathematics? Kepler had exulted, "Why waste words? Geometry existed before the Creation, is co-eternal in the mind of God, *is God Himself.* . . . Geometry provided God with a model for the Creation and was implanted into man, together with God's own likeness and not conveyed through the eyes."[45] Perhaps Kepler went too far, since geometry is no longer considered to be ontologically prior to matter in Einstein's universe. Kepler made ultimate what is merely theophanic. But geometry *is* a manifestation of the Logos in the articulation of the structure of physical reality. As such it is most assuredly a manifestation of God.

Even chance can be seen as a theophany, without our falling under its spell as did Monod. For not only do chance events manifest law-like behavior at the aggregate, statistical level; they are the only way in which all the potentialities of the universe might eventually, given enough time and space, be actualized. "Chance," asserts A. R. Peacocke, "is the search radar of God, sweeping through all the possible targets available to its probing."[46] It is a manifestation of God as the lure of things toward their creative transformation. Chance is not worthy of worship, but there are times when, through fortuitous circumstances or synchronous events, it evokes worship, and we can only thank God in the face of the wonder of it all.

And finally, religion itself with all its trappings—ritual, laws, creeds, doctrines, buildings, calendars, and celebrations—is one of the most virile and deadly of all the *stoicheia* (Gal. 4:3, 9; Col. 2:20), precisely because it lulls us into believing that speaking *about* God is a substitute for relating to God directly. When we let religion replace the actual experience of the living God, we rob ourselves of the immediacy of the numinous reality as a primary intuition. We lose the authority of *knowing,* and fall back on the authority of books or institutions or leaders. Yet Paul, who marshalled one of the most devastating critiques of religion ever penned, nevertheless insists that the law is "holy and just and good" (Rom. 7:12), and sets about organizing a whole new set of religious beliefs, rules, and practices. For law and religion can also be theophanies of God when their springs flow with the living waters of life.

Every search for a single ultimate principle within nature—or even a congregation of them—comes to wreck on the hierarchical complexity of nature itself and the irreducibility of the principles of one level to those of another.[47] The Hebrews insisted that God is not simply one aspect of the world, such as energy, process, selection, number, chance, matter, or order. God is not even to be conceived of as the capstone at the top of the pyramid of being, the "highest" power among the powers of the natural order. God is rather that power that penetrates all being at every level and is revealed at every level, providing the systemic interrelations bonding the whole and the parts. But God's reality is never exhausted in what is made manifest at any given level.[48]

As Meister Eckhart put it, "All creatures are words of God. My mouth expresses and reveals God but the existence of a stone does the same. . . . All creatures may echo God in all their activities. It is, of course, just a small bit which they can reveal." "Even all creatures together, in all they have received, are totally unequal in any comparison to that which is in God, even though all creatures are gladly doing the best they can to express" God. "All creatures want to express God in all their works; let them all speak, coming as close as they can, they still cannot speak [God]. Whether they want to or not, whether it is pleasing or painful to them, they will all want to speak God and [God] still remains unspoken."[49]

Nor can God be reduced to the *stoicheia* taken in their totality. For disorder and turbulence are just as integral to a universe involved in repeated transformations as are order and invariance. As Riggan points out, systemicity confronts us not only in invariant universals, but in the transient particulars as well. God embraces the immutably systemic interrelatedness of order *and* disorder in the universe as what Alfred North Whitehead called the principle of concrescence. And since we cannot possibly obey all the principles of the universe at the same time, the only way to fend off their rival claims is to see them as theophanies systemically integrated within a whole greater than they. The presupposition of an integral life, says Riggan, is obedience to the integrity of that greater Whole and faith that we can mirror it even if brokenly. Stated symbolically, as Israel did through its temple: the holy of holies is dark and it is empty; God negates our attachment to any particular theophany.[50]

If God is conceived as the system of the systems in whom all the parts cohere, then idolatry is the elevation of one of the subsystems to the dignity belonging to the Whole. God cannot be known in totality, but only as manifested through the subsystems. That is why they attract idolatry, for God *is* revealed in and through them, and cannot be known any other way.

The prophetic/Protestant theme, according to Gerd Theissen, has been the critique of any religious expression that identifies God with any specific manifestation of God. Hence the injunction against all images in Israel. Protestantism, however, has tried to make a whole religion out of its prophetic critique. In a secular world where religion is dismissed as infantile regression, disguised resentment, an opiate, or a mystification of the actual material determinants of existence, such one-sidedness is sheer folly. Prophetic criticism always existed in creative tension with vital piety and cultus. Only where God is perceived as manifest *somewhere* can the prophetic injunction against idolizing the medium of God's manifestation have any bite. Only when God is experienced as revealed in the world can the prophet point beyond the worldly means of revelation.[51]

It was appropriate then, according to Philo, that the very sanctuary of God in Jerusalem be constructed of the four elements and filled with symbols of them. There were four kinds of incense, "a symbol of the elements," which in the incense offering are thus permitted to give thanks to their Maker (*Quis her.* 197-200). And the altar itself was dedicated with "the thought of thanksgiving for the elements, for the altar itself contains parts of the four elements," and conveys gratitude for all the "mortal creatures framed from these elements." As long as all the parts of the universe, "the elements and the creatures framed from them," give thanks to God, there is little danger of idolizing the elements themselves (226-27).[52]

These elements are mighty powers—numinous, powerful, eternal, primary, unchanging. Little wonder then that people are overawed, fascinated, drawn toward, and finally make themselves subject to them. Even the redoubtable Seer of the Apocalypse was overwhelmed by such feelings momentarily as he considered the vastness of what an angel had revealed to him: "I fell down to worship at the feet of the angel who showed [the visions] to me, but he said to me, 'You must not do that! I am a fellow servant with you and your brethren the prophets, and with those who keep the words of this book. Worship God' " (Rev. 22:8–9). Small wonder then that those who have glimpsed the unbelievable power latent in the nucleus of a hydrogen atom or have beheld the magnificent simplicity of physical invariances might confuse the glimmer of reflected light with the ultimate Source itself. "Idolatry," Paul Tillich wrote, "is the perversion of a genuine revelation; it is the elevation of the medium of revelation to the dignity of the revelation itself."[53]

When a single *stoicheion* is elevated above the whole of which it is a part, it invites the rebound of the whole against the part in ironic ways. *Irony is the mode divine judgment takes against subsystems that are out of bounds.* We are more familiar with irony at the level of human history. One thinks of the Watergate episode, when President Nixon, unable to trust his own closest aides, installed a taping system that became the source of his own downfall. His aides were charged with conspiracy for breaking the very laws they had enacted in order to deal with Vietnam War protesters, and they were tried in Washington, D.C., before largely black juries who had been the direct victims of the "Southern strategy" these aides had developed to win the 1968 election by neglecting civil rights for blacks.[54]

> The nations have sunk in the pit which they made;
>   in the net which they hid has their own foot been caught.
> The Lord has made himself known, he has executed judgment;
>   the wicked are snared in the work of their own hands.
>   (Ps. 9:15–16)

Irony operates at the level of the elements as well. When we seek to justify ourselves by performing the tenets of some religious law, we can only feel guilty for failing or self-righteous for succeeding—but never at peace with God. When we let religion interpose between us and primary experience, we lose the very reality religion itself describes as ultimate. When we take up astrology as a fatalistic system that predicts our future, we become dependent upon its predictions and create for ourselves a determined world of self-fulfilling prophecies. When the laws of society become ends in themselves rather than the means to the fulfillment of persons, then the laws breed rebellion and circumvention that jeopardize the very social stability that the laws exist to promote. When we treat people like robots or computers that can be quantified and behaviorally conditioned, we get a kind of world that treats us in the same inhuman way. When we poison the air and water in a bid to make fast profits, we are forced to breathe the air and drink the water. When we bring to subatomic realities our own fears and violence, we suffer the rebound of these mighty powers made over into our image. And our mistrust of the Soviets places us in a position where we ironically *have* to trust them. We have to trust that they will not launch a first strike. We have to trust that they will remain rational. We have to trust that their inferior technology and computers will not malfunction the way ours have and "launch on warning" in order to counter our Pershing II missiles now stationed only eight minutes from the heart of Russia.[55]

If we do not act now to reverse this blind rush into night, the final irony may be our self-destruction. Yet even if we act so as to bring upon ourselves annihilation, that too will be a manifestation of the justice and judgment of God. But this is not a foreordained fate. Perhaps the very magnitude of the threat will awaken us to our vassalage. Then perhaps the crowning irony will be instead that the very elements themselves, abused, idolized, and rendered demonic, will have shaken our race from a martial adolescence into a globe-encompassing maturity. Either way, it will not be the "gods of matter" or the "elements of the universe," but we ourselves who decide.

7. The Angels of Nature

We were called a lawless people, but we were on pretty good terms with the Great Spirit, creator and ruler of all. You whites assumed we were savages. You didn't understand our prayers. You didn't try to understand. When we sang our praise to the sun or moon or wind, you said we were worshipping idols. Without understanding, you condemned us as lost souls just because our form of worship was different from yours.

We saw the Great Spirit's work in everything: sun, moon, trees, wind and mountains. Sometimes we approached him through these things. Was that so bad? I think we have a true belief in the supreme being, a stronger faith than that of most whites who have called us pagans . . . living in darkness.

Did you know that trees talk? Well, they do. They talk to each other, and they'll talk to you if you listen. Trouble is, white people don't listen to the Indians so I don't suppose they'll listen to other voices in nature. But I have learned a lot from trees: sometimes about the weather, sometimes about animals, sometimes about the Great Spirit.

Walking Buffalo
A Canadian Stoney Indian

It was not just to the elements of the world that modern culture gave the kiss of death. It was to the whole of nature. How has it come about that every new increment of technology has only further alienated us from the earth? Why has blind fidelity to materialism left us more and more estranged from matter? Matter was regarded as the highest value; why then has it become so cheap? Forsaking heaven, we would build a paradise on earth; why then have we made of earth a putrid bog of poisonous pollution that we are prepared to blow up in defense of our little chunks? What turned the dream so sour?

Perhaps the truest answer is the most painful: because of sin. Greed, lust, avarice, boundless pride, hubris—these, and not some false ideas about the world, are the corrosives that deface and finally crumble every edifice humanity rears toward decency. I do not want to suggest that merely changing our ideas about the world could alter any of that. But the way we see the world does play a substantial role in how we treat it. Put another way, our worldview cannot eradicate our proclivity to sin, but it can make a vital difference insofar as it bridles sin or inspires it.

One can no more *see* one's worldview, when it is functioning properly, than one can see space. Only in the changing of the ages, when the old worldview is already in process of collapse, does it become visible. The very fact that we can discuss our worldview today is itself a sign of its passing. Perhaps the best angle of vision may be gained by contrasting the modern worldview with the medieval cosmology that it replaced.

In the Middle Ages, argues the historian of science Morris Berman, things were never "just what they were," but always embodied a nonmaterial principle that was regarded as the essence of their reality. The universe was alive. Things had "soul." There was no such thing as dead, inert matter. Consequently, people sensed themselves as part of a living, pulsing, interlacing web of existence, which, however brutish and hard, was not devoid of meaning. Owen Barfield has called this "original participation," a kind of consciousness that entails *permeating* matter, not simply (as today) *confronting* it.[1] It was in many respects similar to the perspective of Walking Buffalo.

By contrast, the modern scientific worldview, says Berman, was the dialectical antithesis of original participation. The new science enjoined its practitioners to step outside of nature, to reify it, to reduce it to measurable units. Knowing was redefined; it now consisted not of identifying a thing's sympathetic connections with the larger reality, but of an atomistic analysis by which an entity was subdivided into its smallest components. The universe was no longer conceived as a living whole energized and created by God, but as a vast machine of matter and motion obeying mathematical laws. Now anything that could not be measured had no place in experimental science. The human sense of intrinsic belonging, of a part to play in the whole, of vocation, was rendered untenable in a universe indifferent to human purposes and blind to its own unguided evolutionary future. Laplace learned that in such a world he could do without "that hypothesis," God. Later on, Watson and Skinner would decide that they could do without "that hypothesis," the human self. For if reality is to be reducible to mathematical laws, it must be wholly deterministic, and God and the self, like spirits within matter, were not amenable to deterministic explanation.

Materialism, for all its apparent commitment to matter, was in fact less related to matter than the participating consciousness it replaced. Materialism is highly abstract. Its most fundamental principles are all invisible: gravity, inertial mass, momentum, electrons. It did not object to invisible forces so long as they remained mechanically caused. What materialism would not tolerate, however, was any element of mind in the so-called inert objects that surround us.

Sir Isaac Newton was one of the pivotal figures in the shift from medieval participating consciousness to the philosophy of mechanism. The recent discovery by Lord Keynes of Newton's journals reveals that Newton was a closet alchemist who mined the Hermetic wisdom for his answers and then clothed them in the mechanical philosophy that was coming into vogue among the ruling classes. Newton did not discover gravity, as Gregory Bateson remarked; he *invented* it. The centerpiece of his entire system, gravitational attraction, was in fact the Hermetic principle of sympathetic forces, which Newton saw as a creative principle, a source of divine energy in the universe. Publicly he presented this idea mechanistically; privately, as his journals make clear, he was committed to the notion that mind exists in matter and can control it. Berman points out that "in the modern empirical sense, there was nothing 'scientific' about this shift from Hermeticism to mechanism. The change was not the result of a series of careful experiments on the nature of matter, and indeed, it is no more difficult to visualize the earth as a living organism than it is to see it as a dead, mechanical object."[2]

But the utility of the mechanistic philosophy was proving itself not only in experimental science, but in laissez faire capitalism. The idea of living matter was simply economically inconvenient. In the participative worldview of medieval Europe, one could certainly mine nature's ores, but only with care and devotion. Metallurgy was deliberately compared to obstetrics, and new mines were sunk, until the fifteenth century, accompanied by religious ceremonies in which the miners fasted, prayed, and observed a particular series of rites. But if nature is dead, then there are no restraints on exploiting it for profit. "Once natural processes are stripped of immanent purpose, there is nothing really left in objects but their value for something, or someone, else."[3]

The irony of all this is that participating consciousness does live on in the world of mechanism, but in an estranged way. Just as ex-lovers who refuse to have anything to do with one another really have a powerful type of relationship, so mechanistic consciousness continues to use intuition, tacit knowing, subliminal awareness, and educational *mimesis,* all participational ways of learning; yet it refuses to accord them status in its worldview. Now quantum physics has undermined the very foundations of the materialist/mechanist/determinist worldview, and yet for five decades the scientific establishment has largely managed to ignore its embarrassing implications for the way we regard the world.[4] Faith is a powerful force, even in the face of flagrant disconfirmations, and this is as true for the materialist faith as for any other.

My own developmental experience recapitulates in miniature key elements of this centuries-long process. As an urban teen-ager in Dallas I longed for the woods, and spent every available weekend and much of my summers camping or counseling in camps. Early on I had felt, as did many of my peers, a kinship with all life. God spoke with almost unmediated directness to my open and uncluttered mind. I could sense my belonging to an utterly harmonious whole.

Later, as a college sophomore, my childhood faith graciously blasted by an atheist philosophy professor, I found myself in a forest of virgin fir on the coast of Oregon. Rhododendrons twice my height covered the forest floor, spangled with flowers, under trees so tall they seemed to curve as they converged toward the sky. It was breathtakingly beautiful. It called for a response from my heart that simply was not there. Instead the beauty was an accusation. For the first time I knew myself excluded from the garden. I had lost, with the loss of God, the capacity for participative awareness. I vividly remember feeling like a fish outside its bowl. I had unknowingly withdrawn from my element and now did not know how to return.

A powerful religious experience later that summer, triggered in part by the censure of the trees, temporarily restored me, but could not dike my life against the flood of analytical intellectualism that filled the next years.

Seminary only made things worse, though I remain profoundly grateful for it. The neo-orthodox theology then in vogue freed me from the Harnackian liberalism of my upbringing, and I eagerly took up the new cry that God acts in history. But what, I protested, about nature? Abandon its seductions, I was told. Such sentiments are nothing but Baalism, Canaanite nature religion, fertility cult. The aftermath of World War II required a theology that could make some sort of sense of history's defection from linear progress. History had become a riddle, and the fact that Nazism had contained an element of sentimental nature worship seemed proof of nature's hazards.

And that is pretty much where things remained for almost three decades, until I was introduced to Dorothy Maclean, first through her book, *To Hear the Angels Sing*,[5] later in person. What she had to say about the angels of nature both confounded my earlier theological rationalism and opened the possibility of a second naiveté toward nature, a new kind of participating consciousness: an "animism no longer anthropomorphic," in Sandor Ferenczi's words,[6] or, perhaps more accurately, a consciously spiritual participation no longer physically literalized.

Maclean was one of the three founders of the Findhorn Community in Scotland, along with Peter and Eileen Caddy. Their garden was in the news some fifteen years ago when biologists and horticulturists began making pilgrimages to it in order to try to understand how it could produce such luxurious yields of luscious vegetables and flowers on a barren sand dune.[7] The secret, it turned out, was not in the soil but in the fact that Maclean had allegedly learned to communicate with the angels of the plants in order to determine precisely what they needed to flourish. She never claims to have "seen" an angel. They gave no indication of having a shape or form or sex (much less the male genitals ascribed to the two higher orders of angels in *Jub.* 15:27—and circumcised at that!). Her contact was through written meditations. No automatic writing or mediumship was involved. She would get centered on her higher self through meditation and then address a question to the angel of a particular species of plant. The words she wrote down were thoughts and feelings filtered through her own personality, beliefs, and literary style. She wrote in shorthand, keeping a thesaurus and dictionary at hand in order to express herself as exactly as possible. The process is used widely in spiritual reflection and can be tried by anyone. Whether what she wrote was authentically "given" by an otherness of some sort, or was an empathetic and imaginative entering into the life-space of another being, is, so far as I can tell, impossible to answer. Perhaps the alternatives are false, and the two are really one and the same.

Maclean's impression of these creative essences or "living creative principles" within nature is that they are "overlightings." "Each was not the spirit of the individual plant but was the 'overlighting' being of the species," she writes. "I discovered that the being behind the garden pea held in its consciousness the archetypal design of all pea plants throughout the world, and looked after their welfare. They hold the archetypal patterns of our planet in a sort of inner energy stream of divinity."[8]

I was already familiar with the angels of nature from my study of the New Testament period, but prior to my encounter with Maclean I had always dismissed them as merely bad science, the outmoded superstitions of an antiquated worldview. *Jubilees* (c. 150 B.C.E.) had provided the fullest statement of the angels' functions:

> On the first day [God] created the heavens which are above and the earth and the waters and all the spirits which serve before [God]—the angels of the presence, and the angels of sanctification, and the angels [of the spirit of fire and the angels] of the spirit of the winds, and the angels of the spirit of the clouds, and of darkness, and of snow and of hail and of hoar frost, and the angels of the voices and of the thunder and of the lightning, and the angels of the spirits of cold and of heat, and of winter and of spring and of autumn and of summer, and of all the spirits of [God's] creatures which are in the heavens and on the earth. (2:2, *APOT*)[9]

1 Enoch also speaks of "the spirit" in the thunder, "the spirit of the sea," and of how "the spirit of the hoar-frost is his own angel, and the spirit of the hail is a good angel," and of "the spirit of the snow" and "the spirit of the mist" and "the spirit of the dew" and "the spirit of the rain" (60:15–22; 61:10).[10] The implied worldview is obvious: Every species and thing has its angel.[11]

The Bible itself says very little about nature-angels. The dominant theme is

that God is immediate to every creature, and every creature to God. Nevertheless, angels are a feature of Israelite belief in all strata of the Scriptures, and
were already a part of the pre-Mosaic popular belief.[12] The emergence of
specialized angelic functions in the ordering of nature in the intertestamental
period is simply of one piece with the general process of differentiation in the
godhead characteristic of that whole era. Troops of angelic orders, already identified in the Psalms (see Psalm 148, JB, for instance) were simply assumed as
part of the background belief of the age.[13] That much at least is made clear by
the casual way they are mentioned in the Book of Revelation: "the angel of
water" (Rev. 16:5),[14] "four angels standing at the four corners of the earth, holding back the four winds of the earth, that no wind might blow" (Rev. 7:1), and
"an angel standing in the sun" (Rev. 19:17).[15] Angels of wind and fire are
referred to in Heb. 1:7, which cites the LXX version of Ps. 104:4, and an angel
of water stirs up the pool of Bethzatha in the textual addition in John 5:4.[16]

It is Philo, however, who provides the most striking parallel to the unexpected
angels of Maclean:

> God is one, but He has around Him numberless Potencies (*dynameis*), which all
> assist and protect created being. . . . Through these Potencies the incorporeal and
> intelligible world was framed, the archetype of this phenomenal world, that being
> a system of invisible ideal forms, as this is of visible material bodies. . . . There
> is, too, in the air a sacred company of unbodied souls (*psychōn*), commonly called
> angels in the inspired pages, who wait upon these heavenly powers. . . . Now the
> King may fitly hold converse with his powers (*dynamesin*) and employ them to
> serve in matters which should not be consummated by God alone. . . . [God]
> allowed His subject powers to have the fashioning of some things, though he did
> not give them sovereign and independent knowledge for completion of the
> task. . . . (*De conf.* 171–75)[17]

Maclean's unmodern assertion about the angels of nature as archetypal patterns for whole species thus stands in an ancient and worthy tradition. She herself did not come to an understanding of angels by way of study so much as by
meditative experience. The angels she contacted, she says, are not initiators of
new patterns. This is consistent with the remark of Carolyn Merchant that
nature has no power to enforce its own laws.[18] The angels of nature can ward
off limited damage or adjust to it, says Maclean, but they cannot counter the
massive destructiveness of natural catastrophes or human negligence. It is not
their work to change patterns, but to work with and within existing conditions.
The changing of patterns is the task of the creative Logos, a task in which
humanity can play an increasingly constructive or negative role.[19]

An angel, according to Maclean, can thus be the species pattern of all wild
violets and at the same time speak as the interiority or "within" of a particular

plant. The species-angel maintains the current form (however it has been defined by other forces) and the plant's archetypal possibilities or vocation. The St. John's Wort Angel had this to say:

> Whatever happens, we hold the archetypal pattern immovable. If alteration is necessary, we hold the alteration as part of the pattern. Then it is unchanging, a great steadiness stemming from the eternal peace of God. The incredible activity of our kingdom clusters around the patterns, making sure that they are brought into form perfectly, serving them endlessly. We state this because we would have you realize that you too have the same quality of undeviating devotion to a pattern, which you can hold in rock-like peace under God.[20]

How are we to evaluate all this? No one disputes that such angelology lies deeply embedded in Christian tradition—or for that matter, in Jewish, Muslim, and virtually all religious systems. Our problem is simply that scarcely anyone believes it anymore, and with good reason. Natural science has taken over from this blunderbuss, scattershot proto-science (which even by contemporary Hellenistic standards was primitive) and made the study of rain and grass and wind and hail a matter of rigorous experimental knowledge.

Theology adjusted accordingly. We could learn to live without angels easily enough, since Christ or the Holy Spirit had long since assumed most of their functions. We learned to appreciate myth as symbolic, and separated its existential meaning for human life from its pseudo-scientific explanatory function, discarding the latter as merely the husk around the kernel. I had myself made these adjustments quite successfully, and was engaged in attempting to carry out a consistent demythologization of the angels and, for that matter, all the Powers.

How then do I now find it possible to take the rumors of these angels so seriously? Let me urge three considerations that justify a serious new regard for these ancient messengers of the Creator.

The Angels of Nature and the Emergent New Worldview

The first consideration has to do with *a transformed worldview.* I readily concede that the unverified reports of ancient traditions or a modern mystic are scarcely grounds for scrapping an entire worldview. Today, however, the mechanistic, materialistic worldview has itself become life-threatening. If we are to evolve a more organic, life-enhancing worldview, it will have to be one that restores some sense of participative relationship with nature, without abandoning the critical rigor of modern science. As more scientists abandon the materialist paradigm and begin looking at the world with new eyes, we may begin to observe a remarkable convergence between empirical discoveries and ancient traditions.

In the new world of quantum physics, substance has been made subordinate to events. In the old physics, wholes were regarded as secondary to their parts, and the goal of science was to explain wholes by an analysis of the fundamental substances of which they were made, substances which were not susceptible to change. This led to the isolation of substances as if they were independent of relations and prior to relations, and as if they only entered into relations secondarily. The extension of this notion to human beings in turn reenforced the radical individualism of Western society.

In the new science, however, the complex interactions that comprise events have come to be seen as fundamental, rather than substance. An atom, remark Birch and Cobb, is not a substantial entity but a multiplicity of events interconnected with each other and with other events in a describable pattern. An electromagnetic event cannot be viewed as taking place independently of the electromagnetic field as a whole. "It both participates in constituting that field as the environment for all events and also is constituted by its participation in that field. In abstraction from that field it is nothing at all. It does not have independent existence and then relate to the field. It is constituted by the complex interconnections which its place in the field gives it."[21] The consequences of this view for the way we regard human beings are as far-reaching as in the old paradigm. We are the network of all our relationships, and who we are at any given moment depends on how that field of relationships is constituted.

In such a worldview, it is the *patterning* of energy-fields that is determinative of existence. The language of "angels" will not further science's task of exploring the virtually endless implications of this new insight for our understanding of the universe, but it might help us maintain an inner relationship with that world while it is being explored. For if *internal* relations characterize events, as Birch and Cobb assert, then we can no longer regard anything, even down to the subatomic level, as mere material substance.[22] Even the electron is characterized by its internal relations. Everything possesses an interiority, and while it is scarcely appropriate to describe the interiority of minute events by analogy from human consciousness, mind, or feeling, we can also no longer deny to them an interiority appropriate to their complexity and degree of freedom.[23]

And what tradition has avowed all along is that the angels of nature are the interiority or conscious species-pattern of every physical entity.[24] It is precisely at this point that our individualistic way of looking at things presents an immense hurdle to understanding. Anthropologists and historians of religion invented the names "animism" and "pantheism" to describe what they misperceived as the belief that *a* spirit is confined within *a* thing. But what the "primitive" subjects of their enlightened research meant was probably far closer to the notion that every plant *participates* in a group spirit or group soul that oversees its development.[25] An angel, that is to say, is both immanent within every member of its species and transcendent to it.

We must make restitution to nature by restoring its inwardness. "There was a certain arrogance in stripping the world of its 'within' and stuffing all soul within the subjectivity of human beings, leaving the world a slagheap from which all projections, personifications and psyche had been extracted," writes James Hillman. We are, he says, as much projected upon as ones who project, more "in" life than life is "in" us.[26] The "within" of all things is perceptible to my psyche only because it is given within natural life. Images from our own interior depths are able to mirror the interiority of phenomena "out there" because we are set in life as our medium. Reality seems to be, as Karl Pribram puts it, a holographic domain, in which each organism in some manner represents the universe and each portion of the universe represents in some manner the organisms within it.[27] If the images served up by a materialistic culture treat matter as dead, we not only lose all capacity to bring soul to matter and seek its interiority, but, as we saw in the last chapter, matter itself becomes what we have made it: death-dealing.

One of the redeeming qualities of science is its capacity for self-correction. A recent report on bee behavior by James L. Gould of Princeton provides an amusing illustration of how the empirical method can disconfirm the materialist paradigm, if only the right questions are asked. Gould had long argued that most signs of animal intelligence are the result of innate "prewired" behavior patterns. An experiment that he himself performed, however, has now caused him to question his own assumptions. Gould placed food at progressively removed locations from the hive, increasing the distance each time by a factor of 1.25, or one-and-a-quarter times the distance of the previous move. To his surprise, he discovered that the forager bees began to anticipate where the food source would next be moved, and that when he arrived at his carefully plotted new location, as far as three thousand feet from the hive, he would find the bees circling the spot awaiting the arrival of their food. Somehow the bees had deduced that the distance of the next move would not merely be the same as the distance from the last, but would be increased by a factor of 1.25. They were apparently capable of computing not just simple numerical increases, but geometric sequences!

In reporting this experiment to a symposium at the Smithsonian Institution, Gould remarked with a wry smile, "I wish they'd never done it!" For if animals are not simply governed by prewired instincts, but can actually *think,* then they exercise a degree of freedom and betray an interiority that threatens the very materialist worldview itself.[28] *What* we see in nature is to a very high degree determined by *how we look.* If we look for prewired, determined behavior, we tend to find it. If we change our lenses, as it were, and look for free actions, we tend to find that. Our images of the world have as much to do with our findings as the data we examine, and how we look determines the kinds of questions we ask or fail to ask.[29]

Even when science finally sloughs off the materialist paradigm and begins to respond to nature as alive, the angels of nature will still remain different and more. They belong to a different level of discourse. They are an experiential, not an experimental reality. They are perceived not in the mental, but the imaginal realm. They have no physical reality, no substance. They have no more "being" than the blue of the sky or the life of an oak. They are real, but their reality, as tradition has always insisted, is visionary, and they are only encountered in states of higher consciousness.

Our science is only on the verge of becoming capable of discussing such things; indeed, until now it has not even developed a science of life. It is too early to predict the future evolution of scientific thought on these matters, but the crises of our planet require a transformation of our worldview now, as a simple matter of survival.

The angels, according to ancient tradition, first taught humanity the sciences; but according to one tradition they were good angels, while according to another they were fallen.[30] This ambivalence expresses a profound truth. Whether science is used to enhance or to dehumanize life will depend in large measure on whether it is integrated with religious awareness and values into a unitary view of reality. The language of science and the language of religion are both necessary for describing that reality. Each has its own primary mode. Science tends to *look,* from without; religion tends to *feel,* from within. We need both: the language of science to analyze the workings of the structural processes, and the language of angels and spirits to provide us with a feeling-toned, intuitive relationship with what would otherwise be regarded as soul-less things. Without science we are lost in superstition and speculation; without the angels we are alienated from nature and its symphony of praise to God.

It is not my desire to reduce the ancient belief in angels to an intuitive anticipation of modern biology, to be superseded by the more precise language of biological science. Nor do I want to remythologize science, fuzzing over its analytical precision with poetic similes incapable of empirical demonstration. My concern is to bring together these two quite different languages, mentalities, and realms of experience, to place them in juxtaposition, and to suggest that each provides an indispensable angle for viewing the same reality. We might even discover that the angels constitute the interiority of formative processes, and that the formative processes comprise the "exteriority," the discernible tracings, the vestments of angels. Perhaps then we might begin to recover the sense that reality is in fact one, and sign a truce in the long and costly war between science and religion.[31]

The Angels of Nature and Environmental Justice

The second reason the angels of nature are worth taking seriously is related to the issue of *ecology*. The consequences of the materialist paradigm for the environment have been disastrous. Its only argument for conserving nature was instrumental: we should take care of it because it takes care of us. But the engines of capitalism and socialism alike rolled over such reflections like grass in a mower's path. The demand for quick profits, legitimated by the belief that this life is the only life we have, made exploitation not only permissible but admirable. As a consequence we have done more damage to our planet in the past few generations than in the four thousand previous generations. The problem, we must be clear, is not merely the cumulative result of ever-growing population. We have entered a qualitatively different phase of world history in which our capacity to harm the environment has grown exponentially. We face literal extermination from almost a dozen separate causes, and we do not know if we can change quickly enough to save ourselves from any one of them.

Justice is the ethos of God's world, and when we violate the rights of others we inevitably involve nature in our acts. Environmental justice is linked to social justice. Both depend on an overarching vision of a God who encompasses the whole, in whom all things find their right relation, and in whom all things hold together (Col. 1:15–18). The same violation of that oneness which leads to political exploitation of people leads also to the economic exploitation of land through mineral extraction and cash-crop farming. Behind virtually every war, every border violation, every act of nationalist expansion or national liberation is a struggle for the control of land, its laborers, or its resources. The joy then that leaves the trees of the wood singing is more than joy in being: it is joy in *rectification:*

> Let the heavens be glad, and let the earth rejoice;
> let the sea roar, and all that fills it;
> let the field exult, and everything in it!
> Then shall all the trees of the wood sing for joy
> before the Lord, for he comes,
> *for he comes to judge the earth.*
> He will judge the world with righteousness.
> and the peoples with his truth.
>
> (Ps. 96:11–13, italics mine)

Humanity's failure to see the divine theophany in nature is of the same piece as its refusal to accept the divine theophany mediated through Jesus. "For what can be known about God is plain to them," writes Paul, "because God has shown it to them [in nature]. Ever since the creation of the world [God's] invisible nature, namely, [God's] external power and deity, has been clearly perceived in the things which have been made. So they are without excuse" (Rom. 1:19–20). The signs of God's hand are everywhere around us; even in its violence, nature possesses an awesome beauty. But that is only part of the story. Surely Christopher Nugent is right that nature is as capable of an epiphany of indifference to suffering as it is of harmony. Nature's indifference to human suffering, however, is not an intentional evil, at least not in the sense of deliberate torture. But those who are interested in the power game will inevitably project it out on nature. It was Adolf Hitler, after all, who justified his barbarity with the statement, "Nature is cruel, therefore we too can be cruel."[32] Nature is at best a broken theophany, a veiled epiphany, and even to see God there at all is already a kind of faith.

That comes as a sobering reminder that people are not likely to change their attitudes toward nature unless they have had an encounter with God of an ultimate kind. But for those who have been brought from the death of a world centered in the ego to the life of a world brimming with God, the numinous interiority of nature can open our eyes to the manifestations of God we had missed through nothing more than lavishing all our attention on ourselves:

> Let the floods clap their hands;
>   let the hills sing for joy together
> before the Lord, for he comes
>   to rule the earth.
> He will judge the world with righteousness,
>   and the peoples with equity.
>   (Ps. 98:8–9)

Many in North America are looking to Eastern religions or esoteric traditions to find the spiritual resources to cherish and preserve nature. Yet these very resources have languished, unused, in the very heart of our own tradition, in the angels of nature.

This new-old attitude toward nature inevitably issues in political consequences. Christopher D. Stone has proposed that legal rights be granted to natural objects in the environment and to the environment as a whole. If business corporations have already been granted such rights, why should they be denied to a lake, a river, a mountain, or a forest? Justice William O. Douglas, in a minority opinion to a key Supreme Court decision affecting the environment, accepted Stone's logic. "The ordinary corporation," Douglas wrote, "is a 'person' for purposes of the adjudicatory processes, whether it represents proprietary, spiritual, aesthetic, or charitable causes."

> So it should be as respects valleys, alpine meadows, rivers, lakes, estuaries, beaches, ridges, groves of trees, swampland, or even air that feels the destructive pressures of modern technology and modern life. . . . The river as plaintiff speaks for the ecological unit of life that is part of it. Those people who have a meaningful relation to that body of water—whether it be a fisherman, a canoeist, a zoologist, or a logger—must be able to speak for the values which the river represents and which are threatened with destruction. . . . Those who have that intimate relationship with the inanimate object about to be injured, polluted, or otherwise despoiled are its legitimate spokesmen.[33]

If we do not find ways to achieve environmental justice, and soon, we will find ourselves up against the punishment that *1 Enoch* warned of two thousand years ago:

> And now, do know that your deeds shall be investigated—from the sun, from the moon, and from the stars—for heaven by the angels, on account of your sins (which) were committed upon the earth. . . . Every cloud, mist, dew, and rain shall witness against you; for they shall all be withheld from you, from descending for you; and they shall not give heed, because of your sins. (*1 Enoch* 100:10-11, *OT Ps.*)

And when that judgment comes, according to *Test. Levi* 3(a), "fire, snow, and ice made ready for the day of judgement" will rain upon the earth from the first heaven where they have been stored. Nature will, as it were, settle the score against humanity by means of the recoil of natural phenomena against us.

Has the last judgment already begun?

But the Bible also offers another image, one which we may also with equal freedom choose: the dazzling scene of angelic praises in Revelation 4—7, which Hans-Ruedi Weber has suggested to me should be seen as an "environmental eucharist"—a festival of the synergism, coherence, and cohesion of the entire universe that should not be simply read, but sung, danced, exclaimed. That brings us to the third reason for considering the angels of nature.

The Angels of Nature and Worship

The angels of nature can both broaden and deepen our sense of *worship*. The great Western religions owe the world an apology for giving nature such low regard in official theology. The basis for wonder, praise, and awe for God's creation is there and often celebrated, but the repeated refrain is that God acts in history, in the great revelatory events of peoples. Today we can no longer afford to split creation and redemption. "How can Christianity call itself catholic," asks Simone Weil, "if the universe itself is left out?"[34] The issue should never have been posed as nature versus history, but rather as a choice between history considered from the point of view of nature (the cyclical views of Near Eastern religions) or nature considered from the point of view of history (as in Israel's faith).[35] God is revealed not just in mighty acts of liberation, but in the prodigal variety and lavish beauty of those flowers agricultural civilizations learned to call weeds. The "one God and Father of us all, who is above all and through all and in all" (Eph. 4:6) is manifest in every created thing. At one time such a sentiment would have been labeled pantheism by the orthodox and dismissed. Now it is increasingly recognized as panentheism ("everything is in the divine"; see Col. 1:15–20), and accorded intellectual respect. But do those who now give their assent to the idea really see the vision?

Mechtild of Magdeburg records the event in which her eyes were opened: "The day of my spiritual awakening was the day I saw and knew I saw all things in God and God in all things." And again, "The truly wise person kneels at the feet of all creatures."[36]

Worship will not then be confined to celebration of God's mighty deeds in the past and the anticipation or discernment of those deeds in the present. It will also include the sheer rapturous enjoyment of the beauty of the creation itself. The "congregation" will be seen to be infinitely more vast, stretching to include every created thing as a vibrant, God-praising event. Look at how Psalm 148 calls the roll of those present in the congregation that worships God:

> Let heaven praise Yahweh:
> praise him, heavenly heights,
> praise him, all his angels,
> praise him, all his armies!

> Praise him, sun and moon,
> praise him, shining stars,
> praise him, highest heavens,
> and waters above the heavens! . . .

> Let earth praise Yahweh:
> sea-monsters and all the deeps,
> fire and hail, snow and mist,
> gales that obey his decree,

> mountains and hills,
> orchards and forests,
> wild animals and farm animals,
> snakes and birds,

and only *after* these do we come in:

> all kings on earth and nations,
> princes, all rulers in the world,

> young men and [women],
> old people, and children too!
>
> Let them all praise the name of Yahweh. . . .
>   (Ps. 148:1–4, 7–13a, JB)[37]

Or enter, if you can, into the soul that saw this theophany:

> The pastures of the wilderness drip,
>   the hills gird themselves with joy,
> The meadows clothe themselves with flocks,
>   the valleys deck themselves with grain,
>   they shout and sing together for joy.
>   (Ps. 65:12–13)

If it be soberly objected by some sober exegete that these words are merely poetic, I concede the point entirely, and ask simply whether the poet poetically points to something real. To *see* this way, to bring that much soul to our encounter with the world, requires the recovery of the imaginal or poetic dimension of our existence. If God "did not leave himself without witnesses, for he did good and gave you from heaven rains and fruitful seasons" (Acts 14:17); and if the beasts and birds and plants and fish stand ready to instruct us in theology (Job 12:7–10); then it would be tragic if we shut our eyes to the theophany taking place unceasingly on every side.[38]

The dis-ease of modern society is fundamentally spiritual, and the cure must be as well. The angels of nature invite us to reappraise our entire attitude toward the universe. We need the modern equivalent of the Native Americans' reverence for nature. We must find ways to move beyond observing nature to experiencing ourselves as a part of the nature being observed; to go beyond admiring its beauty to the experience of entering its beauty and being caught up in the ecstasy of nature's epiphany of God. That is, after all, the experiential implication that follows from the Heisenberg principle: the observer is always a part of the field being observed. As we begin to integrate that insight into our lives, we will begin to *see* nature differently: no longer as detached and alienated observers, but as integral aspects of the cosmic dance of praise and delight in God. We will foster the capacity to experience the cosmos as an interiority,[39] and heaven as a quality of existence that can already be entered into in this life—even in the midst of mortal conflict and suffering (Acts 7:55–56).

The very notion of "scenery" is symptomatic of our problem. Nature has become for us a vast museum. National parks can only be entered on payment of a fee, like any museum, and paved roads and roadsigns direct us to the "sights." People Oh! and Ah! at the scenery, but their basic orientation, and the very condition of their presence there, is that of spectators, not participants. The viewer is remote from the view. No doubt some transcend these constraints, but the vast majority is content to observe, catalogue, and even "grade" the sights in terms of an ascending scale of "favorites." How remote such an attitude is from Blake's profound insight: "If the doors of perception were cleansed every thing would appear to man as it is: infinite" ("The Marriage of Heaven and Hell"). When next you gaze at a vista of extraordinary beauty, what will you see: scenery, or a theophany?

The ancient lore of the angels could well help us recover, in our deepest selves, a sense of communion with the world around us. Calling the patterning presences that guide nature "angels" is merely a convention of language, of course. But it is an important one. It is a powerful affront to materialism, since it emphasizes the inwardness of that which the materialist regards as simply the mechanical and chemical processes governing life. It connects the reality we experience back to a long history of such experiences documented over thousands of years among virtually all the peoples of the world. It provides great images which can lead to new environmental attitudes the way no scientific facts ever can. Even if our science is rudimentary, and whole new theories emerge to account for the patterning, emergence and transformations in nature, angels will endure, for they are not premised on the vagaries of scientific opinion but arise from the intuitive, symbolic, imaginal realm of human inwardness. (Since I began sharing these thoughts with others I have been astonished at the number of people who have confided in me their experiences of angels. Because angels are not part of our "available believable," however, *most of them had dismissed the experience and had never previously told anyone.*) Would it not be wise to place the wager, to behave *as if* there are angels patterning and sustaining every material thing? For without some such attitude, what hope have we for the survival of our planet?

It is not an esoteric mystic, but a physicist, Brian Swimme, who urges, "We must address trees. We must address all things, confronting them in the awareness that we are in the presence of numinous mystery." "Remember that the tree doesn't need to be addressed. It is you that needs to address the tree. You are the universe pressing into an awareness of itself. It is your task to become deeply aware of trees, and of all that is."[40]

Even if we do not communicate directly with the angels, we can at least learn to acknowledge their effects. When we are suddenly struck by the beauty of a small stone in the palm of our hands; or when the song of a brook stills the warring inner discord of our souls; or when in a grove of millennial sequoias we feel the hush of a mighty cathedral and the deep stirring of long-dormant praise—then the angels have done their ceaseless work, whether we are conscious of them or not. Maclean writes, "Now flowers are saying, with a new intensity, 'Look, don't think; look directly at us and see God.' " The Landscape Angel of Findhorn, who taught her so much, reminded her, " 'All around you, in every bit of matter, is what has come from, is, and leads to the only One: and within you is the consciousness that can know and express this.' " Another said:

I have a sense of human consciousness saying that God is too mighty to speak through small things. Human consciousness thus seeks to limit God to certain categories, although the atom has proved mighty. Everything, all detail, is important. Every cell and every speck of dust are important and speak in a divine voice. . . . What we are is sufficient, for what we are is what you are: God speaking.[41]

If we understand "angel" to be the code name for the numinous interiority of created things, then when we see a sunset we may find common language inadequate for what has occurred. For if we truly experience the glory of God in this everyday happening, we may need spiritual language to describe the spiritual event. Then perhaps it is far more accurate to say, as J. Bruce Evans suggests, "An angel appeared to me at sunset today"—if in fact, one did.[42] When we can name it thus, and say a Yes to the experience with our whole selves, we become united with the entire universe. By opening ourselves to the divine in one small part we see in it the living reality that animates the whole, and are swept up in a rushing sense of homecoming.

It is true that the early church found it necessary to play down angels in the twilight of Greco-Roman polytheism, when as yet the God of gods had not been grasped as the central religious reality. Angel worship may have been in some sense out of control at Colossae (Col. 2:18), and the Epistle to the Hebrews devotes its first two chapters to checking such belief.[43] The Council of Laodicea in Phrygia (343–81) was obliged to condemn the idolatry of Christians who gave "themselves up in honor of angels." Now, however, it is necessary to revive veneration or reverence for the angels, in order to counter our decline into the twilight world of materialism.

I say this in full awareness of the dangers involved. Superstition is now at floodtide, and some people are only too ready to grasp at anything improbable as a way of giving affront to the tyranny of modern rationalism and scientism. I am not interested in regressing to a world like that of the first centuries of our era, filled as it was with the fear of demons, where vendors hawked amulets to charm away spirits, and every inner prompting was projected out on some power in the cosmos. What we can attempt, however, is to recover the poetic attitude which was able to enlist the then current science in an ecstatic vision of nature as filled with divine presence and purpose. There is nothing to be gained by attempting to restore a worldview of original participation, and a great deal to be lost.

If we are to go all the way through the pilgrimage of our era and out the other side, then ours must be a "second naiveté" based on critical reflection and thoroughly grounded in an empirical approach. We must not go "back to the Bible," but only *forward, by means of the Bible.*

Ours must be an "animism no longer anthropocentric"; we must find soul in matter without simply projecting into it our own souls. And we must recover what was valid in participating consciousness without losing the critical consciousness that we have gained along the way. This requires a dialectical consciousness which is able to maintain a continual oscillation between unity and distance.⁴⁴ The goal is not to return to the one-sided spiritualism of an earlier age or to a sentimental nature-pietism that revels in personal raptures without challenging the polluters, the strip-miners, and the poisoners of nature. The goal is rather to find spirit at the very heart of matter, and a politics to match. Had not Teilhard himself said that it is God and God alone whom we pursue through the reality of created beings? That the light of heaven becomes tangible and attainable to us through the crystal of beings?⁴⁵ Is not the Incarnation itself the message that "corporeality is the ultimate end of all God's ways"?⁴⁶

How then did it come to pass that I, who had some few years ago conceived this study as a thoroughgoing demythologization of the Powers in social science categories, now find myself speaking realistically of angels? Having set sail in pursuit only of scholarly thoroughness and the desire to leave no stone unturned, I through no intention of my own have quite sailed off the map of our two-dimensional universe, *into a universe that is alive.* This new world, teeming with energies and graced with presence, came all unbidden, though witnessed to by Scripture and prepared for by the new physics. And now what are we going to do without that old, flat, mechanical world? It was a kind of solution.

> The angels keep their ancient places;—
> Turn but a stone and start a wing!
> 'Tis ye, 'tis your estranged faces,
> That miss the many-splendored thing.⁴⁷

At least we need not fall into the old trap of overestimating the angels, or of regressing into a new bondage to their transcending powers. Because the angelic realities are encountered within physical things and yet as transcendent to them, it was natural enough that people would have been overwhelmed by them, and feared, placated, and worshiped them. But now we recognize that we too have creative power, that we too (though not yet with the wisdom of the angels) have a part in controlling our world. We can therefore deal with the angels as equals, as fellow sojourners and learners on this planet, as cosmic beings each with different but complementary parts to play in realizing the divine will on earth.

I suppose J. R. R. Tolkien's little hobbits are scarcely weighty enough to anchor so controversial a case as the one I have argued, but they get the last word nonetheless. Merry the Hobbit, after his heroic battle with the Lord of the Nazgulim in *The Lord of the Rings,* ruminates:

> It is best to love first what you are suited to love, I suppose: you must start someplace and have some roots, and the soil of the Shire is deep. Still there are things deeper and higher; and not a gaffer could tend his garden in what he calls peace but for them, whether he knows about them or not.[48]

Epilogue

We are living at the juncture of two ages, when a senescent worldview is contending with its upstart successor and the boundaries of what seems possible liquefy. New superstitions elbow for adherents while jostling up against old superstitions bidding to make a comeback, each preening itself as the solution to the general anxiety of the age. Ancient wisdoms take on sudden incandescence; recent wisdoms lose all credibility. The stone which the builders of the previous worldview rejected may even become the new head of the corner.

I would not wish to argue that Satan, demons, angels, gods, or elements are likely candidates as cornerstones. But the new understanding of the spiritual as the interiority of earthly existence is a very viable candidate, and insofar as these long-neglected Powers throw light on the nature of that virtually lost dimension, they possess a significance far beyond their importance in the New Testament. There they were simply a part of the furniture of the universe. One no more had to argue for their existence then than we today would feel obliged to defend the existence of molecules or quasars. Their place in the ancient and medieval cosmologies was consistent with the consciousness of the times, a consciousness that projected these Powers out onto the screen of the cosmos and granted them ontological status. For that age the devil really "existed" and could assume human shape; demons actually seized people from without and entered them; angels flew between heaven and earth as messengers, sat in the heavenly council representing their nations, or presided over congregations or cities or other corporate entities. People then were as far from perceiving these Powers as the interiority or spirituality of an epoch or institution or nation as most of us are from regarding them as actual personal beings.

We cannot simply revive that ancient worldview without jettisoning much of what humanity has gained in the interval since. But we can reinterpret it. We can and must seek to recover in it the eternal truth revealed through its characteristic thought-forms, images, and presuppositions.

The new age dawning may not "believe in" angels and demons the way an earlier period believed in them. But these Powers may be granted a happier fate:

172

to be understood as symbolic of the "withinness" of institutions, structures, and systems. People may never again regard them as quasi-material beings flapping around in the sky, but perhaps they will come to see them as the actual spirituality of actual entities in the real world. Even if we no longer endow them with human personalities and qualities, we can understand them to be as real as any thing: the invisible, intangible interiority of collective enterprises, the invariant, determining forces of nature and society, or the archetypal images of the unconscious, all of which shape, nurture, and all too often cripple human existence. These mighty Powers are still with us. They are not "mere" symbols—that too is the language of the old worldview that is passing, for we now know that nothing is more powerful than a living symbol. As symbols they point to something real, something the worldview of materialism never learned to name and therefore never could confront.

Volume 3 of The Powers (*Engaging the Powers*) will examine the style of Christian engagement in the struggle with and against the Powers. Its task will be to spell out in practical terms the unique contribution of Christian faith to the struggle to make and keep human life really human in the face of dehumanizing institutions and their apparatus of coercion and control. We will then test the utility of the biblical understanding of the Powers against a representative set of Powers in their everyday institutional or systemic forms, seeking to discern in each case the spirituality behind the forms and the challenge each presents for faith.

The ultimate issue, however, is not whether we comprehend the Powers, but whether we confront them with their apostasy from their heavenly calling. Understanding the Powers is but a step toward encountering them. We unmask them only in order to engage them, in the spirit and power of the One in whom and through whom and for whom they were created: the truly Human Being incarnated by Jesus.

Notes

INTRODUCTION

1. I am using myth here in the best sense, as the privileged narrative by which a community has come to understand and relate to what it holds to be the ultimate meaning of reality. "Myth" as it is used in these volumes has nothing of the old sense of falsehood, unreality, or specious fabrication.

2. Paul Ricoeur finds only four fundamental mythic structures that have played a vital role in Western life (*The Symbolism of Evil* [New York: Harper & Brothers, 1957]). Morton Kelsey identifies seven (*Myth, History and Faith* [New York: Paulist Press, 1974]).

3. Pierre Teilhard de Chardin, *The Future of Man* (New York: Harper & Row, 1964), 271ff.

4. The ancient Hebrews had little to do with evil spirits. Satan is mentioned only three times in the Hebrew Scriptures, all of them quite late, and demons go virtually unnoticed (see J. Maier, "Geister (Dämonen)," *RAC* 9 [1976]: 579–85). Angels belong to all strata of the Bible, but only come into their own in the intertestamental period, under Persian influence. Angelic "principalities" are first mentioned in Daniel, the latest writing in the Old Testament; and the other terms—powers, authorities, dominions, thrones, names, elements of the universe—are never mentioned at all (see *Naming the Powers*). The ancient Greeks for their part had long believed in *daimones* who sometimes did evil, but evil spirits as a *class*, such as we find in the New Testament, do not emerge in Greek thought until the first or second century C.E., when the use of engraved gems, amulets, and spells against demons, phantasms, and night fears suddenly became widespread (E. R. Dodds, *The Greeks and the Irrational* [Berkeley and Los Angeles: Univ. of California Press, 1951], 37–42, 23 nn. 65 and 75, 268 n. 103, 295). See J. Michl, "Engel," *RAC* 5 (1962): 54–58.

1. SATAN

1. Morton Kelsey, "The Mythology of Evil," *Journal of Religion and Health* 13 (1974): 10. Let me clarify two things at the outset. First, there is no discernible difference of meaning between "Satan" and "the devil," apart from the different etymologies of the terms. Satan is Semitic for "accuser," devil is Greek for "slanderer." The words are used interchangeably throughout the New Testament period (see, e.g., Rev. 12:9; 20:2; Matt. 10–11). So also "Beelzebul" equals "Satan" equals "the prince of demons" in Mark 22–23. Second, I have reluctantly decided to refer to Satan as "he," after having tried *s* without satisfaction. I have done so because every archetype must find some

174

image by which to present itself to consciousness, and the satanic seems above all to be *personal* in its assaults on us; and because the form of action we call satanic is most often "agentic" (in David Bakan's term), a type of behavior culturally associated with a crass masculinity unleavened by any feminine qualities whatever. In fact, of course, Satan appears in a variety of forms, including that of women. All in all, "satanic" might be better to use than "Satan," since it avoids the imponderable problem of Satan's metaphysical status.

2. On the decline of credibility of the Satan-image in recent times, see Maximilian Rudwin, *The Devil in Legend and Literature* (Chicago: Open Court Pub. Co., 1931), 114–19; Claude-Edmond Magny, "The Devil in Contemporary Literature," in *Satan,* ed. P. Bruno de Jesus-Marie, O.C.D. (New York and London: Sheed & Ward, 1951), 452; William Woods, *A History of the Devil* (New York: G. P. Putnam's Sons, 1974); Jeffrey Burton Russell, *The Devil* (Ithaca, N.Y.: Cornell Univ. Press, 1977), and the entire issue of *Concilium* 103 (1975).

3. See Paul Ricoeur, *The Symbolism of Evil* (New York: Harper & Row, 1967).

4. Deut. 32:39; see also Isa. 45:6b–7; 1 Sam. 2:6–7. One possible translation of "Yahweh" is "He causes to happen what happens." If, then, everything that happens has been caused by God, evil must also be caused by God. Thus when Pharaoh resisted Israel's liberation, it was not ascribed to his free will or his self-interest or sin, but to God's hardening Pharaoh's heart (Exod. 4:21; 7:3; 9:12; 10:1, 20, 27; 11:10; 14:4, 8, 17; Josh. 11:20, etc.). So also it was Yahweh who sent the evil spirit on Saul (1 Sam. 16:14–16, 23, etc.), and who commissioned a lying spirit to enter the mouths of the four hundred prophets of Ahab (1 Kings 22:22; see also 2 Sam. 17:14).

5. Later tradition could not tolerate Yahweh in the role of would-be murderer. The LXX changed "Yahweh" to "the angel of Yahweh" while Jubilees ascribed the attack to "Mastema," a satan figure (*Jub.* 48:2). This apparent tampering with the text was entirely appropriate, since by the second century B.C.E. Yahweh had been differentiated and "ethicalized," and this function now fell to God's satanic aspect. Likewise in *Jub.* 17:16 Mastema proposes that God should require Abraham to sacrifice Isaac in order to test his love and obedience—a very clear borrowing from Job.

6. See the excellent study by Rivkah Schärf Kluger, *Satan in the Old Testament* (Evanston, Ill.: Northwestern Univ. Press, 1967).

7. Even among these three, only one has the force of a proper name, "Satan" (1 Chron. 21:1). The other two designate a function—"the satan," or "the adversary" who prosecuted defendants in a court of law (Zech. 3:1; Job 1—2).

8. Gerhard von Rad, "Diabolos," *TDNT* 2 (1964): 72–75. The scene is modeled on normal Jewish legal practices.

9. The belief that the high priest represented the whole people of Israel was commonplace, and endured long after the destruction of the Second Temple. See for example *Pirqe R. Eliezer* 70 Ai (Friedlander, 390): " 'When Israel walked into the Holy of Holies'—but only the High Priest could do that." Walther Eichrodt believes Joshua's sins are personal, not Israel's (*Theology of the Old Testament* [Philadelphia: Westminster Press, 1967], 2:205 n. 3), but this is belied by the stress on Yahweh's choice of Jerusalem. Joshua as high priest will be Israel's necessary advocate before God in the soon-to-be restored temple.

10. The voice of the accuser operates independently of religious background or beliefs. It is endemic to the human condition. If you wish to test that assertion for your-

self, pause a moment to write out, carefully, answers to these questions: What is the precise form that this false voice of accusation takes in you? What is it accusing you of? How long has it been accusing you? What does God say to this voice?

11. Rabbi Johanan commented on Job 1—2: "Were it not expressly stated in the Scriptures, we would not dare to say it. [God is made to appear] like a man who allows himself to be persuaded against his better judgment" (*T. B. Baba Batra* 16a). If one reads the Prologue of Job without awareness of the author's intent to polemicize against a perennial but perverse notion of God, the picture that emerges is precisely the one the author attempted to confute!

12. Again, if you wish to locate the experiential reality that is dubbed "Satan" here, reflect in writing on these questions: What in me or in my life needs to be sifted right now? Will I confront this problem consciously and voluntarily, or will I wait for events to overtake me and let Satan do the sifting?

13. This is actually the view of a number of scholars, including Hans Conzelmann, *1 Corinthians,* Hermeneia (Philadelphia: Fortress Press, 1975), 98; and J. Schneider, "Olethros," *TDNT* 5 (1968): 169. The penalty for cohabiting with one's stepmother is defined in the Mishnah as "extirpation" (*kareth*—'cutting off''), which is there spelled out as involving stoning, burning, strangling, or forty stripes (*M. Ker.* 1:1). Pagans were less severe in punishment but no less opposed to sex between a stepmother and her son, as the tragic myth of Phaedra and Hippolytus shows. Paul is engaged not in extirpation but ritual execration (see A. Deissmann, *Light from the Ancient East* [Grand Rapids: Baker Book House, 1965], 302-7). It is unlikely that the Roman authorities in Corinth would have permitted the Christian community to practice ritual lynchings. The Hellenistic Jewish attitude toward cohabiting with one's stepmother is represented by *Pseudo-Phocylides* 179-80 (30 B.C.E.-40 C.E.): "Do not touch your stepmother, your father's second wife, but honor her as a mother" (*OT Ps.* 2:580).

14. Other examples of reproval and shunning are 2 Thess. 3:14-15; 2 Tim. 2:25-26; Titus 3:10-11; and Matt. 18:15-18.

15. I leave open the question of the historicity of this narrative. The concept of Satan remains constant whatever the source. In interpreting this passage, and Satan's role as servant generally, I am indebted to Elizabeth Boyden Howes and seminars with the Guild for Psychological Studies. See especially Elizabeth Howes and Sheila Moon, *The Choicemaker* (Wheaton, Ill.: Theosophical Pub. House, 1977).

16. Sheila Moon's fine phrase, *Joseph's Son* (Francestown, N.H.: Golden Quill Press, 1972), 20.

17. Kluger, *Satan in the Old Testament,* 76.

18. John B. Cobb, Jr., *Christ in a Pluralistic Age* (Philadelphia: Westminster Press, 1975), 84.

19. "Hence, paradoxically, the Devil must cause his own destruction. By bringing the daemonic into the light, the daemonic is stripped of its daemonic character . . . the Devil's very permissiveness is the cause of his destruction" (David Bakan, *Sigmund Freud and the Jewish Mystical Tradition* [Princeton, N.J.: D. Van Nostrand Co., 1958], 232-33). This is true, however, only when choice is struggled for consciously. Goethe articulated the same insight when he spoke of Mephistopheles as "a part of that force which forever wills evil and forever creates good" (*Faust,* Act I, Scene 3). A similar conception is reflected in a myth of the Yakuts, nomadic shepherds of Siberia, in which the creator makes the earth small and beautiful and smooth. Then the evil spirit comes

and begins to tear at it like a dog so as to destroy it. The creator sees him but lets him go on, and while the evil spirit pursues his task, the earth does not cease to grow and the rivers and seas emerge from the cracks he makes. Thus he contributes, in spite of himself, to giving the earth its present size and form (Joseph Henninger, "The Adversary of God in Primitive Religions," in *Satan*, ed. Father Bruno de Jesus-Marie, 115–16).

20. "God has not deprived the devil of his power over the world, because his collaboration is still necessary for the perfecting of those destined to receive a crown" (Origen, *Hom. on Num.*, 13.7).

21. Trevor Ling, *The Significance of Satan* (London: SPCK, 1961), 38.

22. Several modern versions translate, "*If* you are angry," perhaps under the influence of Eph. 4:31 ("Let all . . . anger . . . be put away from you"). But 4:26 is a direct quote of Ps. 4:4 LXX, and while it can conceivably be concessive (BDF, §387.1), the more natural reading is as a simple imperative (following the RSV).

23. The NEB reads, for Eph. 4:26b, "do not let sunset find you still nursing" your anger. Compare its translation of Matt. 5:22: "Anyone who nurses anger against his brother must be brought to judgment." The issue is not then whether one loses one's temper, but whether the grievance is "nursed" until it grows into a power that threatens community relationships.

24. St. Ignatius Loyola, *The Spiritual Exercises*, trans. Anthony Mottola (Garden City, N.Y.: Image Books, 1964), 131–32.

25. This is Charles's reconstruction, *APOT* 2:408 n. 2.

26. The RSV *Apocrypha* reads, "When the ungodly curses his adversary, he curses his own soul." The Greek, however, reads "*the* adversary."

27. Sidney Harris, *Word and Witness*, May 25, 1980.

28. Eccles. 10:20; Luke 20:20. See A. Lods, "Les origines de la figure de Satan, ses fonctions à la cour céleste," *Mélanges syriens offerts à R. Dussaud*, II, *Bibliothèque archéologique et historique* 30/2 (1939): 649–60. See also C. Colpe, "Geister (Dämonen)," *RAC* 9 (1976): 569–70. He notes that demons are described in Mesopotamia, Syria and Asia Minor by the same language as that used of spies, informants, accusers, censors, and secret agents. People sensed a connection between the apparatus of imperial repression and the demonic. It is not a case of displacing to the mythical sphere an experience that is essentially political, thereby mystifying it, but rather of using the well known and thoroughly conscious experience of political surveillance as the clue to a more inchoate but ubiquitous psychic or spiritual experience. See also A. L. Oppenheim, "The Eyes of the Lord," *Journal of the American Oriental Society* 88 (1968): 173–80.

29. According to *1 Enoch* and *Jubilees*, angelic intercourse with women produced giants who killed each other; their spirits survive as demons. The guilty angels were seized by God and bound until the last judgment (*1 Enoch* 1–16; 65:6, 11; 67:12; 85—90; *Jub.* 4:15; 5:1–6; 10:11; see 1 Cor. 11:4–10). This story is *not* the myth of the primordial fall of Satan. That is a post-Biblical motif, alluded to in a late interpolation in the *Life of Adam and Eve* 12—17 (*APOT*); see also *2 Enoch* 29:4–5 (A); *Apoc. Elij.* 15:14–20 (P. Chester Beatty 2018). Satan is cast out of heaven by the fidelity of Christ and his followers (Luke 10:18; Rev. 12:7–12), but this takes place in the midst of history, not before history began. It was not until Milton's *Paradise Lost* that the myth of Satan's fall received its fullest expression.

The Dawn Star (*hēlēl*) in Isa. 14:12 who is cast from heaven for attempting to scale heaven's heights has been popularly associated with Satan's fall, but had no such sense in ancient times. Isaiah thoroughly historicizes the image as a poetic simile for the outrageous self-aggrandizement of the king of Babylon. (See also Ezek. 28:11–19.) Behind Isaiah's image apparently stands a pagan myth, alluded to in a recently discovered Ugaritic text as god of the dawn or morning star. Origen remythologized the tradition when he identified Satan as the Day Star (later called "Lucifer" in the Vulgate). In the New Testament, by contrast, it is *Christ* who is called the Day Star (Luke 1:78; 2 Peter 1:19; Rev. 22:16). See Eichrodt, *Theology of the Old Testament,* 2:208 and 1:460 n. 4; Henry Ansgar Kelly, *The Devil, Demonology and Witchcraft* (Garden City, N.Y.: Doubleday & Co., 1968), 5.

30. Matt. 13:19; John 17:15; 1 John 2:13, 14; 5:18, 19; and as an alternate reading in Matt. 5:39; 6:13; and 2 Thess. 3:3.

31. John 12:31; 14:30; 16:11.

32. Eph. 2:2.

33. 2 Cor. 6:15.

34. Matt. 10:25; 12:24 par.

35. 2 Cor. 4:4.

36. 1 Cor. 10:10.

37. John 8:44.

38. Matt. 13:25, 28, 39; Luke 10:19.

39. Bernard J. Bamberger, *Fallen Angels* (Philadelphia: Jewish Publication Society of America, 1952), 42; Werner Foerster, "Diabolos," *TDNT* 2 (1964): 79. Leo Jung writes, "No Haggadah, no Midrash, contains any hint of an empire independent of, and opposed to, God." An evil Satan is unknown to rabbinic Judaism, for which Satan is strictly a servant of God (*Fallen Angels in Jewish, Christian and Mohammedan Literature* [New York: KTAV, 1974], 32).

40. Mark 3:22 par.

41. Mark 4:15 par.

42. Rev. 2:10.

43. Luke 13:16; Acts 10:38.

44. 1 Thess. 2:18.

45. John 8:44; Acts 5:3.

46. Matt. 13:39; John 17:15; 2 Cor. 2:11; Eph. 6:11; 1 Tim. 5:15; 2 Tim. 2:26; 1 Peter 5:8–9.

47. Luke 22:3; John 6:70; 13:2, 27.

48. John 8:44; Acts 13:10; Rev. 3:9.

49. Acts 26:18; perhaps by implication, Rev. 2:13.

50. Luke 10:18; Rev. 12:7–12.

51. Matt. 25:41; Rev. 20:2, 7, 10.

52. Ling, *The Significance of Satan,* 34.

53. Ibid., 83–84.

54. M. Scott Peck, *People of the Lie* (New York: Simon & Schuster, 1983), 78.

55. " 'The *first nightmare* is the father of all mythology'; without it and its many forms, belief in 'spirits' would never have developed to the extent to which it did" (Jolanda Jacobi, "Dream-Demons," in *Satan,* ed. P. Bruno de Jesus-Marie, 278–79).

56. The universality of symbols for evil has not successfully been accounted for by the theory of cultural interpenetration, for Carl Jung has documented the recurrence of primitive archetypal images in the dreams of modern patients who cannot have had any

knowledge of the symbols beforehand (*The Archetypes and the Collective Unconscious,* CW 9/1 [1971]). Nor can such symbols be wholly attributed to prevailing social or economic arrangements, though the image will no doubt be responsive to such arrangements. (The Satan described by Peck sounds every bit like an Ayn Rand cutthroat capitalist, *People of the Lie,* 204, 207.) For we find myths of an evil spirit who intervenes in creation even among tribes that practiced communal ownership and who had a high degree of social integration, such as the food gathering and hunting eastern Algonquins (the Delaware, the Arapaho, the Gluskabe of the Wawenocks), the central California Maidu and Wintun, the Siberian Koryaks and Samoyedes, the northern Japanese Ainu, or the Mesoamerican Aztecs. See Joseph Henninger, "The Adversary of God in Primitive Religions," in *Satan,* ed. P. Bruno de Jesus-Marie, 116.

57. Peck's definition of Satan (*People of the Lie,* 207).

58. It is often remarked that it is usually only the more spiritually astute who consciously encounter Satan, while those who are busiest doing Satan's will are wholly oblivious to, and usually even disbelieve, his existence. This is not surprising; after all, one does not entice with apples a person who has plunged headlong into the apple barrel. As the Sufis put it, Satan has permeated every pore of their flesh and has nested at the root of each hair of their heads (cited by Peter J. Awn, *Satan's Tragedy and Redemption: Iblis in Sufi Psychology* [Leiden: E. J. Brill, 1983], 155). When one has become so utterly integrated around such collective evils as consumerism or the arms race, one no longer suffers the conflicts that might bring Satan to awareness.

59. James Hillman, *Insearch* (New York: Charles Scribner's Sons, 1967), 90.

60. D. E. Wooldbridge, *The Mechanical Man* (New York: McGraw-Hill, 1968).

61. Bernal, cited by Brian Easlea, *Liberation and the Aims of Science* (Totowa, N.J.: Rowman & Littlefield, 1973), 326–27. I cannot help suspecting that this proposal inspired C. S. Lewis's profound treatment of satanic evil in *That Hideous Strength* (New York: Macmillan Co., [1946] 1975).

62. Cited by Easlea, *Liberation and the Aims of Science,* 261–62.

63. Ibid., 273.

64. Ibid., 267, italics mine.

65. Alfred North Whitehead, *Science in the Modern World* (New York: Mentor Books, 1948), 192.

66. Aleksandr I. Solzhenitsyn, *The Gulag Archipelago* III/Parts V–VII (New York: Harper & Row, 1976), chap. 5.

67. Matt. 6:13; Luke 11:4 by implication. So also, on the basis of psychoanalytic observation, Marie-Louise von Franz: There appears to be in the unconscious something intrinsically evil which derives pleasure from destruction and murder for their own sake ("The Problem of Evil in Fairy Tales," in *Evil,* ed. Curatorium of the C. G. Jung Institute [Evanston, Ill.: Northwestern Univ. Press, 1967], 94–95).

68. We find the same phenomenon in *3 Enoch*. In 4:6, the angels Ùzzah, Àzzah, and Àzaél dwell in the high heavens and accuse humanity before God for its sins. Yet in 5:9 these same angels are identified as the fallen Watchers of Gen. 6:1–4, who taught idolatry and sorcery to humanity and seduced women. Here two apparently contradictory symbols are encompassed as a complementary truth: the accusing angels "fall" when they become too zealous for justice (4:6) or when human beings engage in idolatry (5:7–9, where the angels are retrospectively made the cause of that of which they are the object).

69. David Bakan, *Sigmund Freud and the Jewish Mystical Tradition,* 210–11; idem,

The Duality of Human Existence (Skokie, Ill.: Rand McNally & Co., 1966), 67ff.; and idem, "Psychological Characteristics of Man Projected in the Image of Satan," in *On Method* (San Francisco: Jossey-Bass, 1967), 160–69.

70. Norman O. Brown, *Life Against Death: The Psychoanalytical Meaning of History* (Middletown, Conn.: Wesleyan Univ. Press, 1959), 204–9; cited by Peter Homans, *Theology After Freud* (New York: Bobbs-Merrill Co., 1970), 130–37.

71. Cited by Jean Lhermitte, *Diabolical Possession, True and False* (London: Burns & Oates, 1963), 9.

72. William Stringfellow, in *An Ethic for Christians and Other Aliens in a Strange Land* (Waco, Tex.: Word Books, 1973), 54–57, 132–33, suggests that since we cannot know that we know the will of God, and since so much evil has been done by those who have claimed to know it, we should drop such talk altogether and simply try to be human as best we can, calling on divine grace. I find that attractive but not quite compelling. For I know as little about what "being human" is as I know about the will of God. Both must be revealed to us in their unique specificity at the conjunction of our lives with a given historical moment. What "human" means is still largely unknown (1 John 3:2), though Jesus has revealed the essence of its possibilities. Perhaps our difference could be resolved by saying that the will of God is discovering what it means to be human in a concrete situation. But that remains to some degree at least an act of divine revelation.

73. Satan is a purely mental or spiritual, and not a physical, reality. Satan has no body or material form, but is made manifest through the imaginal dimension (see *Naming the Powers*, 143–44).

74. The early Christians were not unaware of our role in augmenting Satan's power in the world. Chrysostom, for example, argued that the Devil "gained strength, not owing to his own power but from that of man's slothfulness and carelessness." The Devil "is even profitable to us, if we use him aright"; in 1 Cor. 5:5 he is even "a cause of salvation, but not because of his own disposition, but because of the skill of the apostle" (*Hom. on 1 Cor.*, 2: "Against those who object because the Devil has not been put out of the world," in *NPNF* 9:187). "Did [Paul] not oft times command the devil as a captive slave? Did he not carry him about as an executioner?" (*Hom. on Phil.*, 7, *NPNF* 13:216); "If we are fierce toward [the devil], he shall never be fierce towards us. If we are compliant, then he will be fierce" (*Hom. on Eph.*, 22, *NPNF* 13:163). See also *Apoc. Ab.* 23.

75. We can scarcely be certain, since we are dependent on Rufinus's Latin translation, but Origen may not actually have said that Satan *will* be redeemed, but rather that the last enemy will be neutralized, not by its destruction, but by "its ceasing to be an enemy" (*De Principiis* 3.6)—an interpretation of 1 Cor. 15:26 with which we concurred in *Naming the Powers*, 51–52. And if Christ's struggle with satanic powers was not only against them but for their sake, then one cannot exclude the future possibility of their being converted to righteousness due to their possessing the faculty of free will. Origen leaves the issue to the judgment of the reader, noting that "nothing is impossible to the Omnipotent, nor is anything incapable of restoration to its Creator" (*De Principiis* 1.6.2; 1.8; 3.6.5; see James W. Boyd, *Satan and Mara: Christian and Buddhist Symbols of Evil* [Leiden: E. J. Brill, 1975], 60–61).

76. The Sufi masters recognized that Satan was being scapegoated by humanity for its own deeds and nicknamed him "Satan the Stoned." Some even held out for Satan's final redemption. See Peter J. Awn's moving *Satan's Tragedy and Redemption: Iblis in Sufi Psychology*.

77. I learned this from Morton Kelsey.

78. Mark 3:22 par.

79. Mark 3:19–21; John 10:20.

80. John 7:20; 10:20.

81. Mark 2:7 par.

82. Mark 2:23–28 par.; 3:1–6 par.; 6:2, 5; Luke 13:10–17; 14:1–6; John 5:1–18; 7:21–24; 9:1–41.

83. Mark 5:24b–34 par.; 7:24–30//Matt. 15:21–28; Mark 10:1–12 par.; 12:41–44//Luke 21:1–4; Matt. 13:33//Luke 13:20–21; Matt. 26:6–13//Mark 14:3–9; Luke 7:36–50; 10:38–42; 13:10–17; John 4:1–42.

84. Mark 10:13–16 par. Marcion's copy of Luke adds to the list of crimes for which Jesus was executed in 23:2, "and for causing the women and children to revolt (*apostrephonta*)."

85. Mark 2:13–17 par.; Matt. 11:19//Luke 7:34; Matt. 10:3; 21:31–32; Luke 7:29; 7:36–50; 15:1; 18:9–14: 19:1–10·

86. There is a heady but dangerous truth in Friedrich Nietzsche's statement, "The great epochs of our life come when we gain the courage to rechristen our evil as what is best in us" (*Beyond Good and Evil,* trans. Walter Kaufmann [New York: Vintage Books, 1966], 86).

87. William Blake, *Jerusalem,* plate 52, in *The Complete Writings of William Blake,* ed. Geoffrey Keynes (London: Oxford Univ. Press, 1966), 682.

88. Clyde Z. Nunn documents the sharp increase in belief in Satan's existence (those "absolutely certain" up from 37 percent to 50 percent from 1964 to 1973, and now, according to recent polls, higher) at a time when belief in God appeared to be declining within the culture as a whole. The collapse of the era of progress under the landslide evils of our age has produced an odd kind of inverse faith. Churchgoers comprise the highest percentage of believers in Satan. They blame Satan for the crisis of modern society, yet they are also strongly committed to the present social order and identify criticisms of it as satanic. This is a far cry from the scriptural notion that Satan is the "god of this world" and lord of the status quo. Nunn's study also shows a striking correlation between intolerance and belief in Satan. This leads to the identification of nonconformists and opponents as evil and the desire to exterminate them (by capital punishment, holy wars, massive retaliation, revenge) or to shun "sinners" (whom they identified as divorcees, gays, blacks, Hispanics, socialists, etc.). See Nunn, "The Rising Credibility of the Devil in America," *Listening: Journal of Religion and Culture* 9 (1974): 84–100.

89. See, for example, Jung's *Psychology and Religion: West and East*, CW 11, (1977), index entries under "devil" and "Satan."

90. Justin Martyr, *1 Apology* 1.54, 57; 2.5.

91. Dreams are referred to well over a hundred times in Scripture as sent from God; in only a dozen or so passages are they discredited as false prophecies or nonsense.

92. Edward Langton, *Satan, A Portrait* (London: Sheffington & Son, 1945), 72–73.

93. The Egyptian demon cult of the *zar* provides an interesting cross-cultural comparison. Anthropologist Cynthia Nelson suggests that the *zar* ceremony psychologically reinforces the inferior status imposed on women in that Muslim society. All the evil spirits are male, she notes, and it is they who possess a woman, dominate her, and make demands of her. She can make no demands of the spirit, nor can she ever be delivered from it. She can only hope, by means of the rites of the *zar,* to pacify it. Dancing violently to the tempo of drum, tambourine, and flute, the supplicant yields her body to

the demon who possesses her. During the dance, women are able for a few moments to shed traditional inhibitions placed on them, on the ground that they are not responsible for their behavior.

The "demon" here is real, all right, but it would appear to be the introjection of the male-dominated society as a demonic form. The ceremony both reinforces that domination (the male demon "can never be driven out"), and provides a kind of harmless, even pleasurable catharsis of violent pent-up feelings and normally repressed hungers. The "demon" is the actual spirituality of a cruel patriarchal culture; it is no figment of their imaginations. In contrast to witchcraft or Satanism, which provide an underground structure of protest and defiance, the rite of the *zar* merely reinforces the social inequality of women by mystifying its real source: the demonic interiority of male-dominant society. (See Christopher S. Wren, "In Cairo, Dance of a Cult Pacifies Demons," *New York Times,* July 9, 1979, A4; William Sargant, *The Mind Possessed* [Philadelphia: J. B. Lippincott, 1974], 137–38.)

94. One former Satanist whom I know (she is now a deeply committed Christian) grew up Roman Catholic, desiring to become a priest. Finding that route barred as a woman, she became a nun. Subsequently she left her order, became a prostitute, and finally joined a satanist church. There at least a woman could be a priest and officiate at the ritual. Clear injustice and male domination played a major role in her development, but, as she herself points out, so did a tremendous unredeemed power-drive. Having suffered the torments of hell, she is now studying to be a Protestant minister.

95. See also Rev. 4:6. The image in Revelation of a lake of fire burning in heaven is not at all unique in Jewish and Christian apocalyptic. *2 Enoch,* for example, places hell and its fires, not under the surface of the earth, but in the third of seven heavens, along with Paradise (*2 Enoch* 8—10)—a conception reflected in the parable of Lazarus and the rich man as well (Luke 16:23—the rich man can see Lazarus in Abraham's bosom from where he roasts in Hades, since both are in the third heaven). In *2 Enoch* 7 Satan and the Watchers who consorted with women are imprisoned in the fifth heaven awaiting the last judgment, while other apostate angels are bound in the second heaven (*OT Ps.* 1:114 n. i). The Slavonic text of *3 Baruch* 16:4 seems to locate Paradise and Hell together, ostensibly in the fifth heaven. The *Midrash on Psalm* 90:12 (196a) is even closer to Revelation; it states that Paradise is on God's right hand and Gehinnom (Hades) on the left (so also Matt. 25:33, 41).

96. There is in Hinduism a remarkable parallel to John's image of Satan burning forever before God in the lake of fire. Krishna has a great fight with Kamsa the evil serpent, in which the champion of righteousness defeats the evil usurper and dances on its heads (compare Rev. 12:3—Satan the ancient dragon has seven heads). John Stratton Hawley remarks, "As Krishna dances he symbolically draws energy from the snake and turns it to creativity . . . he dances, and through him the whole world becomes play" ("Krishna's Cosmic Victories," *Journal of the American Academy of Religion* 47 [1979]: 209).

97. "For analysis does not undo the *effects* of repression. The instincts that were formerly suppressed remained suppressed; but the same effect is produced in a different way. Analysis replaces the process of repression, which is an automatic and excessive one, by a temperate and purposeful control on the part of the highest mental faculties. In a word, *analysis replaces repression by condemnation*" (Freud, *Collected Papers* 3:285; cited by Homans, *Theology After Freud,* 155–56). Peter Lamborn Wilson cites

the alchemical doctrine that the volatile spirit of mercury must be "killed" or fixed by the stable solar principle of sulphur, just as the lithe and sinuous dragon must be "slain" by the Angel of the Sun, Michael. The symbolism, he says, is this: "The vital spirit is by nature chaotic and chthonic [earthly], but the intellect cannot operate without its power. To 'kill' the dragon is not to eliminate it but to tame it, to leash it, to order it, to use its power towards spiritual ends" (*Angels* [New York: Pantheon Books, 1980], 82).

98. T. S. Eliot, *Four Quartets* (New York: Harcourt Brace Jovanovich, 1971), 59.

2. THE DEMONS

1. Wilhelm Reich, *Character Analysis,* 3d ed. (New York: Simon & Schuster, 1972), xxvi.

2. This narrative is blessed with brilliant exegetical studies. Especially noteworthy are Jean Starobinski, "The Gerasene Demoniac," in *Structural Analysis and Biblical Exegesis,* R. Barthes, et al., ed. (Pittsburgh: Pickwick Press, 1974), 57–84; Franz-J. Leenhardt, "An Exegetical Essay: Mark 5:1–20," 85–109 in the same volume; Paul W. Hollenbach, "Jesus, Demoniacs, and Public Authorities: A Socio-Historical Study," *Journal of the American Academy of Religion* 49 (1981): 567–88; and René Girard, "Generative Violence and the Extinction of Social Order," *Salmagundi* 63–64 (Spring–Summer 1984): 204–37.

3. J. F. Craghan, "The Gerasene Demoniac," *Catholic Biblical Quarterly* 30 (1968): 522–36. Isa. 65:1–15 contains what could be read by the church as an allusion to Jesus' entering the Decapolis (65:1); those "who sit in tombs, and spend the night in secret places; who eat swine's flesh" (v. 4); "who say, 'Keep to yourself, do not come near me' " (v. 5); and also possibly vv. 7, 12, 15. The LXX adds to v. 3b, "burning incense upon bricks *to demons (tois daimoniois) which have no existence*"; and to v. 11, "who set a table for *the demon (tō daimoni;* Heb., "Fortune"). These resonances may have lent color and even a few details to the narrative in Mark 5, but they are scarcely fundamental to the narrative.

4. Josephus refers to Gadara as possessing territory that "lay on the frontiers of Tiberius" (*Life* 42; see also possibly *War* 3.37), that is, the Sea of Galilee; and elsewhere he mentions that the "territory of the Gerasenes" extended at least as far as Ragaba, fourteen miles to the west of Gerasa (*Ant.* 13.398).

5. Gergesa may be an allusion to the Old Testament Girgashites, who may have dwelt in this region (Joseph Wallfield, "Mark V 1 and 9: From Sources to Meanings," unpublished manuscript, courtesy of the author).

6. So large a herd of swine, whether historical or not, would only be believable in a story set on Gentile soil. For Jewish and Jewish Christian hearers of the tale, the destruction of the pigs would have provoked howls of delight.

7. Josephus, *War* 1.104, 155–57, 396; 2.97, 458–80; 4.413, 486–90, 503; *Ant.* 13.397–98; 15.354; *Life* 42–43. See also Carl Kraeling, *Gerasa, City of the Decapolis* (New Haven, Conn.: American Schools of Oriental Research, 1938); D. E. Pellett, "Decapolis," *IDB* 1:810–12.

8. The Decapolis may have been among those "Syrian" cities on which Crassus (d. 53 B.C.E.) had levied taxes in preparation for the Parthian war. He required them also to meet quotas for troops; yet "he released from the obligation those who gave him

money, and so lost their respect and was despised by them" (Plutarch, *Crassus* 17.5). Julius Caesar's assassination brought new exactions beyond their ability to pay. See Robert O. Fink, "Jerash in the First Century A.D.," *Journal of Roman Studies* 23 (1933): 109–24.

9. Josephus, *War* 4.486–90.

10. Kraeling, *Gerasa,* 49 n. 106; A. H. M. Jones, *The Cities of the Eastern Roman Provinces* (Oxford: Clarendon Press, 1937), 230.

11. See, in addition to the work cited in n. 3, Girard's *Violence and the Sacred* (Baltimore: Johns Hopkins Univ. Press, 1985); idem, *Des choses cachées depuis la fondation du monde* (Paris: Grasset, 1978); and idem, *Le bouc émissaire* (Paris: Grasset, 1982).

12. Girard, "Generative Violence," 210.

13. Leenhardt, "An Exegetical Essay," 96.

14. "Constantly reinforced throughout the empire, imperial rule was a recurring cause of riot and revolution. . . . The *polis* had been understood throughout Greek history to be 'one big family' or 'an all-in-all partnership,' and ardent devotion to this ideal remained a higher allegiance than obedience to Rome, and frequently led to violence" (James M. Fennelly, "The Primitive Christian Values of Salvation and Patterns of Conversion," in *Man and His Salvation,* ed. Eric J. Sharpe and John R. Hinnells [Manchester: Manchester Univ. Press, 1973], 116).

15. Origen, still within a wholly mythological context, saw a connection between demons and their geopolitical location. One must therefore address them in the local languages to cast them out; for of "the various demons upon the earth, to whom different localities have been assigned, each one bears a name appropriate to the several dialects of place and country" (*Against Celsus* 1.24 [*ANF* 4:406]).

16. Gerd Theissen, *Sociology of Early Palestinian Christianity* (Philadelphia: Fortress Press, 1978), 101–2.

17. Psychic "invasion" by demons frequently parallels physical invasion by an alien culture, as in the Cargo Cults and the Native American Ghost Dances. In East Africa in 1916, J. J. Dannholz reported cases of possession in which the "spirit" was, among other things, a *European.* Possession among that tribe was "not known in former times, but seems to have made a recent appearance," spreading from the coast (where contact with Europeans was greatest) to the interior (T. K. Oesterreich, *Possession and Exorcism* [New York: Causeway Books, (1921) 1974], 137). Among the Ba-Ronga people, primitive sorcery and magic died down under the influence of Portuguese colonial administration, but a new phenomenon arose in their place: the belief that the spirits of the dead could enter into the living and cause sickness and even death (Junod, cited by ibid., 379). Did these "spirits of the dead" represent the tribal culture for which European civilization sounded the death knell, and was its demise bringing in its wake psychic crises that manifested themselves in psychosomatic illness and even death?

18. Hollenbach, "Jesus, Demoniacs, and Public Authorities," 575, 581. See also John Pairman Brown, "Techniques of Imperial Control: The Background of the Gospel Event," in *The Bible and Liberation: Political and Social Hermeneutics,* ed. Norman K. Gottwald (Maryknoll, N.Y.: Orbis Press, 1983), 357–77; and Colleen A. Ward and Michael H. Beaubrun, "The Psychodynamics of Demon Possession," *Journal for the Scientific Study of Religion* 19 (1980): 201–7.

19. Girard, *Violence and the Sacred,* 13. See also Liliane Frey-Rohn, "Evil from a

Psychological Point of View," in *Evil*, ed. the Curatorium of the C. G. Jung Institute (Evanston, Ill.: Northwestern Univ. Press, 1967), 179.

20. Girard, "Generative Violence," 218, 221. Derrett rightly notes that the description of the pigs' behavior is altogether unpiglike. Pigs do not flock, but are highly independent. The man's screams would have sent them in all directions (J. Duncan M. Derrett, "Contributions to the Study of the Gerasene Demoniac," *Journal for the Study of the New Testament* 3 [1979]: 2–17). Their lemming-like behavior is itself uncanny—or is it the embroidery of Jewish narrators unfamiliar with their ways?

Demons abhor water, according to *Test. Sol.* 5:11–12. Drowning, however, does not imply their destruction so much as their being returned to the collective unconscious.

21. "Deviance," observes Kai Erikson, "is not a property *inherent in* certain forms of behavior; it is a property *conferred upon* these forms by the audiences which directly or indirectly witness them. The critical variable in the study of deviancy, then, is the social audience rather than the individual actor, since it is the audience which eventually determines whether or not any episode of behavior or any class of episodes is labelled deviant" ("Notes on the Sociology of Deviance," in *The Other Side. Perspectives on Deviance* [New York: Free Press, 1964], 10–11). See also his classic study of deviancy, *The Wayward Pilgrims. A Study of Social Deviance* (New York: John Wiley & Sons, 1966).

22. Quotations cited by Lionel Rubinoff, *The Pornography of Power* (Chicago: Quadrangle Books, 1968), 36–42.

23. George Rosen, *Madness in Society* (London: Routledge & Kegan Paul, 1968).

24. Starobinski, "The Gerasene Demoniac," 83.

25. Louis Sass, "The Borderline Personality," *New York Times Magazine*, August 22, 1982, 12ff. The subtitle is revealing: "A new diagnosis of mental illness that is stirring up controversy in psychological circles is a metaphor for our unstable society."

26. Walter Reich, "The World of Soviet Psychiatry," *New York Times Magazine*, January 30, 1983, 25.

27. Rosen, *Madness in Society*, 109. Individualism, far from protecting against mass influences, strips people of the buffers of local, ethnic, and tribal traditions and leaves them exposed to the fads and fashions of mass culture. See Jacques Ellul, *Propaganda* (New York: Vintage Books, 1973).

28. Cited without reference by Denis de Rougemont, *The Devil's Share*, Bollingen Series 2 (New York: Pantheon Books, 1945), 140–41.

29. Referring to Hitler, Jung wrote in 1936, "One man, who is obviously 'possessed,' has infected a whole nation to such an extent that everything is set in motion and has started rolling on its course towards perdition. . . . A god has taken possession of the Germans. . . . A hurricane has broken loose in Germany while we still believe it is fine weather. . . . When it is quiescent, one is no more aware of the archetype Wotan than of a latent epilepsy" ("Wotan," in *Civilization in Transition*, CW 10 [1970], 185–87). Elsewhere Jung speaks of the Nazi debacle as "the first outbreak of epidemic insanity" ("After the Catastrophe" [1945], ibid., 212). On the dreams of his German patients, "The Fight with the Shadow," ibid., 219. H. G. Baynes's *Germany Possessed* (London: Jonathan Cape, 1941) is a superb analysis of Nazism as collective possession. The author's overanalysis of Hitler is irritating at times, but so keen is his insight that he predicted, five years before Hitler's death, that Hitler would, like Nero, be expected to

return after his death (the Hitler *redivivus* myth). In the introduction to Baynes's book, Hermann Rauschning wonders whether perhaps "Hitler is not himself the expression of the shadow-side of our whole civilization" (p. 13).

30. James Hillman, "Anima Mundi: The Return of Soul to the World," *Spring* (1982): 76.

31. "It was as exorcisers that Christians went out into the great world, and *exorcism formed one very powerful method of their mission and propaganda. It was a question not simply of exorcising and vanquishing the demons that dwelt in individuals, but also of purifying all public life from them"* (Adolf von Harnack, *The Mission and Expansion of Christianity in the First Three Centuries* [New York: G. P. Putnam's Sons, 1908], 1:131, italics his). It would appear then that the early Christians clearly perceived the relationship between personal and collective possession, and saw their task as countering both. On the relationship between baptism and exorcism, see Otto Böcher, *Christus Exorcista. Dämonismus und Taufe im Neuen Testament* (Stuttgart: Kohlhammer, 1972), esp. 170–80.

32. Thomas M. Franck and Edward Weisband, cited without reference by William Appleman Williams, *Empire as a Way of Life* (New York and London: Oxford Univ. Press, 1980), ii.

33. Martin Luther King, Jr., "Beyond Vietnam," reprinted in *Sojourners* 12 (January 1983): 12.

34. Ernest Becker, *The Denial of Death* (New York: Free Press, 1973), 133.

35. Carl Jung, "The Psychological Function of Belief in Spirits," *The Structure and Dynamics of the Psyche*, CW 8 (1969), 308–15.

36. Cited by Gordon Rupp, *Principalities & Powers* (Nashville: Abingdon Press, 1952), 24.

37. As told to me by Dr. Raimundo Valenzuela of Santiago, Chile, who was present at the meeting.

38. Peter Berger, "The Devil and the Pornography of Modern Consciousness," *Worldview* 17/12 (1974): 36–37. The quotation appeared in italics in the original.

39. The Shepherd of Hermas (2C) was one of the first to explore naming the negative emotions "demons." He lists quick-temper, evil-speaking, sorrow, unbelief, lust, etc. (*Mand.* 2:2; 5:1, 2, 3, 7; 6:2; 9:9; 10:1; 12:2; *Simil.* 9:23). This attempt to develop a psychology of the spiritual life without owning the projections proved wholly inadequate. Jesus was more astute; he did not ascribe "evil thoughts" to outer demons, but to our own hearts (Mark 7:21–23 par.)—what I am calling the inner personal demonic. Nevertheless there may be cases where a person *is* seized by a "Spirit of Hatred" that goes far beyond the limits of the personal, or a "Spirit of Lust" which has been, at least in part, "caught" from the sexual sickness of our society, itself the result of alienation, loneliness, and the public attitude that people are for consumption. In such a case exorcism might indeed prove helpful.

40. Alfred Romer as quoted in *The Choice Is Always Ours,* ed. Dorothy Berkley Phillips, Elizabeth Boyden Howes, and Lucille M. Nixon (Wheaton, Ill.: Re-Quest Books, 1977), 119.

41. Angelus Silesius, *The Cherubic Wanderer,* trans. Willard R. Trask (New York: Pantheon Books, 1953), 31.

42. Rainer Maria Rilke, *Letters to a Young Poet,* trans. M. D. Herter Norton (New York: W. W. Norton, 1954), 69. One way you can help your own "unclean spirit" might be to write a dialogue with it, having first invoked your own awareness of God's healing

presence by perhaps lighting a candle. Ask your unclean spirit to name itself. Ask what help it needs from you. Offer it your love. Demand its blessing.

For practical guidance in spiritual exercises such as this, see Elizabeth Howes and Sheila Moon, *The Choicemaker* (Wheaton, Ill.: Theosophical Pub. House, 1977).

43. "When we meet a demonic other, it pays to watch carefully how it reacts if we respond with the New Testament counsel to love our enemies. What does this other do with the libido and attention we give it? Does it use this energy to transform itself into a more positive expression? Or does it just swallow and devour this energy and grow fat on it and ask for more? If that is the case, then we can be sure we are feeding a demon. . . . What do we do then? We starve it. We give nothing—no libido, no interest, no attention, no energy, no blood, no warmth, no life. We save all of that for the conscious side" (Ann B. Ulanov, "The Psychological Reality of the Demonic," in Alan M. Olson, *Disguises of the Demonic* [New York: Association Press, 1975], 146–47).

44. M. Scott Peck, *People of the Lie* (New York: Simon & Schuster, 1983), 202. More might be known about possession had scientists early in the century not defined the phenomenon as nonexistent and simply ignored it. One of the greatest scientists of that day, William James, vehemently objected: "The refusal of modern 'enlightenment' to treat possession as a hypothesis to be spoken of as even possible, in spite of the mass of human tradition based on concrete experience in its favor, has always seemed to me to be a curious example of the power of fashion in things scientific" (cited without reference by John Richard, *But Deliver Us From Evil* [London: Darton, Longman & Todd, 1974], 91).

Andrew Canale has pointed out to me that my discussion is not confused enough, because the phenomenon itself is, if it is anything, confusing, and our categories must reflect that fact. There does seem to be something intermediate between the inner personal demonic and the outer personal demonic, something more virulently evil than the personal shadow, and more personal and focused on one individual than the collective shadow projected on a scapegoat. Those who have encountered this aspect of the demonic insist that it seems to exist independently of groups, personalities, or institutions, and that it feels like a real being of some kind. It is important then that my categories be taken purely heuristically, as tentative, preliminary helps toward the long-range task of understanding this phenomenon scientifically. The fact is that everyone who has written on this subject has had to do so from a severely limited data base. Until we have better documentation we will simply continue to flounder about in relative ignorance. Pending the establishment of some such institute as Peck has suggested, St. Luke Health Ministries (4215 Loch Raven Blvd., Baltimore, Md. 21218) has agreed to be a repository for documentation of encounters with the demonic in all its manifestations (including the less dramatic forms). No material should be submitted without the approval of the persons concerned, but without their names, and care should be taken to ensure anonymity. The name and address of the person submitting the data should be included.

45. The disciples did have trouble with one case, that of the "epileptic" boy (Mark 9:14–29 par.).

46. Mark 1:22–28; Luke 4:33–37; Mark 1:34; Luke 4:41; Mark 3:11–12; Matt. 12:15–16; Mark 5:2–8 par.; 9:20.

47. How does mental illness relate to possession? Some have argued that they are the same. See, for example, the exchange between M. J. Sall ("Demon Possession or Psychopathology: A Clinical Differentiation," *Journal of Psychology and Theology* 4 [1976]: 286–90) and Paul J. Bach ("Demon Possession and Psychotherapy: A Theologi-

cal Relationship," ibid., 7 [1979]: 22–26); and Sall's rejoinder (ibid., 27–30). Jesus' exorcisms apparently brought instantaneous relief; the psychoses and neuroses known to us, by contrast, only yield to protracted therapies, if at all. M. Scott Peck believes that possession is qualitatively different from mental illness, due to the palpable evil of the former. He argues that the proper question is not, Is this person possessed or mentally ill? but rather, Is this person just mentally ill, or mentally ill and also possessed? In addition, there are people who have so conformed themselves to the demonism of society that they manifest no symptoms that could bring their possession to light. These Peck dubs "people of the lie" (*People of the Lie,* 192).

Many cultures have distinguished between diseases of the mind and possession. Besides the ancient Greeks, one could cite the Melanesians and the African Ba-Ronga (Oesterreich, *Possession and Exorcism,* 268, 280).

48. The classic study is Oesterreich, *Possession and Exorcism.* See also, besides those previously cited, Morton Kelsey, *Discernment* (New York: Paulist Press, 1978); D. P. Walker, *Unclean Spirits, Possession and Exorcism in France and England in the Late Sixteenth and Early Seventeenth Centuries* (Philadelphia: Univ. of Pennsylvania Press, 1981); and Karl Kertelge, "Jésus, ses miracles et Satan," *Concilium* 103 (1975): 45–53, out of a host of other studies.

49. Jung, "Archaic Man," in *Civilization in Transition,* 2d ed., CW 10 (1970), 67–68, italics mine. Again, "Nothing that is autonomous in the psyche is impersonal or neutral. Impersonality is a category pertaining to consciousness. *All autonomous psychic factors have the character of personality,* from the 'voices' of the insane to the control-spirits of mediums and the visions of the mystics" (Jung, "Mind and Earth," in *Civilization in Transition,* 42, italics mine). Autonomous complexes do appear to "possess" the personality, because they "behave quite independently of the ego, and force upon it a quasi-foreign will" (Jung, "On the Doctrine of Complexes," in *Experimental Researches,* CW 2 [1973], 601–2). There is an enormous number of references to the demonic in Jung's Collected Works, constituting a virtual phenomenology of the demonic. See among others "On the Psychogenesis of Schizophrenia," in *The Psychogenesis of Mental Disease,* CW 3 (1960), 243; *Psychological Types,* CW 6 (1971), 109; *Symbols of Transformation,* CW 5, 2d ed. (1976), 255; "Psychological Aspects of the Mother Archetype," *The Archetypes and the Collective Unconscious,* 105.

50. Lucan, *The Civil War* 6.508ff.

51. The linguist W. J. Samarin has done preliminary work on the problem (*Tongues of Men and Angels* [New York: Macmillan Co., 1972]), with negative results.

52. The prioress who started the whole craze and spread it through the convent by the power of suggestion did so, by her own uncoerced confession in later life, deliberately and spitefully in order to destroy a priest who had spurned her sexual advances. See Aldous Huxley's fascinating account, *The Devils of Loudun* (New York: Harper & Brothers, 1952).

53. This is the judgment of Joseph Crehan, S. J., cited by Richard, *But Deliver Us From Evil,* 70. Huxley, who accepts the reality of some sort of psychic dimension, does not regard it very highly. Mediumistic trances, he writes, simply mean "merging in spirit with every Tom, Dick and Harry of a psychic world, most of whose inhabitants are no nearer to enlightenment than we are, while some may actually be more impenetrable to the Light than the most opaque of incarnate beings" (*The Devils of Loudun,* 73). This judgment is consistent with ancient wisdom as well. Iamblichus (c.

250–c. 330), a Neoplatonist who practiced theurgy, admits that inexperienced practitioners sometimes call up the wrong god, or worse still, one of those evil spirits called *antitheoi* (antigods) (*De myst.* 177.7ff.). He himself is said to have unmasked an alleged Apollo who was in reality only the ghost of a gladiator (Eunapius, *Vit. soph.* 473). False answers are attributed by Synesius to such intrusive spirits who "jump in and occupy the place prepared for a higher being . . ." (*De insomn.* 142A; see E. R. Dodds, *The Greeks and the Irrational* [Berkeley and Los Angeles: Univ. of California Press, 1951], 298).

54. The Bible treats apparent epilepsy as demon-induced (Mark 9:14–29 par.), a diagnosis that Hippocrates (4C B.C.E.) had strenuously opposed centuries before. Anyone who has watched a grand mal seizure will sense the appeal of the demonic interpretation. However, since surgical severance of the corpus callosum in the brain can relieve severe epilepsy, Hippocrates would appear to have been on firmer ground, at least in terms of the *cause*. The *effects* are, of course, "demonic," but how helpful is such a term when the real strides made in winning acceptance for epileptic children in schools have come through treating it simply as a physical problem, and nothing "diabolical" at all? Did the church find epilepsy so hard to heal "by prayer and fasting" (Mark 9:29, "and fasting" being a later addition not attested in the better manuscripts) because it was *not* in fact demonically induced? Jesus for his part simply seems to wait for the seizure to pass (9:20–27). It would be helpful if we had the boy's subsequent medical history.

55. T. K. Oesterreich, "The Genesis and Extinction of Possession," in *Exorcism Through the Ages,* ed. St. Elmo Nauman, Jr. (New York: Philosophical Library, 1974), 134, italics his.

56. One very astute Pentecostal minister told me, "We teach people how to 'act out' possession so that when life-pressures or serious problems well up, they can gain the attention they need and be taken seriously by being exorcised. We teach people who cannot afford therapy and are not verbally gifted how to get help."

57. Oesterreich, *Possession and Exorcism,* 352.

58. Julian Jaynes, *The Origin of Consciousness in the Breakdown of the Bicameral Mind* (Boston: Houghton Mifflin, 1976), 339–60, esp. 348–50.

59. I have found, in reading for and writing this chapter over a period of years, that each time I immerse myself in the subject, spooky, bizarre, unhinging things begin to happen. A friend confided that he had had the same experience while writing a book on the Jonestown mass suicide. He felt himself being physically inundated by an evil force which wanted to control his body and intended to destroy him. Why only *then,* however? Were we not made vulnerable by our very preoccupation with the demonic? For this reason the church warned against too much curiosity into "the deep things of Satan" (Rev. 2:24). Not everyone who enters the abyss returns.

60. Jean Lhermitte, *Diabolical Possession, True and False* (London: Burns & Oates, 1963). See also his "Pseudo-Possession," in *Satan,* ed. P. Bruno de Jesus-Marie, O.C.D. (New York and London: Sheed & Ward, 1951), 280–99.

61. Cited by Henry Ansgar Kelly, *The Devil, Demonology and Witchcraft* (Garden City, N.Y.: Doubleday & Co., 1968), 94. But then, Paris was a major cultural center!

62. Athanasius is representative of the early church's attitude when he says that Christians "chase them [demons] away and mock at their captain the devil" (*De Incarnatione* 53.3–5). Jesus would not allow the demons to speak (Mark 1:22–28; Luke 4:33–37; Mark 1:34; Luke 4:41; Mark 3:11–12; Matt. 12:15–16). This was later reinterpreted by

the early church as a part of the messianic secret, but originally it was probably just sound procedure in exorcism. St. Anthony comments that since Jesus refused to allow demons to speak even when they told the truth, as in confessing him Son of God, or to quote Scripture, "so let us, too, neither listen to them, regarding them as so many strangers, nor pay any attention to them, though they rouse us to prayer and talk about fasting. . . . We must not fear them even though they appear to attack us and to threaten death. In reality, they are weak and can do nothing but threaten" (Athanasius, *The Life of St. Anthony*, trans. Robert T. Meyer [Westminster, Md.: Newman Press, 1950], sections 26–27, pp. 42–43). The seventeenth-century *Rituale Romanum* concurred, adding that the demon should only be allowed to answer essential questions, and by no means be permitted to volunteer information. But many curious exorcists then and now have ignored this advice, with disastrous results, especially during the witch mania, when demons named innocent people in the community as the cause of possession.

One exorcist told me that she had at first asked demons questions. Once a demon threatened to kill both her and her patient, and taunted her that she was not strong enough to get rid of him. God, however, was, and easily. Now she orders the spirits to come out without speaking and with no nonsense, bluffing, displays, or pleas for mercy. She is critical of those who overdramatize the power of demons. "If you expect a show you get one," she says, "If you don't, you don't." Just as Satan is constellated as God's servant or God's enemy by our choices, so also the demons are potentiated or subjugated depending on whether we believe that God is sovereign over them or not.

63. *Ekballō*, "to cast out," is used some thirty-seven times in the Gospels in reference to exorcism.

64. Eduard Schweizer, *The Good News According to Mark* (Richmond: John Knox Press, 1970), 231–33.

65. *Center Peace*, published by the Center on Law and Pacifism, P.O. Box 308, Cokedale, Colo. 81032.

George McClain, in developing a service of exorcism for members of the United Methodist Church, New York Conference, outside the South African embassy in New York City, distinguished these elements:

1. Explicit naming of the institution embracing and possessed by evil.
2. Declaration of its subjection to the power of Jesus Christ.
3. Renunciation of its power over us.
4. Public confrontation with the institution, in which the institution is boldy called from its idolatry to its new vocation (in this case, confrontation involved arrests).
5. Performance of these acts with authority; that is,
   a. believing that power to do this is given by Christ, and
   b. confidence that our prayer and casting out is not just symbolic but will make an objective difference.

The words of exorcism were:

We act today, in the name of Jesus Christ, to break the power of sin and death.

We declare that in Jesus Christ the power of apartheid is broken and in the fullness of time will fall.

We therefore renounce any power that apartheid in South Africa may have over our personal lives, over the United Methodist Church, its agencies and conferences, over our investments or programs, or over our local churches and our ministries within them.

And in the power of the Spirit, we covenant to continue to struggle against apartheid at home and abroad, that the might and glory of God may be manifest among the nations.

66. Natural science offers us analogues of possession, so it is at least neither unnatural nor unscientific to speak this way. Rabies perpetuates itself by inducing a frenzy in its victims that results in biting attacks on others (cows and humans are exceptions to this behavior). Thus one host creates another. And Donald R. Perry recently discovered a killer fungus that releases its spore, or reproductive body, into the humid air of a tropical rain forest. On landing on an insect's body, it bores its way through a weak spot in the animal's shell-like exterior and proliferates inside its body. At some stage the fungus interferes with the nervous system of the insect and it may go berserk before it dies. Sometimes it appears to be frozen in midstride. Soon after, mushrooms emerge from its carcass, and more fungus spores are released to continue the cycle. Perry asks, "Does the fungus, in some quasi-demonic fashion, take over the nervous system of its victim? Mycologists—scientists who study fungi—have noted that most carcasses consumed by this type of fungus are found on vegetation at heights from which released spores are most likely to fall on new prey. They therefore suggest that the fungus causes its victims, before they die, to climb to locations favorable for the dispersal of the fungus' spores!" He concludes, "If the entomogenic fungi do 'possess' the insect mind in this way, the implications are enormous" ("The Creeping Killers," *Science Digest* 92 [February 1984]: 82).

3. THE ANGELS OF
THE CHURCHES

1. William Brownlee, "The Priestly Character of the Church in the Apocalypse," *New Testament Studies* 5 (1958–59): 224–25; Hugh Martin, *The Seven Letters* (Philadelphia: Westminster Press, 1956), 42–43. So also, among others, Theodor Zahn and Johannes Weiss.

2. Nine of the seventy-five uses of *aggelos* in the Book of Revelation occur in reference to the "angels of the churches" in 1:20—3:22. Every other use of the term outside the letters refers explicitly to heavenly agents, as for example 10:1: "Then I saw another mighty angel coming down from heaven, wrapped in a cloud, with a rainbow over his head, and his face was like the sun, and his legs like pillars of fire." Would that we had such bishops! Origen significantly refers to the angels of the churches as their *invisible* bishops (*Hom. on Luke,* 13).

3. Most scholars have rejected the notion of human "messengers." See, e.g., I. T. Beckwith, *The Apocalypse of John* (New York: Macmillan Co., 1913), 445–46; Paul Minear, *I Saw a New Earth* (Washington, D.C.: Corpus Books, 1968), 41. The "angels of the churches" are equivalent to the seven stars in the right hand of the "one like a son of man" (1:16, 20). These angels may also be equivalent to the "seven spirits of God" (3:1). We know from Jewish apocalyptic literature that angels and spirits were often interchangeable. Bishops in the New Testament, on the other hand, are never exalted above the congregation or regarded as an embodiment of it (Gerhard Kittel, "Aggelos," *TDNT* 2 [1964]: 86–87).

4. A treatment of personal guardian angels belongs in this book, but I am not currently capable of doing the theme justice. The value of angels in the transformative proc-

ess has been profoundly treated by Elizabeth B. Howes, "The Living Presences," in *Intersection and Beyond,* vol. 2 (San Francisco: Guild for Psychological Studies Pub. House, 1986). She speaks of the personal angel as the essential bridger of the chasm between the human being in his or her narrower self and the indwelling God of the deeper self, where the message personifies something new arising from the depth of the unconscious.

5. 1 Tim. 5:21 may also allude to the angels of the churches. "In the presence of God and of Christ Jesus and of the elect angels I charge you to keep these rules without favor, doing nothing from partiality." These elect angels seem in some way to have particular concern for the church, and may be those in the heavenly council appointed for their care—which is to say, the angels of the churches.

6. Gregory of Nazianzus, *Or.* 42 ("The care of this Church has been entrusted to an angel. And other angels are in charge of other Churches, as St. John teaches in his Apocalypse"); Origen, *Hom. on Luke,* 23 ("I have no doubt that there are angels in our assembly, too, not only the Church in general, but each church individually"); so also his *Hom. on Luke,* 13; Basil, *Comm. on Isa.*, 1.46; Gregory of Elvira, *Tract.* 16; Hippolytus, *De Antichr.* 59; Eusebius, *Comm. on Ps.* 47; 50. See Jean Daniélou, *The Angels and Their Mission* (Westminster, Md.: Newman Press, 1953), 55–56 for additional references.

7. There are but a few exceptions where plural "yous" are used, and in each case it is because only a *part* of the congregation is being addressed: 2:10 (in part), 13 (in part), 23, 24, 25. Most striking is 2:10—"Do not fear what you [sing.] are about to suffer. Behold, the devil is about to throw some of you [plural] into prison, that you [pl.] may be tested, and for ten days you [pl.] will have tribulation. Be faithful unto death, and I will give you [sing.!] the crown of life." This surprising shift back to the singular suggests that the whole congregation's reward rides on the fidelity of the few. How would it change the way you underwent imprisonment if you knew that not only *your* crown, but that of the whole congregation, depended on your fidelity? How would it affect a congregation's response if it knew that its whole future depended on these suffering few?

8. A vision of the angel of a church would come from the imaginal realm, and could be an authentic apprehension of the church's spirituality, whatever one decides about its metaphysical status.

9. To be sure, every church is under obligation to make known to the world the sovereignty of the God declared by Jesus. But each church addressed in Revelation is given a different task, in light of the specific history and problems it faces. Pergamum is urged simply to hold on in the face of the accelerating hostility of an affronted paganism and its acolytes, and to rid itself of heresy (Rev. 2:12–17). Smyrna faces martyrdom (Rev. 2:8–11). Ephesus has lost its first love (2:1–7). Thyatira is too tolerant of a prophetess whom John castigates for being sympathetic to views previously championed by Paul (2:18–29). Sardis is on the point of death and urged to repent (3:1–6); Philadelphia is the very picture of health and is encouraged to hold fast (3:7–13). And lukewarm Laodicea, utterly self-deceived about its vitality, is in danger of being spewed out of Christ's mouth altogether unless it acknowledges its pitiable, naked state (3:14–22). Each, within the general call to be the church, has its own unique task in each historical moment, and each is addressed accordingly. There is thus no one model of an "obedient" or a "successful" church that applies equally to all. It may be a church's vocation to die on behalf of others. Perhaps another achieves its goal not by resolving conflict but *through*

it. The specific task can only be known, then, by revelation. That poses a real dilemma for those who believe that revelation ceased in the first century.

10. Reported in *Christian Century* 97 (December 10, 1980): 1215. Almost a quarter of the churches studied had fired pastors before.

11. James Hopewell was, at the time of his death, using myths from all cultures to help congregations discover the deep structure of their life together. See his "The Jovial Church: Narrative in Local Church Life," in *Building Effective Ministry,* ed. Carl S. Dudley (San Francisco: Harper & Row, 1983), 68–83; and his forthcoming book, tentatively titled *Congregation* (Philadelphia: Fortress Press).

12. The issue of merger raises the question whether a church can have more than one angel. I am inclined to think not. Like some people, the angel may be extremely complex, or schizophrenic, or possess multiple personalities, but there is still only one collective entity, however fractured. When two congregations merge, however, there is a period when the new congregation is like a two-headed monster. If the merger is successful, they are absorbed into each other and a new angel is produced.

13. "The spiritual vision of the sensible or sensible vision of the spiritual is a vision of the invisible in a concrete form apprehended not by one of the sensory faculties, but by the Active Imagination, which is the organ of theophanic vision" (Henry Corbin *Creative Imagination in the Sufism of Ibn 'Arabi,* Bollingen Series 91 [Princeton, N.J. Princeton Univ. Press, 1969], 145).

14. Origen, *De Oratione* 31.4; *Hom. on Luke,* 23; see Jean Daniélou, *Origen* (New York and London: Sheed & Ward, 1955), 241. In the liturgy of St. John Chrysostom there is a prayer for angelic presence in worship: "O Master, our Lord and our God, who hast established in the heavens orders and hosts of Angels and Archangels for the service of thy glory: grant that thy holy Angels may enter with us here, serving with us, and glorifying us with thy goodness" (in *Eucharistic Prayers from the Ancient Liturgies,* ed. Evelyn Underhill [London: Longmans, Green & Co., 1955], 27). And Gregory of Nazianzus (d. 389), as he was leaving his beloved church in Constantinople, allayed his anxieties for those formerly under his charge by bidding the angel of his church farewell and begging it to see "that there be no hindrance to bar its people on their way to the heavenly Jerusalem" (*Or.* 32; see also Basil, *Ep.* 2.238).

15. "The assumption that the human psyche possesses layers that lie *below* consciousness is not likely to arouse serious opposition. But that there could just as well be layers lying *above* consciousness seems to be a surmise which borders on a *crimen laesae majestatis humanae* [high treason against human nature]. In my experience the conscious mind can claim only a relatively central position and must accept the fact that the unconscious psyche transcends and as it were surrounds it on all sides" (Carl Jung, *Psychology and Alchemy,* CW 12 [1980], 137).

16. Sociologists of business corporations have begun to approach something of a sense of the corporate Gestalt. See for example Terence E. Deal, *Corporate Cultures* (Reading, Mass.: Addison-Wesley Pub. Co., 1982).

17. Eusebius, *Hom. on Eph.,* 1.

18. It is Christ who reveals the reality and vocation of the church, not the angels: "angels have no message because they themselves are the message" (Robert Avens, *The New Gnosis: Heidegger, Hillman, and Angels* [Dallas: Spring Publications, 1984], 46).

In the Fifth Book of Ezra 2:42–47 (Christian, c. 200), Ezra sees a vision of "a young man, tall of stature, towering above all the rest, and he set a crown upon the head of each one of them [the saints] and he waxed ever taller" (*NT Apoc.* 2:695). An angel identifies the young man as Christ. Apparently the more Christians there are who have "conquered," the larger the spirit of Christ grows as a reality to be reckoned with in the world. He is "in heaven," to be sure, but this "heaven" is on Mt. Zion (v. 42), not in the sky. The faithfulness of the church on earth actually augments the spiritual power and presence of the inner spirit that enlivens it.

19. Hence each letter ends by equating Christ with the Spirit who speaks to the churches (2:7, 11, 17, 29; 3:6, 13, 22). John may even equate Christ with the Angel of the Christian Church, since in 1:1 it is an angel who reveals the message, while in 1:10–20 it is Christ.

4. THE ANGELS OF
THE NATIONS

1. Gil Eliot, *Twentieth Century Book of the Dead,* cited by Gordon Zahn, "The Bondage of Liberation," *Fellowship* 43 (June 1977): 6.

2. Rev. 14:6. John uses similar expressions seven times, always in a different word order (5:9; 7:9; 10:11; 11:9; 13:7; 17:15).

3. The data for equating the angels of the nations with the gods of the nations and both with the "sons of God" is given in *Naming the Powers* (26–35) and in chap. 5 of this volume (109–12). Deut. 4:19 had asserted that Yahweh had given the heavenly bodies to be worshiped by the pagans as gods, but they were not autonomous powers. They belonged to the divine council presided over by Yahweh. So the Psalmist sings, "I give thee thanks, O Lord, with my whole heart; before the *gods* I sing thy praise" (Ps. 138:1; the LXX reads "angels," the Hebrew, *elohim,* "gods"). "For who in the skies can be compared to the Lord? Who among the sons of gods is like the Lord, a God feared in the council of the holy ones" (Ps. 89:6–7, RSV marginal reading). See also Pss. 86:8; 95:3; 96:4; 97:7, 9; Exod. 15:11; 22:28 (reading with the LXX "gods" not "God"); Deut. 3:24; I Kings 8:23, etc. At Qumran, 1QM 1; 14; 15; 1QH 12; 15; 4QShirShab; 4Q181; 11QMelch. So also the Targum of Pseudo-Jonathan to Gen. 11:7–8.

4. The translations of the KJV, RSV, and JB are literally correct but confusing, rendering *sar* as "king" or "prince" but not making clear that the heavenly regents or guardian angels of Persia and Greece are meant, as the parallelism with Michael makes clear (also using *sar*). The NEB helpfully translates *sar* as "angel prince" in Dan. 10:13. *Sar* is also used of the angelic commander of the heavenly army of Yahweh in Josh. 5:14.

5. The angels of the nations can be disobedient, vengeful, lazy, and preoccupied (*1 Enoch* 89:51—90:13), and will be judged accordingly (Isa. 24:21–23; 1 Cor. 6:3). See *Naming the Powers,* 29 n. 48; 132 n. 28.

The fact that pagans, or for that matter more recently, Pan-Germanist, Nazi, and national security state ideologues have appealed to the "national soul" in order to justify their geopolitical schemes, no more invalidates the idea of angels of nations than the fact that Latin American dictators insist that they are acting in defense of "Christian civilization" invalidates Christianity. The nation has a soul; various demagogues will naturally try to declare a monopoly on its definition. *They must,* in order to succeed. This makes all the more crucial the prophetic task of unmasking these usurpations of the nation's divine vocation.

6. André Lacocque, *The Book of Daniel* (Atlanta: John Knox Press, 1976), 209.

7. See *Naming the Powers*, 131–40. The War Scroll of Qumran vividly depicts the "war in heaven" that rages alongside earthly war: "On the day when the Kittim fall, there shall be battle and terrible carnage before the God of Israel, for that shall be the day appointed from ancient times for the battle of destruction of the sons of darkness. At that time, *the assembly of gods* and the hosts of men shall battle, causing great carnage; on the day of calamity, the sons of light shall battle with the company of darkness amid the shouts of a mighty multitude and *the clamour of gods and men . . ."* (1QM 1, italics mine). The Kittim (Romans) are explicitly identified as "Satan's host"; Satan is in effect the angel of Rome, just as in Revelation 12—13.

Angels of the nations were a common element in the cosmology of the ancient Roman world for Jews, Christians, and pagans alike. For additional references in the early church writers see Jean Daniélou, *The Angels and Their Mission* (Westminster, Md.: Newman Press, 1953); J. Michl, "Engel IV (Christlich)," *RAC* 1 (1962): 164–65.

8. This is how one general in World War I described morale after a setback: "Influences which have remained mysterious proceeded to spread that state of mind [defeat] from the rear into the army. . . . Towards the end of May, an insidious propaganda crept into the families, the stations, the depots, wherever the service could be reached. . . . The supreme command itself was caught by an uneasiness. It felt itself surrounded by this dull and unseizable ferment which might set tumbling with one single blow the results of such efforts" (cited by Alfred Vagts, *A History of Militarism* [New York: W. W. Norton & Co., 1937], 300).

9. These views on the angels loosely correlate with medieval and modern views of the nature of the state, ranging from those who identified the state with the kingdom of God on earth to those like Hobbes who thought the state a necessary evil rendered indispensable by the even greater evil of human sin, to those of a more liberal temperament who regard the state as capable of relative degrees of good or evil depending on the system and leadership involved, to those who see the state as nothing but a machine for the oppression of one class by another, in the democratic republic no less than in the monarchy (Lenin). Such wide disparities of interpretation result not just from philosophical differences but from where one is located in society in terms of identity, power, and wealth. To ask whether the *angel* of a nation is good or evil, or to ponder whether *states* as such are good or evil, is to ask the same question, posed in the first case from the point of view of the "within" or interiority of the nation, in the second from that of its acts in the world.

10. See Hermann Keyserling's *Europe* (New York: Harcourt, Brace & Co., 1928); idem, *America Set Free* (New York: Harper & Brothers, 1929); idem, *The Travel Diary of a Philosopher* (New York: Harcourt, Brace & Co., 1925); idem, *South American Meditations on Hell and Heaven in Man's Soul* (London: J. Cape, 1932). Keyserling's depictions of national psyches drew the warm approbation of no less a reviewer than Carl Jung (*Civilization in Transition*, CW 10 [1970], 479–501), and several attempts at such depictions by Jung himself (ibid., 502–30 and *Memories, Dreams, Reflections* [New York: Vintage Books, 1965], 238–88). Alexis de Tocqueville's *Democracy in America*, 2 vols. (New York: Alfred A. Knopf, 1945) is a classic. Laurence Durrell's notion of a *Spirit of Place* (New York: E. P. Dutton, 1969) was taken up and elaborated by the biologist René Dubos (*A God Within* [New York: Charles Scribner's Sons, 1972]). See also Andrew H. Malcolm, *The Canadians* (New York: Times Books, 1985); Cyril Fox, *The Personality of Britain: Its Influence on Inhabitant and Invader in Prehistoric*

and Early Historical Times (Cardiff: National Museum of Wales, 1932); and Glyn Daniels, "The Personality of Wales," in *Culture and Environment. Essays in Honour of Sir Cyril Fox* (London: Routledge & Kegan Paul, 1963), 7–23. H. G. Baynes, in *Germany Possessed* (London: Jonathan Cape, 1941), provides an able if at times overdrawn analysis of the spirit of Germany between the wars; and Gregory Bateson's *Steps to an Ecology of Mind* (New York: Ballantine Books, 1972), 88–106, is a groundbreaking attempt to apply insights of cultural anthropology to Western nations.

Esoterics have written extensively on the theme. See, e.g., Alice Bailey's *The Destiny of Nations* (New York: Lucis Publishing Co., 1949); Seyyed Hossein Nasr's summary of Islamic thought on the planets as agents of God governing the climate of various regions which thus give rise to different civilizations (*An Introduction to Islamic Cosmological Doctrines* [Boulder, Colo.: Shambhala, 1978], 88–89); David Spangler's "Conversations with John" (Elgin, Ill: Lorian Press, 1980); Dorothy Maclean's "Nations and Oversouls" (Elgin, Ill.: Lorian Press, 1981); and Adam Bittleston's *Our Spiritual Companions* (Edinburgh: Floris Books, 1980).

Some esoteric writers distinguish between folk angels and national angels, the former pertaining to a unique racial or ethnic group in its interaction with the land, the latter applying to the spirit of what are often quite arbitrary and changeable national entities. The distinction is valid, and has special relevance to Europe or Africa, where folk and national spirits do not coincide. But in the United States or Canada, where the folk spirit virtually died with the extermination or expulsion of the native settlers, a new folk spirit and national spirit have grown up together.

11. The emperor Julian (d. 363) is typical of his age in holding that all peoples possess a distinct character, language, and laws, determined by its presiding spirits. "If some presiding national god, and under him an angel and a demon and a hero and a special class of spirits as subordinates and agents to greater powers, had not established the differences in laws and nations, tell me, whatever else has produced these?" (*Against the Galileans* 143B). The Demiurge "has divided the peoples among various gods, whose business it is to watch over the different nations and cities. Each of these gods rules over the portion that has fallen to him in accordance with his nature. . . Every nation reproduces the national characteristics of the deity ruling it" (ibid., 115D).

12. "If at any time I declare concerning a nation or a kingdom, that I will pluck up and break down and destroy it, and if that nation, concerning which I have spoken, turns from its evil, I will repent of the evil that I intended to do to it. And if at any time I declare concerning a nation or a kingdom that I will build and plant it, and if it does evil in my sight, not listening to my voice, then I will repent of the good which I intended to do to it" (Jer. 18:7–10).

13. Pss. 82:8; 96:7–10; Acts 17:26.

14. Jer. 10:7.

15. Pss. 22:28; 47:8.

16. Pss. 7:8; 9:8–20; 59:5; 110:6; Isa. 2:4; 14:26; 34:2; 60:12; Jer. 1:5, 10; 10:10; 12:17; 25:12, 15–16, 31; 27:8; 46:28; Ezek. 29:12; 30:23; Joel 3:2; Zeph. 3:6; Matt. 25:32; Rev. 19:15.

17. Pss. 67:4–5; 94:10.

18. Pss. 22:27; 67:3; 86:9; 102:15; 117:1; Isa. 2:2–4; 66:18–19; Jer. 3:17; Zech. 2:11; 8:22–23; Rev. 15:4.

19. Martin Buber, "The Gods of the Nations and God," *Israel and the World* (New York: Schocken Books, 1948), 197–213.

20. I am not sure that modern nations are as conscious of their guiding spirit as Buber alleges, but at least the Kingdom of Portugal once was. In the heyday of the Portuguese empire, King Manoel I (1495–1521) petitioned the Pope to sanction the Feast of the Angel of Portugal on the third Sunday in July.

21. Buber, "The Gods of the Nations and God," 200, italics mine. This capacity to evoke hostility by simply existing is nothing new for Judaism. *Test. Levi* 5:6 quotes the archangel Michael (?) as saying, "I am the angel who intercedeth for the nation of Israel that they may not be smitten utterly, for every evil spirit attacketh it" (*APOT*).

22. *Ethnē* in Greek can mean "Gentiles," "heathen," or "nations." For the Greek reader of the New Testament, its ambiguity presented no problem since the context or syntax dictated its proper nuance. Whenever a *racial* distinction is intended, the idea of "non-Jews" prevails (hence "Gentiles," as in Rom. 9:24). Whenever a *religious* distinction is paramount, the translation "heathen" or "pagans" is appropriate (as in 1 Cor. 12:2 or 5:1). When the *political* entity that characterizes a people is implied, "nation" is the correct translation (Acts 28:19). But in a large number of cases, the distinction between racial and political entities is not clear, due to the unique combination of race, religion, and politics in Israel's own life. The *ethnē* are thus "the others," as opposed to Israel. In these cases the translation I have used is "Gentile nations."

23. Gerhard von Rad, *Old Testament Theology* (New York: Harper & Row, 1962), 1:161–65.

24. Contrast this statement by Bishop William R. Cannon in his Episcopal Address to the 1984 General Conference of the United Methodist Church in the U.S.A.: "People alone as individuals can be redeemed, not institutions, structures of society, or forms of government. . . . Neither the United States nor the Soviet Union will exist in heaven. . . . The church is not to be a mirror of the world but a reflection of heaven" (*United Methodist Reporter,* May 4, 1984, 3). We are all too familiar with the kind of social ethic such an attitude fosters.

The same paradoxical or contradictory image of the destruction and yet survival of the nations at the endtime is reflected in *Ps. of Sol.* 17 (1C B.C.E., Jewish), where the "unlawful nations" are destroyed "with the word of his mouth" and shattered "with an iron rod" (17:24), and yet later serve Israel as slaves (17:30) and are treated with compassion (17:34) (*OT Ps.* 2:667–68).

25. William Stringfellow, *An Ethic for Christians and Other Aliens in a Strange Land* (Waco, Tex.: Word Books, 1973), 83–84, 114.

26. Origen, *Comm. on John,* 18.59. In other places Origen declares that Christ's coming has abrogated the rule of the angels over the nations and has placed the nations under his own rule. This led to the reproach by his adversaries that Christians had become "a new race of people without country or tradition, in league against religious and civil institutions" (*Against Celsus* 8.2). The *Epistle to Diognetus* 6.7–8 shows just how far some Christians were willing to carry the sense of having transcended national definition.

27. Origen, *Hom. on Luke,* 12. Here also he says, "Before the birth of Christ these angels could be of little use to those entrusted to them and their attempts were not followed by success." On the whole subject see Jean Daniélou, *The Angels and Their Mission* (Westminster, Md.: Newman Press, 1953), 15ff., 232; and idem, "Les sources juives de la doctrine des anges des nations chez Origène," *Recherches de Science Religieuse* 38 (1951): 132–37.

28. The god Juppiter promises Rome, according to Virgil, "I set no boundary in space

or time; I have granted them dominion, and it has no end. . . . But you, Roman, must remember that you have to guide the nations by your authority, for this is your skill, to teach the ways of peace, to show mercy to the conquered, and to wage war until the haughty are brought low" (*Aeneid* 1.278–79; 6.851ff.). Compare U.S. Senator Albert J. Beveridge's famous "star of Empire" address of 1900: "And just as futile is resistance to the continuance today of the eternal movement of the American people toward the mastery of the world. This is a destiny neither vague nor undesirable. It is definite, splendid and holy" (cited by Robert T. Handy, "The American Messianic Conscious ness: The Concept of the Chosen People and Manifest Destiny," *Review and Expositor* 73 [1976]: 56).

29. Cited by Reinhold Niebuhr, *Moral Man and Immoral Society* (New York: Charles Scribner's Sons, 1932), 105. For a fuller treatment of American messianic imperialism see Ernest Lee Tuveson, *Redeemer Nation* (Chicago/London: Univ. of Chicago Press, 1968); Robert N. Bellah, *The Broken Covenant* (New York: Seabury Press, 1975); Martin Marty, *Righteous Empire* (New York: Dial Press, 1970); Robert Jewett, *The Captain America Complex,* 2d ed. (Philadelphia: Westminster Press, 1984); William Stringfellow, *The Politics of Spirituality* (Philadelphia: Westminster Press, 1984), and John Patrick Diggins, *The Lost Soul of American Politics* (New York: Basic Books, 1984).

30. Andrew Bard Schmookler, *The Parable of the Tribes* (Berkeley and Los Angeles: Univ. of California Press, 1984), his italics. So also Sue Mansfield, *The Gestalts of War* (New York: Dial Press, 1982), chaps. 2–4.

31. Schmookler, *The Parable of the Tribes,* 62.

32. Cited by Stoughton Lynd, *Nonviolence in America: A Documentary History* (Indianapolis: Bobbs-Merrill, 1966), xxx–xxxi.

33. Compare the attitude of Abraham Lincoln:

May we not justly fear that the awful calamity of Civil War, which now desolates the land, may be but a punishment, inflicted on us, for our presumptuous sins, to the needful end of our national reformation as a whole People? We have been the recipients of the choicest bounties of Heaven. We have been preserved, these many years, in peace and prosperity. We have grown in numbers, wealth and power, as no other nation has grown. But we have forgotten God. We have forgotten the gracious hand which preserved us in peace, and multiplied and enriched and strengthened us; and we have vainly imagined, in the deceitfulness of our hearts, that all these blessings were produced by some superior wisdom and virtue of our own. Intoxicated with unbroken success, we have become too self-sufficient to feel the necessity of redeeming and preserving grace, too proud to pray to the God that made us!

It behooves us then, to humble ourselves before the offended Power, to confess our national sins, and to pray for clemency and forgiveness.

(Lincoln's *Works* I:382; VI:156; cited by John Patrick Diggins, *The Lost Soul of American Politics,* 330).

34. Martin Luther King, Jr., "Beyond Vietnam," reprinted in *Sojourners* 12 (January, 1983), 12. The poem by Hughes is from the same speech. In a recent address, James Baldwin concluded an indictment of American racism with this remark: "It is impossible not to love your country. It is possible to disagree with it, to have to leave it, to never make peace with it. But nothing can make it less than my country" (as reported by *The Berkshire Eagle,* April 5 1984, 18).

35. There is also another group that needs to forgive their nation. It is the veterans who fought in the most unpopular war the United States has ever waged—the first war in history to be actively opposed by a significant and finally overwhelming proportion of the citizens of the country waging that war. Having risked their lives, many of them maimed physically and psychologically, these soldiers returned home to disgrace, not honor, shunned by a public that only wanted to forget. Forgiveness by these will be far harder, but even if only for themselves, forgiving must come before healing—and a sense of their own forgiveness—can take place.

36. Martin Luther King, Jr. repeatedly stressed the importance of national loyalty, and not for purely pragmatic reasons. "I oppose the war in Vietnam because I love America," he confessed. "I speak out against it not in anger but with anxiety and sorrow in my heart, and above all with passionate desire to see our beloved country stand as a moral example to the world. I speak out against this war because I am disappointed with America. There can be no great disappointment where there is no great love" ("The Casualties of War," cited by Coleman Barr Brown, "Grounds for American Loyalty in a Prophetic Christian Social Ethic" [diss., Union Theological Seminary, New York, 1979], 162).

37. One actually finds occasional recognition of the soul of the state, as in this statement by J. Sullivan Cox in 1846: "There is a moral sense—a soul in the state, which longs for something more than the tariffs, the bank, and the bankrupt bills of a temporizing present; which looks for some celestial beacon to direct the course of popular movement through the eternal future" (cited by Ernest Lee Tuveson, *Redeemer Nation*, 125). So also more recently Robert N. Bellah: "No one has changed a great nation without appealing to its soul, without stimulating a national idealism" (*The Broken Covenant*, 162).

38. Brown, "Grounds for American Loyalty," 367.

39. Ibid., 147. "*Acceptance* of American identity is a prerequisite to the awful responsibility of effective participation in the American identity conflict. Indeed . . . acceptance of American identity conflict—and full participation in that conflict—is integral to the meaning of social ethical responsibility for Americans" (ibid., 348).

5. THE GODS

1. Carl Jung, *Alchemical Studies*, CW 13 (1968), 37.

2. The early church was as circumspect in appropriating pagan philosophy as it was in rehabilitating the pagan gods. Most Christians of the first two centuries regarded *all* philosophy as intrinsically atheistic (see Col. 2:8), and those few enterprising intellectuals who took the risk of expressing Christian beliefs within the current philosophical traditions were vigorously opposed by most of their colleagues (Robert L. Wilken, *The Christians as the Romans Saw Them* [New Haven, Conn.: Yale Univ. Press, 1984], 78-79).

3. I am following G. B. Caird's helpful discussion in *Principalities and Powers* (Oxford: Clarendon Press, 1956), 2-8.

4. Isa. 40:12-28; 41:21-29; 43:10; 44:6-20; 45:14-17, 20-23; 46:9. Isa. 40:13-14 and 41:28 may even polemicize against the notion of a heavenly council.

5. Jer. 5:7; 10:2-16.

6. Jer. 23:18, 22; see also Isa. 63:9. Ps. 8:5 should probably read, "Yet thou hast

made him little less than gods," since the LXX, Syriac, and Targum translate "angels" here, indicating that the members of the heavenly court were in mind (Gerald Cooke, "The Sons of (the) God(s)," *Zeitschrift für die Neutestamentliche Wissenschaft* 76 [1964]: 22–47. "Sons of" is a widespread Semitic means of classification, meaning "of or pertaining to the following category." "Sons of God" or "sons of gods" thus means merely "those who are of the realm of the gods, who partake of divinity," lesser deities, godlings. Some of Israel's "angels" clearly began their careers as astral gods (see Job 38:7; Isa. 24:21).

7. See also Ps. 89:5–10, where the writer applies to Yahweh the myth of Baal's victory over Chaos and Canaanite imagery of the heavenly council. The Hebrew of v. 6b reads "sons of gods." See also Job 1:6; 2:1; 5:1; 15:15; 38:7; Gen. 6:2; Pss. 86:8 ("There is none like thee among the gods, O Lord"); 96:4–5; 97:7–9; 103:19–22; 135:5; Deut. 3:24; 1 Kings 8:23. Yahweh is "God of gods" also in Pss. 84:7; 136:2; *Apoc. Abr.* 8:3; Bel and the Dragon 7 (LXX). Gods other than Yahweh are frequently acknowledged in the Old Testament (Judg. 11:24; 1 Sam. 26:19–20; 1 Kings 11:5, 7, etc.). Israelite religion assumed that worship of these gods was appropriate for pagans (Deut. 32:8; 4:19), but no Israelite was to do so. As Yehezkel Kaufmann points out, Jonah does not fulminate against the Ninevites for their idolatry but for their violent injustices (3:8); nor is there the slightest hint of disapproval of the sailors praying each to his god (1:5). No law in the Torah forbids belief in pagan gods, or the telling of their myths. Nowhere in Scripture are the pagan gods said to be nonexistent. Indeed, the Israelites seem to have known very little about the surrounding religions, reducing what were rather high religions to fetishistic worship of wood and stone idols (*The Religion of Israel* [Chicago: Univ. of Chicago Press, 1960], 13–17, 129). Kaufmann concludes from this that Israel had no commerce with the gods of paganism at all, but to sustain his case he ignores or understates the data already adduced in this chapter, especially the role of the heavenly council.

8. Cooke, "The Sons of (the) God(s)." The plural of Gen. 1:26 cannot be a "plural of majesty" or "royal 'we' " (referring only to God), unless we interpret that royal "we" as taking in the entire heavenly council. So also Gen. 3:22 would have read "like us" instead of "like one of us" had it referred to God alone. Josephus interprets the "let us" of Gen. 11:7 in a polytheistic sense (*Ant.* 1.118); and the Hebrew of Eccles. 12:1, no doubt alluding back to Gen. 1:26, reads, "Remember your creator*s* (LXX—"Creator") in the days of your youth." George Foot Moore is thus justified in saying, regarding Gen. 1:26, that "Let us make humanity in our image, after our likeness" means that we are not just made in the image of God but of the gods as well—a conclusion not far from John 10:34 (*Judaism* [Cambridge: Harvard Univ. Press, 1962], 1:447).

Hebrew usage of what I would prefer to call the "conciliar 'we' " is paralleled in Ugaritic lore, where Asherah declaims to the assembly of El, "Let us make (N.) king," and in El's decree to the assembly, "Our king is 'Al'iyan Baal; our judge without peer" (Texts 49:I: 20, 26; 51:IV: 43, 44; cited by Frank M. Cross, Jr., "The Council of Yahweh in Second Isaiah," *Journal of Near Eastern Studies* 12 [1953]: 274–77. For the Greeks see Wilken, *Christians as the Romans Saw Them*, 180).

9. Kaufmann, *The Religion of Israel*, 21–59.

10. Norman Gottwald's designation (*The Tribes of Yahweh: A Sociology of the Religion of Liberated Israel 1250–1050 B.C.E.* [Maryknoll, N.Y.: Orbis Books, 1979], 679).

Neither term is quite right. What Israel had in effect was henotheism in international relations (Yahweh is God of Gods) and mono-Yahwism in its internal life (Thou shalt worship Yahweh your God; him only shall you serve). "Henotheism" means "one (*heis*) god," specifically, belief in one supreme God over other gods. "Monolatry," which implies that only one God is accorded worship (*latreia*), though others may be acknowledged as existing, is also a valid designation.

11. B. W. Anderson, "Hosts, Host of Heaven," *IBD* 2:655–56. Cooke ("The Sons of [the] God[s]") demonstrates that this concept of divine beings in Yahweh's heavenly council is to be found in all periods of Israel's history. It also appears frequently at Qumran. See, e.g., 1QM 1 (The "assembly of gods" = the heavenly hosts); hence God is "God of gods," 1QM 14. See also 1QM 15; 18; 1QH 12; 15; 1QShirShab; 4Q181 (the elect will be rewarded by being "counted with Him in the community of the gods as a congregation of holiness in service for eternal life and [sharing] the lot of His holy ones"); 11QMelch (where Melchizedek is referred to as *elohim*—not a proper name so much as a generic category, "divine being"—who takes "his place in the divine council: in the midst of the gods he holds judgment"). The same usage is continuous with other Jewish writings of the period, such as the addition to Daniel, "Song of Three Children" ("Bless the God of gods," line 68), and repeatedly in Philo (for example, *De dec.* 64; *De spec. leg.* I.13–20; 307). Artapanus (3–2C B.C.E.) daringly depicts Moses as the teacher of Orpheus, as the founder of Egyptian animal-god cults, and as worthy of god-like honor by identification with Hermes (Eusebius, *Praep. Evang.* 9.27.4, 6; *OT Ps.* 2:898–99). Synagogue worship continued the language of the Psalms; God is "King of the gods" and "God of holy ones" (Hellenistic Synagogal Prayers from Book Seven of the *Apostolic Constitutions* 7.33.2 and 7.35.9 [*OT Ps.* 2:677, 681]). *Pseudo-Phocylides,* despite the evasions of his modern editor (*OT Ps.* 2:574–82), refers to the heavenly bodies and to deceased people as gods (71, 75, 104, 162), though he does deny that eros is a god (194) (1C B.C.E.–1C C.E.). See also *The Sentences of the Syrian Menander* 263–64 (*OT Ps.* 2:599, Jewish, 3C C.E.?).

12. See also Mic. 4:5, which should be translated as future in both clauses: "For all the peoples *will* walk each in the name of its god, but we *will* walk in the name of the Lord our God for ever and ever." Since the context is eschatological, this suggests that the appointment of gods over the nations is not a temporary or evil expedient but a permanent aspect of the divine economy.

13. Origen interpreted this verse as forbidding Christians to blaspheme or desecrate pagan statues or temples (*Against Celsus* 8.38). Rom. 2:22 implies that Jews and Christians alike were enjoined from damaging or robbing temples (R. P. C. Hanson, "The Christian Attitude to Pagan Religions up to the Time of Constantine the Great," *ANRW* II.23.2 [1980]: 951).

14. The LXX translates "sons of God(s)" by "angels" in Pss. 8:5; 97:7; 138:1. The Targum of Job at Qumran (column xxx, line 5, Job 38:7) does the same.

15. Philo, *De gig.* 6.16. See *De fuga* 212: "Angels are God's household-servants, and are deemed gods by those whose existence is still one of toil and bondage." Also, *De spec. leg.* I.13–20.

16. The Orphics had already distinguished between "good" and "evil" *daimones* (Werner Foerster, "Daimon," *TDNT* 2 [1964]: 3), but this pertained not to their nature so much as their specific mission. They were judged good or evil in terms of what they

brought to humanity. Later pagan writers (e.g., Porphyry, 3C C.E.) developed the evil aspect of the *daimones,* in response to the general spirit of the age, but on the whole the ambivalence of the daimons was maintained in the Greek milieu.

17. Henry Ansgar Kelly, *The Devil, Demonology and Witchcraft* (Garden City, N.Y.: Doubleday & Co., 1968), 12–13.

18. *1 Enoch* 19:1 (fallen angels lead people astray "into sacrificing to demons as gods"); see also 99:7; *Jub.* 1:11; 22:17 ("they worship evil spirits"). The Jews may have taken the idea from Persian religion; the demotion of other gods to the status of angels or demons had already been hit upon by Zoroastrianism as early as 600 B.C.E. (Jeffrey Burton Russell, *The Devil: The Perception of Evil from Antiquity to Primitive Christianity* [Ithaca, N.Y.: Cornell Univ. Press, 1977], 105).

19. Hans Conzelmann, *1 Corinthians,* Hermeneia (Philadelphia: Fortress Press, 1975), 142.

20. In Gal. 4:8 Paul expressly denies the *divinity* of the gods ("you were in bondage to beings that by nature are no gods") but acknowledges their reality as powers capable of holding people in bondage. They are creatures, indeed even weak and beggarly elements (4:9), and therefore unworthy of worship and impotent before the liberating power of the one true God. But here, as we shall see in the next chapter, Paul is explicitly referring to the "elements of the universe," which in this context he identifies as Jewish and Gentile religious rules, rituals, and practices. They are *not* gods in essence, but have been inappropriately granted an ultimacy they do not deserve.

21. Here Paul seems to be combining the Greek and Palestinian views of demons into one. The gods are *daimones* insofar as they are pagan gods, and they are "demons" insofar as they enslave their devotees and separate them from God.

22. F. C. Conybeare, "The Demonology of the New Testament," *Jewish Quarterly Review* 8/9 (1896/97): 608. See for example, Tertullian, *Apology* 23; Justin, *1 Apol.* 5.64; *Dial.* 30.

23. W. Kern, S. J., "Die antizipierte Entideologisierung oder die 'Weltelemente' des Galater-und Kolosserbriefes Heute," *Zeitschrift für Katholische Theologie* 96 (1974): 200ff.

24. Vv. 15, 17, 23, 27, 55. See also Isa. 40:18–20; 44:6–20; 46:1–7; Wisd. of Sol. 13—14; Bel; Jos., *Ant.* 10.50.

25. "The god himself was a statue. The statue was not *of* a god (as we would say) but the god himself" (Julian Jaynes, *The Origin of Consciousness in the Breakdown of the Bicameral Mind* [Boston: Houghton Mifflin, 1976], 178). As this immediacy of symbol and god began to collapse, due to the rise of personal consciousness, rites were developed to attempt to imprison the souls of *daimones* or angels in statues with the help of herbs, gems, and odors, so that the statue might speak and prophesy. And for some it seems to have worked; in Rome, Nero prized a statue which warned him of conspiracies (Suetonius, *Nero* 56).

26. Maximus Tyrius 8.10; cited by W. R. Halliday, *The Pagan Background of Christianity* (Liverpool: Liverpool Univ. Press, 1955), 7–8. Celsus condemned Christian polemic against idols as ludicrous. "If they [Christians] merely mean that the stone, wood, brass, or gold which has been wrought by this or that workman cannot be a god, they are ridiculous. . . . For who, unless he be utterly childish in his simplicity, can take these for gods, and not for offerings consecrated to the service of the gods, or images representing them?" (in Origen, *Against Celsus* 7.62 [*ANF* 4:636]).

27. Cited by Photius, *Bibl.* 215. For a general discussion, E. R. Dodds, *The Greeks and the Irrational* (Berkeley and Los Angeles: Univ. of California Press, 1951), 292–95 and 306 n. 87.

28. Campbell Bonner, "Religious Feeling in Later Paganism," *Harvard Theological Review* 30 (1937): 139. The worship of images disturbed even such pagans as Heraclitus of Ephesus, Zeno, Chrysippus, Varro, and Porphyry (R. P. C. Hanson, "The Christian Attitude," 911–12). Christianity rode to political power on the backs of the "Christian" emperors, it is true, but it did not consolidate that power through anything like the persecutions from which it itself had emerged incalculably strengthened. Polytheism produced few martyrs, and was not annealed, purified, or revitalized by being marginalized. It simply collapsed, despite the last-ditch efforts of the Emperor Julian, or the evangelical entreaties of Aelius Aristides, or the fact that it held a monopoly on virtually all the religious real estate of the entire Mediterranean basin.

29. James M. Fennelly, "The Primitive Christian Values of Salvation and Patterns of Conversion," in *Man and His Salvation*, ed. Eric J. Sharpe and John R. Hinnells (Manchester: Manchester Univ. Press, 1973), 117–118.

30. Hermann Kleinknecht, "Theos," *TDNT* 3 (1965): 67.

31. Ibid., 68.

32. "Now it is an axiom of psychology that when a part of the psyche is split off from consciousness it is only *apparently* inactivated; in actual fact it brings about a possession of the personality, with the result that the individual's aims are falsified in the interests of the split-off part" (Carl Jung, "The Psychology of the Child Archetype," *The Archetypes and the Collective Unconscious*, CW 9/1 [1971], 164).

33. Cited by Norman Cohn, *Europe's Inner Demons* (New York: New American Library, 1975), 68–71.

34. Jung, *Alchemical Studies*, 37.

35. Euripides, *Bacchae*. This is a translator's reconstruction of the lacuna at line 1329; I have been unable to discover whose. It is, however, consistent with and a summary of the entire play.

36. Jung, "Concerning the Archetypes and the Anima Concept," *The Archetypes and the Collective Unconscious*, 66, 58.

37. Ibid., 48; "Psychological Aspects of the Mother Archetype," ibid., 79–80. Rupert Sheldrake's theory of morphogenetic fields may prove to be a more persuasive explanation of the transmission of archetypes than is Jung's appeal to the "germplasm" (now called DNA). See *A New Science of Life* (Los Angeles: J. P. Tarcher, 1981), 28–29.

38. Jung, "General Aspects of Psychoanalysis," in *Freud and Psychoanalysis*, CW 4 (1961), 232. Philo was apparently the first to use "archetypes" for the Platonic "ideas." Once he speaks of them as having been falsely deified by pagans and worshiped as gods (*De conf.* 172–73). Generally, however, he regards them as an aspect of the creative Logos. Augustine seems to equate gods, angels, and Platonic ideas in *The City of God* 10.1.

39. Jung, *Symbols of Transformation*, CW 5 (1970), 64; Ira Progoff, *Jung's Psychology and Its Social Meaning* (Garden City, N.Y.: Doubleday & Co., Anchor Books, 1973), 182. To head off any misunderstanding let me emphasize that God, the gods, and the spiritual realities generally are not merely functions of our psyches. They are both inner and outer realities. But they can only be known through the psyche; indeed, nothing can be known by us except through the psyche. The fact that the *ways* in which the

psyche makes these realities known to us can now to some extent be understood does not mean that the divine has been "reduced" to an aspect of the psyche. Quite the contrary, the psyche is merely the channel through which revelation in all its forms is mediated.

40. Progoff, *Jung's Psychology,* 186ff.

41. Jung, "The Concept of the Collective Unconscious," 44; idem, *Aion,* CW 9/2 (1979), 179.

42. The unconscious is naturally polytheistic, and mythology draws heavily from its images. Since the integration of opposite energies in the self is frequently symbolized in dreams by incestuous intercourse between mother and son, father and daughter, brother and sister, it was inevitable that this conjunction of the opposites be depicted thus in mythology as well. Rationalists and moralists were scandalized at the prurient behavior of the gods, and indeed it was scandalous, if literalized and read as a model for human imitation. The mistake lay in wrenching the stories out of their proper domain as symbols of unconscious processes.

43. Jacob is a good case in point, for he does not know how to name his assailant. Is it a "man" (Gen. 32:24), or a spirit of the ford (according to some scholars, the earliest form of the tradition), or an angel (Hos. 12:4), or God (Gen. 32:30)? Perhaps the blessing cannot be gained until we are able to see the assault of the god/angel/*daimōn* as somehow *sent by God,* necessary for the integration of the self. See my "On Wrestling with God: Using Psychological Insights in Biblical Study," *Religion in Life* 47 (1978): 136–47.

44. Curtis Bennett, *God As Form* (Albany: State Univ. of New York Press, 1976). It is incomprehensible to me that Bennett could have written this work without reference to the work of Jung or Hillman.

45. Bennett, *God As Form,* 31.

46. Kern, "Die antizipierte Entideologisierung," 204.

47. See Rainer Maria Rilke, "The Sonnets to Orpheus," first series, no. 5, in *Duino Elegies and the Sonnets to Orpheus,* trans. A. Paulin, Jr. (Boston: Houghton Mifflin, 1977), 93. In the original the pronouns are masculine.

48. Homer, *Odyssey* 4.260–61.

49. Jung, "The Archetypes of the Collective Unconscious," in *The Archetypes and the Collective Unconscious,* 30.

50. The earliest document that I have found (excluding Gnostic writings) is the twelfth-century Jewish *Zohar,* which speaks of "gladly carrying out the religious duty to have conjugal intercourse before the Presence" (I.49b; III.81a; in *Zohar,* ed. by G. G. Scholem [New York: Schocken Books, 1971], 35–37, 115–16).

51. Ephraem (306–73) listed the gods as the first of the ranks of heavenly hosts: (1) gods, thrones, dominions; (2) archangels, principalities, authorities; (3) angels, powers, cherubim, seraphim (*Op. Syr.* [Rome, 1737] I, p. 270 [on Deut. 1:13]).

52. Paul Ricoeur's remarks on this subject are still an unmined treasure of insights for the question of religious pluralism (*The Symbolism of Evil* [New York: Harper & Row, 1967], 248, 308–30).

53. James Hopewell has demonstrated the utility of Greek myths in helping congregations discover the mythic story that has dominated and determined their own corporate life. See Hopewell, "The Jovial Church: Narrative in Local Church Life," in *Building Effective Ministry,* ed. Carl S. Dudley (San Francisco: Harper & Row, 1983), 68–83.

54. Schmookler, *The Parable of the Tribes*, 97.

55. 1 Cor. 8:5-6; Gal. 4:9 (au. trans.).

56. Rom 1:23; see Acts 7:40-43; 12:22-23; 14:11-18; 17:23; 28:6. How can we explain Acts 19, where the message of Paul, with its sexual restraint and disciplined life, was able to eclipse the worship of Artemis, with its sexual permissiveness, its affirmation of nature, and its awesome image of Artemis herself, with her sixteen breasts? Jung's view is that people inundated by the unconsciousness of paganism turned in desperation to Christianity's one-sided spiritualism in order to break the bondage that the gods exercised over their lives. This flight from the world and nature successfully allowed Christian civilization to build up an inner, spiritual world which could sustain the onslaught of sensory experience. This conquest of the world of the senses brought to birth the peculiarly abstract quality of Western thinking, in which thought was unfettered from the emotional effect of sense impressions. This would lead in time to a new and independent relationship with nature. With the collapse of Christendom, the world would finally be deprived not only of its gods but its soul as well (Jung, *Symbols of Transformation*, 74-78).

57. Murray Stein, "Hephaistos: A Pattern of Introversion," in *Facing the Gods*, James Hillman et al. (Irving, Tex.: Spring Publications, 1980), 84-85. It is as a clinical psychiatrist and not as a speculative philosopher that Jung speaks when he says, "It must be reckoned a psychic catastrophe when the *ego is assimilated by the self*" (*Aion*, CW 9/2 [1979], 24, his italics).

58. Jung, "Psychological Aspects of the Mother Archetype," 103-4. The proponents of a "new" polytheism have not, it seems to me, taken sufficient account of the dangers. It is sobering to recall that the two great prophets of a return of the gods—Hölderlin and Nietzsche—were possessed by them and driven mad. The new polytheism has the unbalanced quality of a compensation, a pendulum swing. But writers such as James Hillman have done a great service in identifying the contemporary presences of the gods. See, among his many works, *Archetypal Psychology* (Irving, Tex.: Spring Publications, 1983), and his frequent articles in the journal *Spring*. David L. Miller's *The New Polytheism* (Irving, Tex.: Spring Publications, 1981) and his *Christs* (New York: Seabury Press, 1981) also explore polytheism, with very little acknowledgment of the hazards involved when moderns, wholly unprotected by the rituals, myths, and supports of the old city-state cultus, dabble with the gods. His more recent article in *Facing the Gods*, "Red Riding Hood and Grand Mother Rhea: Images in a Psychology of Inflation," 87-99, shows more awareness. Curtis Bennett, in *God As Form*, seems to take an almost fatalistic view toward compulsion by the gods. They cannot be resisted, even when one's will is set against them. One can only succumb (45-46). No wonder pagans fled to Christianity! Other writers on the new polytheism include Charles E. Scott, "On Hillman and Calvin: The Gods Formed a Circle Around the One True God and Danced. Then They Fought and Did Many Other Things," *Soundings* 63 (1980): 61-73; and Edward C. Whitmont, *Return of the Goddess* (New York: Crossroad, 1984), who warns against using the goddess archetype to rationalize magical regression. The most sensible, careful and sober treatment of the contemporary role of the gods I have seen is Jean Shinoda Bolen, M. D., *Goddesses in Everywoman* (San Francisco: Harper & Row, 1984), who identifies seven feminine archetypes and offers wise guidance for learning from them.

59. Hans-Ruedi Weber, *Experiments with Bible Study* (Geneva: World Council of

Churches, 1981), 22–23. Jewish mysticism sought to protect the aspirant by describing the hostility of the angels to humans attempting to ascend to the divine throne. This hostility was in fact a divine service, intended to protect the holy against profanation. In Gnosticism this motif degenerated into the idea that the archons guarding the portals of the seven heavens are evil and opposed to God (Ithamar Gruenwald, *Apocalyptic and Merkavah Mysticism* [Leiden: E. J. Brill, 1980], 89). Behind both conceptions, but increasingly lost as the image declined into intellectualized dogma, was the very real mystical experience of the numinosity of the archetypes and their actual destructive capacities when related to without adequate awareness.

6. THE ELEMENTS OF
THE UNIVERSE

1. This chapter builds on the analysis provided in *Naming the Powers*, 67–77. For a justification of the definition given here, and for detailed exegesis of the relevant New Testament texts, see that earlier discussion.

2. William Hoffer, "A Magic Ratio Recurs Throughout Art and Nature," *Smithsonian* 6 (December 1975): 110–12. Wolf Strache's *Forms and Patterns in Nature* (New York: Pantheon Books, 1973) uses the photographic essay to document the way the same designs and patterns are repeated in nature. Marie-Louise von Franz adduces other examples, and postulates that the natural integers are the archetypal patterns that regulate the unitary realm of psyche and matter (*Number and Time,* trans. Andrea Dykes [Evanston, Ill.: Northwestern Univ. Press, 1974]). See also Tobias Dantzig, *Number: The Language of Science,* 4th ed. (London: George Allen & Unwin, 1962); and H. E. Huntley, *The Divine Proportion. A Study in Mathematical Beauty* (New York: Dover, 1970).

3. I have adapted this image from Ralph Wendell Burhoe, "Introduction to the Symposium on Science and Human Values," *Zygon* 6 (1971): 98 n. 30. In Paul's day the elements most idolatrously overestimated were the fundamental structures of religion, such as rituals, rites, traditions, and laws, Jewish and pagan alike (Gal. 4:3, 9; Col 2:20), though Paul clearly perceived the threat of a religious philosophy that posited ultimacy in the most basic constituents of nature as well (Col. 2:8, 10). Our situation today is just the reverse. While many people continue "holding the form of religion but denying the power of it" (2 Tim. 3:5), the greater idolatry is instanced by modern science, with its cryptoreligious grail-quest for the ultimate particle. In this chapter we will focus on idolatry in science while acknowledging the continuing need to combat it in religion.

4. Ralph Wendell Burhoe, "Natural Selection and God," *Zygon* 7 (1972): 60, italics mine.

5. Ralph Wendell Burhoe, "The Phenomenon of Religion Seen Scientifically," in *Changing Perspectives in the Scientific Study of Religion,* ed. Allan W. Eister (New York: John Wiley & Sons, 1974), 32. While I would argue that the gods were a great deal more than just unknown forces of nature (see chap. 5), I believe that Burhoe is correct insofar as the gods of which he speaks participated in natural events.

6. E. E. Von Bount, M. D. Shepherd, V. R. Wall, W. P. Ganong, and M. T. Clegg, "Penetration of Light into the Brain of Mammals," *Annals of the New York Academy of Sciences* 117 (1964): 217–24, cited by Robert E. Ornstein, *The Psychology of Consciousness* (New York: Viking Press, 1972), 212. On color, Lindsey Gruson, "Color Has Powerful Effect on Behavior, Researchers Assert," *New York Times,* October 19, 1982, Cl.

7. Pazuzu, the southwest wind in Babylon that brings malarial mosquitos from the marshes, was depicted with a monstrous head with a goat's horns atop a naked, emaciated human's body. Four wings and the claws of a beast of prey indicate the speed with which it dives down on its victims, plunging sharp nails into their flesh. "I am Pazuzu, son of Hanpa," says the inscription, "king of the evil spirits of the air. I swoop with violence from the mountains, spreading fever as I go." True, the Babylonians were unable to identify the physical cause of their malady, but they certainly described its effects accurately. Cited by Henry Ansgar Kelly, *The Devil, Demonology and Witchcraft* (Garden City, N.Y.: Doubleday & Co., 1968), 4.

8. Ornstein, *Psychology of Consciousness,* 213–16. See especially A. P. Krueger, "Preliminary Consideration of the Biological Significance of Air Ions," in *The Nature of Human Consciousness,* ed. Robert E. Ornstein (San Francisco: W. H. Freeman & Co., 1973), 408–20. Gravity is also suspected of having an effect on psychological states through physiological structure (David Sobel, "Gravity and Structural Integration," in Ornstein, ibid., 397–407).

9. John A. Eddy, "The Case of the Missing Sunspots," *Scientific American* 236 (May 1977): 80–92; Robert H. Dicke, "Solar Luminosity and the Sunspot Cycle," *Nature* 280 (July 5, 1979): 24–27. S. R. C. Malin and B. J. Srivastava have established a correlation between changes in the sun's magnetic field and the incidence of heart attacks (*Nature* 277 [February 22, 1979]: 646–48).

10. There is no evidence that the stars or planets were called *stoicheia* prior to the third century c.e. (*Test. Sol.* 8:1–4; 18:1). The power-term used for the heavenly bodies was instead *dynameis* ("powers"), and each was set under the authority of a guardian (*archōn*). See *Naming the Powers,* 162–63. Hence the frequent identification of the New Testament *stoicheia* with "astral spirits" is completely unwarranted. For further discussion of astrology see my article, "The 'Elements of the Universe' in Biblical and Scientific Perspective," *Zygon* 13 (1978): 238–40; Franz Cumont, *Astrology and Religion Among the Greeks and Romans* (New York: G. P. Putnam's Sons, 1912); and Clinton V. Morrison, *The Powers That Be* (London: SCM Press, 1960), 77–80.

11. Clement of Alexandria, *Exhortation to the Greeks* 5, trans. G. W. Butterworth (LCL). This statement by the pagan Albinus is characteristic of his whole epoch: "There are other divinities, some for all the elements: there are some in the aether, some in fire, some in the air and others in water. These divinities have been given sway over all sublunary things, all things on earth" (*Ep.* 15.7). Jews and Christians simply changed "divinities" to "angels" and affirmed the same thing. See for example Origen: "There are angels in charge of everything, of earth, water, air and fire: all the elements alike" (*Hom. on Jer.,* 10.6; see also *Hom. on Num.,* 14.2; Athenagoras, *Apol.* 10).

12. Even when Aristotle rejected the four physical elements as the first principles of the universe, he substituted a different quaternity: hot and cold, dryness and moisture (see *Naming the Powers,* 74 n. 81).

13. Jung, "Psychology and Religion," in *Psychology and Religion: West and East,* CW 11 (1977), 54–57. For a fuller discussion of quaternity, see "A Psychological Approach to the Doctrine of the Trinity," ibid., 107–200.

14. Jung, *Psychology and Alchemy,* CW 12 (1980), 245.

15. Jung, *Symbols of Transformation,* CW 5 (1976), 76.

16. Ibid., 77.

17. John Davy, "Man and the Underworld," in *The Golden Blade* 32 (1980): 55–56. I have found much to ponder in this essay, even where it goes beyond what I can readily

assent to.

18. Morris Berman, *The Reenchantment of the World* (Toronto: Bantam Books, 1984), 255.

19. Davy, "Man and the Underworld," 55–56; Jung, *Psychology and Alchemy*, 304.

20. Cited by Jung, *Psychology and Alchemy*, 246, 270–71. Douglas Sloan, though appreciative of attempts by physicists like Fritjof Capra to reconcile science with Eastern spirituality, notes that the attempt is made without any fundamental critique of physics as we know it. Physics is accepted as instrumental and quantitative; Eastern spirituality "is dragged down to a lower level, deprived of its own inner identity, and ends up lending sanction and support to a Western science that goes on its way unchallenged and unchanged." This is a kind of cultural strip mining, in which selective aspects of Eastern thought are appropriated to legitimate Western science and provide it with much-needed depth. The scientist is only required to broaden his or her perspectives, not to undergo arduous and unremitting personal purification and transformation, *as all Eastern traditions demand.* Nor is it clear why Capra chose to compare the energy patterns of modern physics with the nirvanic harmonies of Buddhism rather than with the forty thousand hells of the Mahayana doctrine. "The latter would seem, on the face of things, to be more descriptive of the chief products of modern physics . . . atomic bombs and an exceedingly poisonous substance, plutonium, perhaps more aptly named than has been recognized, after the god of death and the underworld" (*Insight—Imagination. The Emancipation of Thought and the Modern World* [Westport, Conn. and London: Greenwood Press, 1983], 135–38 n. 53).

21. Diogenes Laertius 10.139.

22. Berman, *The Reenchantment of the World*, 3, 18, 105, 118, 124, 152.

23. Cited by Marshall McLuhan and Barrington Nevitt, *The Executive as Dropout* (New York: Harcourt Brace Jovanovich, 1972), 108.

24. "That there is something beyond the borderline, beyond the frontiers of knowledge, is shown by the archetypes and, most clearly of all, by numbers, which this side of the border are quantities but on the other side are autonomous psychic entities, capable of making qualitative statements which manifest themselves in *a priori* patterns of order" (Jung, "Flying Saucers: A Modern Myth," in *Civilization in Transition*, 410–11).

25. Ernest Gellner's humor puts it all in perspective. No Puritan could have been closer to the thought of sin, he says, no Victorian more intimately and pervasively embattled with the idea of sex, than were these thinkers with the idea of *nonsense*. It is not perhaps an unworthy preoccupation, "but why is it so persistent? Why—and this is the crucial question—do they feel the danger of falling into nonsense to be so pervasive, so close, so haunting, and the goal of speaking sense to be so enormously desirable, so very difficult to achieve? Why do they not, like earlier generations, treat talking sense as the natural and secure birthright of sane men of good faith and sound training, and the talking of nonsense as a real but not very significant danger, like slipping on a banana skin?" ("The Crisis in the Humanities and the Mainstream of Philosophy," in *The Devil in Modern Philosophy*, ed. I. C. Jarvie and Joseph Agassi [Boston: Routledge & Kegan Paul, 1974], 17–18).

26. *The Education of Henry Adams* (Boston: Houghton Mifflin Co., 1906). For a deft critique of the misuse of the second law in "scientific mythologies" see Stephen Toulmin, *The Return to Cosmology* (Berkeley and Los Angeles: Univ. of California Press, 1982), 33–49.

27. Jacques Monod, *Chance and Necessity* (New York: Vintage Books, 1972); John A. Miles, Jr., "Jacques Monod and the Cure of Souls," *Zygon* 9 (1974): 33–34; Toulmin, *Return to Cosmology*, 140–55.

28. Theoretical physicist David Bohm remarks, *"Nature will respond in accordance with the theory with which it is approached.* Thus, in ancient times, men thought plagues were inevitable, and this thought helped make them behave in such a way as to propagate the conditions responsible for their spread. With modern scientific forms of insights man's behaviour is such that he ceases the insanitary modes of life responsible for spreading plagues and thus they are no longer inevitable" (*Wholeness and the Implicate Order* [London: ARK Paperbacks, 1983], 6, italics mine).

29. Conversations with David Spangler and Dorothy Maclean.

30. White Eagle, *Spiritual Unfoldment* II (Hampshire, England: White Eagle Publishing Trust, [1969] 1981), 67, 78–79.

31. Ibid., 73, 62. The earliest text I know that personifies the elements is Joannes Stobaeus's fifth-century *Ecl.* I.403, 9–405, 25, where the elements are displeased with human beings and petition God against them (Gerhard Delling, "Stoicheō-stoicheion," *TDNT* 7 [1971]: 676).

32. Mathew Fox, "Creation-Centered Spirituality from Hildegard of Bingen to Julian of Norwich," in *Cry of the Environment,* ed. Philip N. Joranson and Ken Butigan (Santa Fe: Bear & Co., 1984), 101; and Gregory Bateson, *Steps to an Ecology of Mind* (New York: Ballantine Books, 1972), 434. Just as the human race was judged by the element water in the days of Noah, so tradition warns that it will be judged by the element fire in the time to come (2 Peter 3:10, 12).

33. Cited by Brian Easlea, *Liberation and the Aims of Science* (Totowa, N.J.: Rowman & Littlefield, 1973), 255.

34. Arthur Koestler, *The Ghost in the Machine* (New York: Macmillan Co., 1968), 17.

35. See Arthur Koestler and J. R. Smythies, *Beyond Reductionism: New Perspectives in the Life Sciences* (New York: Macmillan Co., 1969), especially the chapters by Ludwig von Bertalanffy and Victor Frankl; Ludwig von Bertalanffy, *General System Theory* (New York: George Braziller, 1968); David Bakan, "Idolatry in Religion and Science," in *On Method* (San Francisco: Jossey-Bass, 1967); and A. R. Peacocke, *Creation and the World of Science* (Oxford: Clarendon Press, 1979), chap. 2.

36. Roger S. Jones, *Physics as Metaphor* (New York: New American Library, 1982), 115–16; Berman, *The Reenchantment of the World,* 324–25 n. 14. Even if physicists finally were to succeed in discovering "the ultimate material, the final stuff from which all the complexity of existence emerges," in Heinz R. Pagels's awestruck terms (*The Cosmic Code* [New York: Simon & Schuster, 1982], 251), that would still not provide what scientists went looking for—the basis for a totally reductionist explanation of the universe in materialistic terms. For there is no reason why the morphogenetic fields of atoms should be considered to have a privileged position in the order of nature; they are simply the fields of morphic units at one particular level of complexity (Rupert Sheldrake, *A New Science of Life* [Los Angeles: J. P. Tarcher, 1981], 85). Besides, as Paul Davies argues, none of the subatomic particles are really particles in the common meaning of the term; they are *levels of description.* They may not even be "things" at all. Looked at non-reductionistically, in reference to the shroud of energy surrounding them, we must finally regard every particle as somehow made up of every other particle in

an endless Strange Loop, where no particle is more elementary than any other (*God and the New Physics* [New York: Simon & Schuster, 1983], 159, 163). Enrico Fermi made the revealing comment, when he realized that the quest for the ultimate particle had resulted in the discovery of an infinite number of hadrons, that had he known this was to become the outcome of nuclear physics, he would have studied zoology (Pagels, *Cosmic Code,* 219).

37. M. Charles Birch, "Can Evolution Be Accounted for Solely in Terms of Mechanical Causation?" in *Mind in Nature: Essays on the Interface of Science and Philosophy,* ed. John B. Cobb, Jr. and David Ray Griffin (Washington, D.C.: University Press of America, 1978), 13–18.

38. Roger Sperry, "Changed Concepts of Brain and Consciousness: Some Value Implications," *Perkins Journal* 37 (Summer 1983): 25.

39. See p. 207 n. 11 above.

40. E. E. Waddington, "Whitehead and Modern Science," in *Mind in Nature,* 143.

41. So JB note. Compare the similar passage in *1 Enoch* 2:1-3, where the heavenly luminaries are regarded as the source of order and regularity.

42. Fritjof Capra, *The Tao of Physics* (New York: Bantam Books, 1980), 281.

43. George Riggan's fundamental statement is in his "Epilogue to the Symposium on Science and Human Purpose," *Zygon* 8 (1973): 476. Much of what I learned from Riggan took place in courses we taught together in Hartford Seminary's Church and Ministry Program, 1975-77.

44. Burhoe, "Natural Selection and God." Burhoe believes that nature and natural selection reveal a God who can be the center of the rebirth of a universal religion for a scientific and technological world. In science, nature itself finally becomes the creator, guide, judge, and sustainer of life, and reveals the nature of God. "It is this doctrine of elements [sic!] intrinsic to nature as the source, creator and judge of man which has been growing in the scientific and public mind in the century since Darwin" (p. 35). Well-meaning as the program is, it threatens to fall back into a worship of the *stoicheia.* Elsewhere Burhoe is more cautious; see his "The Human Prospect and the Lord of History," *Zygon* 10 (1975): 365.

45. Cited by Brian Easlea, *Liberation and the Aims of Science,* 51, italics mine. In Hebrew speculation the first essences or elements were not the four physical elements, but rather the letters of the Hebrew alphabet, which also doubled as numbers. God created the world, not by building with earth, air, fire, and water, but by the word. The almost infinite combinations of these alphabetical numbers account for the whole of the created world, including the Throne of Glory itself and the Divine Throne Chariot on which God rides. The analogy with DNA is startling. Hugo Odeberg comments that these letter-numbers are "a sort of spiritual atoms." The whole world was created from the twenty-two Hebrew letters and the seventy principle words, making ninety-two first elements or cosmic principles of creation. See *3 Enoch* 41:1-3; 13:1-2; and Odeberg's introduction in *Third Enoch* (Cambridge: Cambridge Univ. Press, 1928), 17-18. For a highly suggestive attempt to relate science and religion through number, see Arthur M. Young, *The Reflexive Universe* (San Francisco: Delacourt Press, 1976).

46. Peacocke, *Creation and the World of Science,* 94.

47. I am using "hierarchy" not in the sense of ranked importance, superiority, or preference, but in the more neutral sense of relationships of ascending complexity, without judgment as to relative importance. Perhaps an organismic image would be better,

such as Paul's in 1 Cor. 12:14–31. Clearly we are speaking not of straight stairstepping but rather of a clustering of sub-hierarchies, without clear reference as to their relative values. "Levels" are not so much bureaucratic aspects of nature but *modes or domains of explanation* (Lawrence LeShan and Henry Margenau, *Einstein's Space and Van Gogh's Sky* [New York: Macmillan Co., 1982], 122). Similarly God is no longer to be conceived of as located at the pinnacle of the hierarchy of being, but as equi-present within all being at every point.

48. God is the aspect of systemic interrelatedness in all systemic processes, and remains constantly that, in that sense transcending the process. In a trinitarian schema one could point to the "Father" as creator of the systems, the "Son" as the system of the systems, and the "Holy Spirit" as systemicity, on analogy with Augustine's metaphor for the trinity: lover, loved, love.

49. Matthew Fox, *Breakthrough. Meister Eckhart's Creation Spirituality in New Translation* (Garden City, N.Y.: Doubleday & Co., Image Books, 1980), 57–59.

50. "Call it the evolving cosmos, call it mansoul, or call it *god,* the superposition of states of the cosmos, in its logically primordial aspect, transcends any possible state of its actual evolution while containing all qualities possible of manifestation— commensurable and incommensurable alike. Yet the cosmic system exists nowhere else than in the transient components of its evolving states. Viewed transcendentally, the cosmic superposition is immutable, omnipotent; viewed immanently, it participates in the hopes, joys, sufferings, and failures alike of mankind and of all creation. In the polarity of transcendence and immanence it remains forever a self-surpassing system, surpassed by none of its self-transcending subsystemic components" (Riggan, "Epilogue," 480).

51. Gerd Theissen, *A Critical Faith* (Philadelphia: Fortress Press, 1979), 16.

52. See also *Mos.* II.88; *De cong.* 117.

53. Paul Tillich, *Systematic Theology* (Chicago: Univ. of Chicago Press, 1951), 1:133.

54. Elizabeth Dodson Gray, *Green Paradise Lost* (Wellesley, Mass.: Roundtable Press, 1979), 75.

55. Kermit D. Johnson, "The Sovereign God and 'the Signs of the Times,' " *Christian Century* 100 (August 17–24, 1983): 741.

7. THE ANGELS OF
NATURE

1. Morris Berman, *The Reenchantment of the World* (Toronto: Bantam Books, 1984).

2. Ibid., 117. Samuel Beckett puts the issue neatly in perspective. The Newtonian universe, he says, was not reality itself; "it was a story Europe told itself for many decades" (from his *Embers,* cited by Amos N. Wilder, *The Parables of Jesus and the War of Myths* [Philadelphia: Fortress Press, 1982], 67).

3. Ibid., 27; Carolyn Merchant, *The Death of Nature* (San Francisco: Harper & Row, 1980), 3–4.

4. Berman, *Reenchantment of the World,* 134–36. Speaking as a neurophysiologist, Nobel laureate Roger Sperry guesses that 99.9 percent of his colleagues hold to some form of the "modern behavioral science out of which comes today's prevailing objective, mechanistic, materialistic, behaviouristic, fatalistic, reductionistic view of the nature of mind and psyche." This kind of thinking, he notes, "is not confined to our laboratories

and classrooms. . . . It leaks and spreads, and though never officially imposed on the societies of the Western world, we nevertheless see, everywhere we turn, the pervasive influence of creeping materialism" (*Science and Moral Priority* [New York: Columbia Univ. Press, 1983], 29–30).

5. Dorothy Maclean, *To Hear the Angels Sing* (Middleton, Wisc.: Lorian Press, 1980 [P.O. Box 147, Middleton, Wisc. 53562]). H. K. Challoner's *Regents of the Seven Spirits* (Wheaton, Ill.: Theosophical Pub. House, 1976) is a more esoteric approach to angels.

6. Berman, *Reenchantment of the World,* 141.

7. For a full account, see Dorothy Maclean, *The Findhorn Garden* (New York: Harper & Row, 1975).

8. Maclean, *To Hear the Angels Sing,* 50, 73. Since the word "angel" had such a stereotyped image in her mind, contrary to her impression of the lightness, joy, and formlessness given by these beings, she decided to call them "devas" (Sanscrit: "shining ones"); though more recently she has returned to the term "angels" since "devas" in Zoroastrianism designated evil spirits, whereas the angels she encountered were uniformly good.

9. Rabbinical sources fixed the creation of the angels on the second or fifth days, in order to counter too high a regard for them. They thus made it clear that angels had absolutely no role in the creation of the world, but are merely creatures along with everything else (*Bereshith Rabba* 1:1). Gabriel is set over fire, Michael over snow, Jurqemi over hail. Other angels preside over wind, water, rain, the ripening of fruits, pregnancy, and death (references to rabbinic sources in Peter Schäfer, *Rivalität Zwischen Engeln und Menschen: Untersuchungen zur rabbinischen Engelvorstellung* [Berlin and New York: Walter de Gruyter, 1975], 56–59). *Test. Adam* 4:2 (2—5C c.e.; *OT Ps.* 1:995) ascribes to the archangels, as the second from the lowest order of angels, direction over "everything in this creation according to the plan of God, whether powers or animals, birds, or creeping things, or fish, and to speak briefly and in short, whatever exists in this creation, besides human beings, they care for it and guide it." The third order, the archons, make all the variations in the atmosphere (clouds, rain, snow, hail, dust, blood [?], thunder, lightning). The fourth order, the authorities, administer the sun, moon, and stars.

10. See also *1 Enoch* 82:7-20 (angels over seasons); 66:2 and 69:22 (spirits over water, winds, zephyrs, etc.); the Qumran Hymns (1QH 1—winds as angels); *4 Ezra* 8:21 (angels of wind and fire); 6:41 (spirit of the firmament); *2 Enoch* 19:1-6 (angels over seasons, years, rivers, seas, fruit, grass, everything bubbling); 15:1-4; 16:7; *3 Enoch* 14:3 (angels of fire, hail, wind, lightning, whirlwind, thunder, snow, rain, day, night, sun, moon, planets, constellations); Targum to 1 Kings 19:11-12 (angels of winds and earthquakes).

11. *Test. Adam* 4:2; Origen, *Against Celsus* 8:31; *Gospel of Bartholomew* 4.31-45 (*NT Apoc.* 1:498-99). The same view prevailed in Judaism (*Bereshith Rabba* 10:6) and in Islam. Mohammed said that every raindrop that falls is accompanied by an angel (cited without reference by Peter Lamborn Wilson, *Angels* [New York: Pantheon Books, 1980], 38). Angels and troops of Allah are appointed for the nurturing of plants, the generation of animals, and the composition of minerals (Seyyed Hossein Nasr, *An Introduction to Islamic Cosmological Doctrines* [Boulder; Colo.: Shambhala, 1978], 92). For other references in early Christian writings, see J. Michl, "Engel," *RAC* 1 (1962): 137-38; and in world literature, see Gustav Davidson, *A Dictionary of Angels* (New York: Free Press, 1971).

12. Walther Eichrodt, *Theology of the Old Testament* (Philadelphia: Westminster Press, 1967), 2:194, 25; see also Claus Westermann, *God's Angels Need No Wings* (Philadelphia: Fortress Press, 1979). The Sadducees no doubt played down the role of angels, but Acts 23:8 may exaggerate; not even the most convoluted exegesis could turn every angelic messenger in the Torah into a human messenger (Gerhard Kittel, "Aggelos," *TDNT* 1 [1964], 80 and n. 33). In what follows I will limit myself to references to angels that seem to reflect actual human experiences of a numinous sort. For that reason I will leave aside the philosophical use of angels as a bridge between the immaterial God and the material universe, such as we find in medieval philosophy. The neat list of hierarchies of angels developed by Pseudo-Dionysius the Areopagite (500 C.E.) has had enormous influence on Christianity, but betrays a systematic quality that owes more to philosophic tidiness than to experience. (The first circle contained Seraphim, Cherubim, and Thrones; the second, Dominions, Virtues, and Powers; the third, Principalities, Archangels, and Angels. As I argued in *Naming the Powers* the New Testament knows nothing of this differentiation, and treats Dominions, Principalities, and Powers somewhat interchangeably. And "Thrones" in the New Testament refers either to the authority invested in the chair or, by metonymy, to its current occupant, and not to a kind of spiritual being.)

In addition I will ignore those references to angels in Scripture which are simply figures of speech without reference to actual experiences (for example, 1 Sam. 29:9; 2 Sam. 14:17, 20; 19:27; Zech. 12:8; Gal. 4:14). And I will leave for a future study or another hand the large number of references to angels as messengers, instruments of judgment, hosts of Christ at his return, and as guardians of individuals. In short, the three chapters on angels in this book scarcely exhaust the subject.

13. "In the main Christ and His Apostles appropriated the Angelology of Judaism," writes J. T. Marshall. Jesus does not say much about them, "but when we *classify* His utterances, we find that they constitute almost a complete Angelology; and so far as it goes, it is in harmony with the Jewish beliefs of the period. The Jews believed all that the NT says of angels, but they also believed much more" (*Dictionary of Christ and the Gospels,* ed. James Hastings [Edinburgh: T. & T. Clark, 1906], 1:57). Paul, though he insisted on our superiority to angels (1 Cor. 6:3), nevertheless assumes their continued activity (1 Cor. 4:9; 11:10; 13:1; 2 Cor. 11:14; Gal. 1:8; 3:19; 1 Thess. 4:16; 2 Thess. 1:7). Elsewhere we are considered their *equals* (Luke 20:36; Rev. 22:9). The incarnation did not supersede their efforts, but finally made them effective (Origen, *Hom. on Luke,* 12).

14. This could be simply a shorthand way of referring to the third angel of 16:4 who pours out the phial on the waters. In that case, however, it should have been called "the angel of *blood,*" for that is what his phial turns the waters into. And *1 Enoch* 66:2 speaks explicitly of angels who "were over the powers of the waters"; 69:22 of "the spirits of the water"; *2 Enoch* 19:4 of "angels that are over rivers and seas." This is the apocalyptic thought-world to which the Book of Revelation belongs, and provides the best clue to its meaning.

15. This angel is probably to be taken as the angel responsible for the sun, as it is described in other writings from the same period: *Asc. Isa.* 4:18; *2 Enoch* 15:1 (not in B); *3 Enoch* 14:3 ("the angel of the sun"); 14:4.

16. Otto Böcher, *Christus Exorcista* (Stuttgart: Kohlhammer, 1972), 23.

17. Philo again, on the archetypal or pattern-holding function of the angelic powers: "For particulars within a class are of their nature such as to come into being and pass

out of it again, but to the potencies (*dynameis*) which give their form to these particulars is allotted an existence indestructible" (*De cher.* 51). So also, more recently, William Blake: "The forms of all things are derived from their Genius, which by the Ancients was called an Angel & Spirit & Demon" (*All Religions Are One,* plate 4, in Morton D. Paley, *William Blake* [New York: Greenwich House, 1978], 15).

18. Merchant, *The Death of Nature,* 11.

19. Ancient tradition concurred in this judgment that the angels are not themselves energetically creative. They did not assist God in creating the world initially, but were created on the second or fifth days (see n. 10 above).

20. Maclean, *To Hear the Angels Sing,* 165.

21. Charles Birch and John B. Cobb, Jr., *The Liberation of Life* (New York and Cambridge: Cambridge Univ. Press, 1981), 87; see 84–91.

22. Ibid., 88. Internal and external aspects can be found in every occasion or entity whatever. There are no purely inner or mental or spiritual occasions and no purely external or physical ones. There are only occasions in which the element of self-origination is relatively important and others where it is negligible.

23. See in this regard the fascinating theories of Arthur M. Young, *The Reflexive Universe* (San Francisco: Delacorte Press/Seymour Lawrence, 1976). The nineteenth-century philosopher Gustav Theodor Fechner commented that we have no more cause to attribute consciousness or mentation solely to beings with central nervous systems than to argue that because violins and pianos make sounds with strings, sound cannot be produced any other way (William James, *A Pluralistic Universe* [New York: Longmans, Green & Co., 1909], 164–67).

24. Aquinas, the "angelic doctor," spoke of angels as "pure intelligences," impersonal power, each angel an entire species unto itself (Etienne Gilson, *The Philosophy of St. Thomas Aquinas* [Freeport, N.Y.: Books for Libraries Press, 1971], 175–76). Philo is strikingly similar: Angels are "unbodied souls . . . all mind through and through, pure intelligences" (*De spec. leg.* I.66). This same regard for the divine care lavished on every created thing is strong in Sufism, where the angels are called "lords of the species." 'Abd al-Karim Jili formulated the relation of angels to material things thus: "Each sensible thing has a created Spirit [Angel] by which its Form is constituted. As Spirit of that form, it is related to the form as a meaning is related to a word" (cited by Henry Corbin, *Creative Imagination in the Sufism of Ibn 'Arabi,* Bollingen Series 91 [Princeton, N.J.: Princeton Univ. Press, 1981], 22, 245).

25. See Rupert Sheldrake, *A New Science of Life* (Los Angeles: J. P. Tarcher, 1981), 17–32.

26. James Hillman, "Anima," *Spring* (1973): 122–23.

27. Karl Pribram, "What the Fuss Is All About," *Revision* (Summer-Fall 1978): 17; see also the challenging manifesto by John Biersdorf, "The Coming Revolution in Theology," *haelan* (Spring-Fall 1982): 6–18.

28. Bayard Webster, "Are Clever Animals Actually Thinking?" *New York Times,* May 31, 1983, C4. Birch and Cobb (*Liberation of Life,* 123–29) note that planarian worms betray behavior analogous to anxiety, since like rats they suppress their feeding when placed in a new environment. Bats clearly manifest mental activity in their capacity to form "cognitive maps" of an area. Indeed, they pay more attention to their maps than they do to new echoes from newly placed objects. Hence they may collide with obstacles suddenly placed in their environment, or turn back from the former location of objects

that have been suddenly removed. For additional data on bees and birds, see D. Griffin, *The Question of Animal Awareness: Evolutionary Continuity of Mental Experience* (New York: Rockefeller Univ. Press, 1976); and idem, *Animal Thinking* (Cambridge: Harvard Univ. Press, 1984).

29. See Roger S. Jones's provocative *Physics as Metaphor* (New York: New American Library, 1982). Jones succeeds wonderfully in relativizing the materialist metaphor of reality, but pays an unnecessarily high price. By refusing Ernest Becker's wager for God, Jones opts for radical subjectivity, in which the universe and things are *wholly* the creation of our imaginations. The logical quicksand he lands himself in is inescapable: if there is no objective referent, no absolute reality which, though finally unknowable, can at least be approached and approximated by thought, how can he assert that his own view is true? How could we test it? Is it all then a matter of preference? Then why is he trying to persuade us?

30. *Jub.* 4:15–22; *1 Enoch* 7–9.

31. William James predicted in 1909, "Let empiricism once become associated with religion, as hitherto, through some strange misunderstanding, it has been associated with irreligion, and I believe that a new era of religion as well as of philosophy will be ready to begin" (*A Pluralistic Universe,* 314).

32. Christopher Nugent, *Masks of Satan* (London: Sheed and Ward, 1983), 170—an excellent book.

33. Cited by Morton Mintz and Jerry S. Cohen, *Power, Inc.* (Toronto: Bantam Books, 1977), 753. The authors propose a constitutional amendment which will make possible class-action suits on behalf of large groups against the government and/or nongovernmental power centers (742-62).

34. Simone Weil, *Waiting for God* (London: Fontana Books, 1959), 116. This disparagement of the creation took place despite St. Bonaventure's description of the visible world as *corpus angelicum,* the body of angels (Ladislaus Boros, *Angels and Men* [New York: Seabury Press, 1977], 104).

35. Norman Pittenger, *The Lure of Divine Love* (New York: Pilgrim Press, 1979), 184. The "Hymn to the Cosmic Christ" in Col. 1:15–20 only appears to begin with the creation of the world; its real starting point is the historic event of Jesus of Nazareth.

36. Mathew Fox, O.P., "Creation-Centered Spirituality from Hildegard of Bingen to Julian of Norwich," in *Cry of the Environment,* ed. Philip N. Joranson and Ken Butigan (Santa Fe: Bear & Co., 1984), 94. Fox also cites Meister Eckhart: "Every creature is a word of God and a book about God." "If I spent enough time with a caterpillar, I would never have to prepare a sermon because one caterpillar is so full of God" (p. 90).

37. The Psalms cited in this chapter refer to angels but do not specify the angels of nature. They do, however, depict created things as capable of offering praise to God, which assumes that they possess an interiority, and it is this interiority that I have identified with the angels of nature.

38. Other texts celebrating God's self-revelation through nature include Job 38—41; Pss. 19:1–6; 66:1–4; 69:34; 96:1–2; 98:7–9; 103:22; 145:10; 150:6; Isa. 40:12–31; Acts 17:24–27. Early Christians also depicted the nonhuman orders of nature at worship. See for example *Test. Adam* 1–2 (2–5C C.E.), which states that doves praise God in the second hour of the night, fish and fire and all the lower depths in the third, and the waters above the heaven in the fifth. By day, birds praise God during the third hour, beasts during the fourth, fire (again) and the waters below during the eighth. Richard

H. Hiers points out that the other creatures not only praise Yahweh, but pray for deliverance in time of need. Thus in the story of Jonah, the king of Nineveh calls on people, *herds, flocks,* and *beasts* to fast from food and water, and to be covered with sackcloth; "and let them cry mightily to God" (Jon. 3:7-8) ("Ecology, Biblical Theology, and Methodology: Biblical Perspectives on the Environment," *Zygon* 19 [1984]: 49).

39. Marianne Jacoby, "Psychotherapy in a Nonhuman Cosmos," *Spring* (1972): 22. A Valentinian interpolation into the apocryphal Acts of John (95:12-17) depicts Christ speaking on the eve of his death:

> I would pipe
> so you must all dance at the wedding, Amen.
> I would mourn,
> so you must all play at funerals, Amen.
> Heaven is singing along with us, Amen.
> The zodiac above is dancing with us, Amen.
> Whoever is dancing is in tune with the universe, Amen.
> He who does not dance, does not realize what is happening, Amen.

40. Brian Swimme, *The Universe Is a Green Dragon* (Santa Fe; Bear & Co., 1985), 131-34.

41. Maclean, *To Hear the Angels Sing,* 188, 214, 217. Wallace Stevens shared the same angelic epiphany:

> Yet I am the necessary angel of the earth,
> Since, in my sight, you see the earth again,
> Cleared of its stiff and stubborn, man-locked set. . . .

(Quoted by Stephen Crites in a delightfully literate manifesto of the Seraphic Audubon Society, in whose ranks this chapter should accord me honorary membership ("Wallace Stevens' Necessary Angel," *Soundings* 64 [1981]: 302).

42. J. Bruce Evans, *The Human Odyssey* (Baton Rouge, La.: Fellowship Ministry Press, 1979), 157. I would not want to close this chapter without recommending Paul Winter's *Missa Gaia,* or Earth Mass (Living Music Records, Inc., Box 72, Litchfield, Conn. 06759), which so beautifully conveys St. Francis's attitude toward nature.

43. The "heresy" combated by the Epistle to the Hebrews may have arisen over the problem of defining the relation of angels to the Logos. If everything in nature has an angel as its pattern or initial aim, then angels are nothing other than the specific initial aim which the Christ or Logos provides to every particular thing. They are the Logos-made-specific; patterning, patterned. How easy it would be then by extension to speak of the Logos as the Angel of the angels. Indeed, Heraclitus the Stoic (1C c.e.?) had identified *logos* and *angelos* through Hermes (*Quast. Hom.* 28, p. 48, 8); and Philo had done the same ("the Angel, who is the Word," *Leg. all.* III.177; *De som.* I.115, 142, 148, 190, 239; *De mut.* 87; *De agr.* 51; *De sob.* 65; *De conf.* 28, 146; *De fuga* 5). Such a view was opposed by the author of Hebrews because it failed to do justice to the psychic experience of early Christians that Christ had in some sense entered the godhead itself; and possibly also because the angels are not, like the Logos, agencies of creative transformations.

44. The same dialectical method for interpreting Scripture which I delineated in *The Bible in Human Transformation* (Philadelphia: Fortress Press, 1973) can be usefully applied to the understanding of any text, the "text" of the world included.

45. Pierre Teilhard de Chardin, *The Divine Milieu* (New York: Harper & Row, 1960), 42.

46. Friedrich Christoph Oetinger (d. 1782); cited by Gilles Quispel, *The Secret Book of Revelation* (New York: McGraw-Hill, 1979), 109.

47. Francis Thompson, "The Kingdom of God," in *The Works of Francis Thompson* (London: Burns & Oates, 1913), 2:226.

48. J. R. R. Tolkien, *The Return of the King,* volume 3 of *Lord of the Rings* (New York: Ballantine Books, 1965), 179.

Index of Authors

Index of Passages

221

APOCRYPHA

PSEUDEPIGRAPHA
(in OTPs or APOT)

RABBINIC LITERATURE

EARLY CHRISTIAN THEOLOGIANS